The Opinion Connection

The Opinion Connection
Polling, Politics, and the Press

Albert H. Cantril

in collaboration with
Susan Davis Cantril

A Project of the
National Council on Public Polls

PRESS

A Division of Congressional Quarterly Inc.
Washington, D.C.

Copyright © 1991 Congressional Quarterly Inc.
1414 22nd Street, N.W., Washington, D.C. 20037

Printed in the United States of America

Cover design by Carol Crosby Black

Library of Congress Cataloging-in-Publication Data

Cantril, Albert Hadley, 1940-
    The opinion connection : polling, politics, and the press / Albert
H. Cantril ; in collaboration with Susan Davis Cantril.
        p.   cm.
    "A Project of the National Council on Public Polls."
    Includes bibliographical references and index.
    ISBN 0-87187-583-7
    1. Public opinion polls.   2. Public opinion--United States.
3. Presidents--United States--Election--1988.   4. Press and
politics--United States.   I. Cantril, Susan Davis.   II. National
Council on Public Polls (U.S.)   III. Title.
HM261.C285   1991
303.3'8--dc20   90-21965
                                                              CIP

To Four of the Founders

Hadley Cantril
Archibald M. Crossley
Lloyd A. Free
George H. Gallup

Table of Contents

Foreword

In the wake of the 1988 presidential election, thoughtful people have raised serious questions about the quality of our politics. Concern has been expressed about the process of candidate selection, the length of campaigns, the nature of political advertising, and the influence of television. And, as polls have become an inextricable part of our political process, many questions also have been asked about what constructive role they play.

Many of us in the field of public opinion research have been troubled by the criticism about the polls, which rose to a crescendo following the 1988 election. We have always believed that opinion polling serves a fundamental public purpose: bringing the voice of the people into the processes of our political, social, and economic life. But the criticism heard from serious quarters cannot be answered merely with a stirring defense of the polls, although it would be tempting to do so.

As an association of public opinion research organizations dedicated to the improved conduct and reporting of polls, the National Council on Public Polls (NCPP) thought it would be both timely and in the public interest to assist in underwriting an independent exploration of the issues and criticisms that have been raised.

To that end we sought out an author knowledgeable about polling itself and also its relationship to the media and the electoral process.

Albert Cantril fits the bill perfectly. His experience spans the worlds of public opinion research, government service, and the nonprofit sector; he is a former president of NCPP; and he has written extensively on polling and politics. Most important, he is not associated with any polling or news organization. From the beginning it was agreed that the author would have complete discretion as to the direction of the inquiry, recognizing that NCPP might not agree with every word produced. Thus, Cantril brings independent, and—as this book demonstrates—informed, judgment to the task at hand.

The purpose of this book is twofold. First, it represents a broad-gauged, scholarly but real-world examination of modern polling: the good and the bad, the new criticisms and the old chestnuts, the use and misuse of polling by news organizations. Second, the book provides a concise guide to the elements in the design, conduct, and reporting of polls that are essential for polling to contribute to an understanding of our times.

In preparing this manuscript, Cantril has reviewed an extensive body of literature and interviewed more than two dozen leading political reporters, news editors, news executives, and pollsters.

The book brings to pollsters, journalists, scholars, and the politically attentive lay audience a thorough examination of political polling: its role in the political process, its relationship to the media, and how it serves a larger public purpose.

Burns W. Roper, Chairman
Harry W. O'Neill, President

National Council on Public Polls

Acknowledgments

Few exercises compete with writing a book when it comes to providing reminders of how dependent one is on the insights, good will, and thoughtful critique of friends and colleagues.

With gratitude and the hope their comments have been faithfully reflected, I have drawn upon interviews with: Herbert Alexander, Ben Bagdikian, Douglas Bailey, Ken Bode, Benjamin C. Bradlee, Hal Bruno, Adam Clymer, Mark J. DiCamillo, E. J. Dionne, Jr., Katherine Fanning, Mervin Field, Ed Fouhy, Lloyd A. Free, George Gallup, Jr., Sheldon Gawiser, Jeffrey Gralnick, Peter Hart, Deborah Hensler, Karlyn Keene, Mary Klette, Andrew Kohut, the late and much missed I. A. (Bud) Lewis, Larry McCarthy, Warren Mitofsky, Richard Morin, Kirk O'Donnell, Thomas O'Donnell, Harry O'Neill, Charles W. Roll, Jr., Burns Roper, Humphrey Taylor, Rosita Thomas, Richard Wirthlin, and Cliff Zukin.

In researching and writing this book, I have culled the academic literature for empirically grounded insights on the topic at hand. In this regard I am especially indebted to Malcolm Hamilton and his able colleagues at the library of the John F. Kennedy School of Government at Harvard University.

Several individuals have provided useful background materials for which I am most grateful: Kathleen Frankovich, Michael Kagay, Karlyn Keene, Andrew Kohut, Gary Langer, Paul Lavrakas, Warren Mitofsky,

Ralph Murphine, Humphrey Taylor, and Rosita Thomas. Others helped along the way: Mildred Barton, Francis Bourne, Anne Doyle Kenney, Bernard Roshco, and Eileen Shanahan.

At CQ Press the encouragement and good counsel of Joanne Daniels and David Tarr are much appreciated as are the energies of Jerry A. Orvedahl, Steven B. Kennedy, and others involved at various stages in production of the book.

The initiative for this project came from the National Council on Public Polls (NCPP). Representatives of member organizations have been attentive to questions raised about the role of the polls in our political process. They agreed that what was needed was a wide-ranging exploration of the dimensions and impact of public opinion research as an institution in its own right.

The national council's support for a portion of the costs of this project is gratefully acknowledged. However, more important has been its encouragement of unfettered inquiry. The manuscript has benefited from comments of knowledgeable individuals active in NCPP, but in no sense has it been constrained by them. While the book is a "project of the National Council on Public Polls," it is no consensus statement. In fact, I have received vigorous dissent from more than one colleague on points herein. Special appreciation is due for the level-headed judgment of Burns Roper and the good faith with which Harry O'Neill served as NCPP liaison to the project.

An author is fortunate when colleagues find time to put a critical eye to the argument and exposition of a manuscript. Without implicating them for the deficiencies that remain, let me express a deep debt for the careful reading of the draft manuscript by Lloyd Free, Bill Kovach, Charles W. Roll, Jr., Burns Roper, and two anonymous reviewers. It is much the better for their reading.

Others have read individual chapters or commented in their areas of expertise. Collectively their reactions have enriched the veracity, rigor, and nuance of the argument. I speak of: Joan S. Black, Charles D. Cowan, Dan Fenn, Sheldon Gawiser, Andrew Kohut, Gladys and Kurt Lang, Warren Mitofsky, Harry O'Neill, Glenn Roberts, and Harold Washburn.

This book would not have been possible without the encouragement, example, and counsel of the four individuals to whom it is affectionately dedicated.

Most important, my colleague through the endeavor has been my wife, Susan Davis Cantril. Drawing on experience in practical politics, television news, and opinion research, she has collaborated at every step. The argument of every page is the stronger for her involvement and its exposition a good deal more precise.

Albert H. Cantril
Cambridge, Massachusetts

The Polls at Fifty: A Midlife Crisis?

Viewers of ABC's "World News Tonight" must have been just as puzzled as Peter Jennings was on Monday night, August 15, 1988. As the Republican National Convention was kicking off in New Orleans, Jennings told a nationwide audience:

> Listen to this. On Friday, we reported the results of an ABC News/*Washington Post* presidential poll, which showed that the race had really tightened up, that George Bush was actually ahead of Dukakis by 49 to 46 percent. We told you on Friday that there was a larger margin of error than usual, that for all practical purposes, the race could be dead even.
>
> Last night, using the same methodology we have always used, and using the same polling sample size, listen to this. We're told that 55 percent of those that we asked prefer Dukakis and 40 percent prefer Bush. Do you believe that there could be such a swing overnight? Quite frankly, with a two-man set yet so undefined to the electorate at large, we are not sure what the heck is going on.[1]

1

What was going on? In the rush to get a poll story on the air as part of its Friday, preconvention newscast, ABC broadcast results before interviews with a full cross section of the public had been completed. The reported 49-46 Bush lead rested on interviews with only a third of the intended sample of more than one thousand. Moreover, some parts of the country had not been contacted. Then, two nights later, ABC conducted a separate overnight poll in which a complete sample of 382 registered voters was interviewed.

ABC's regular polling partner, the *Washington Post,* had joined in the poll. But while ABC released incomplete results Friday night, the *Post* declined to publish the results from the partial sample. It waited until the poll was completed as planned, including additional attempts to contact people least likely to be at home. The *Post*'s report, based on the complete sample of 1,119, was published almost a week after ABC's premature release. It showed Dukakis ahead of Bush, 49-46, more in line with what other polls were picking up at the time.[2]

ABC stuck by its numbers. When asked in retrospect whether he would handle matters differently next time, ABC's polling director said, "No, but I'd hope to have better luck. I'd hope I wouldn't have events shifting under me so that the figures are hard to explain." [3] While he had some doubts that a shift to Dukakis of such great magnitude could take place in only two days, he contended that "a shift occurred and we measured it approximately." [4]

The sequence of events, to which we will return in a later chapter, frames in stark fashion the issues at the heart of this book. What is required to achieve reliable poll results? When are the conclusions drawn from a poll valid? How should methodological considerations concerning poll quality be reconciled with the journalistic imperative to break a story? In their use of polls are news organizations reporting news or creating it? How are pollsters and the press accountable to the public? What effect does the reporting of polls have on the electorate and the lifelines of a campaign—money, media attention, and staff morale? In short, what function do, and should, polls play in our political process?

Polling and the Political Process

Final preelection polls in 1948 predicted the defeat of incumbent president Harry Truman by Republican candidate Thomas Dewey. In the aftermath of Truman's victory by almost five percentage points, the issue was credibility: could *any* polls be trusted? Newspapers canceled subscriptions to the Gallup Poll, and the Roper Poll reported a dip in business.[5] The image of Truman holding aloft the *Chicago Tribune* with its banner headline, "Dewey Defeats Truman," was ample spur to pollsters to change their sampling methods and to interview up until the last moment.[6]

While the occasional and sometimes highly visible preelection poll is off the mark these days, the ability of opinion research to gauge the state of voter sentiment is now widely accepted. Polls have become part of the warp and woof of American politics and of the coverage of politics by news organizations. The question is no longer whether polls as a whole can be trusted but rather when a given poll can be trusted. This places a special burden on all who report polls to acquire the knowledge needed to assess the quality of a poll's methodology and the limits to which its findings can be generalized.

The importance of accuracy in election polls, however, cannot be minimized. Because the results of an electoral poll can be checked against the outcome of an election, the polling technique can be validated, giving polls credibility when no other source of outside validation is available. Were preelection polls not reasonably accurate, who would believe opinion measurements about, for example, the proportions of the public holding various nuanced views on issues like abortion or gun control?

Now that the issue of credibility of polling has been redefined from whether to when polls are reliable, a related issue has emerged. As the techniques and insights of opinion research have been adopted widely by both politics and journalism, the issue is increasingly the legitimacy of polling: what is the intrinsic value of opinion polling in our society and our democratic system of government?

The electoral campaign of 1988 was distinctive in American presidential politics. For the first time in two decades an incumbent was not running for reelection. This forced a scramble within each party to define the center of political gravity. In the early months, as candidates vied for their party's nomination, the probable outcome within either party was far from clear.

Soon after the parties had settled on their standard bearers, it became clear that both George Bush and Michael Dukakis had unusual latitude in defining the contours of the campaign. Unlike earlier presidential elections, no single issue consumed the public's attention as had the war in Vietnam in 1968, the murkiness of the Watergate coverup in 1976, or the hostage situation in Iran that haunted President Jimmy Carter in 1980. Moreover, both Bush and Dukakis were relatively unknown to most of the American people.

One consequence of this unique set of circumstances was that the techniques of modern politics came into sharper relief as the electorate watched the campaign unfold. "Media events," "sound bites," "targeting," "tracking polls," and "comparative ads" were laid bare as the instruments of politics. Prison furloughs, the Pledge of Allegiance, and other symbols had to pass for its substance.

The polls were implicated as misgivings about the process were spelled out. The nastiness of the 1988 race was of particular concern. One week before the election, for example, Seattle TV commentator Jim Compton wrapped up a special broadcast on the polls noting:

> Polls have become the handmaiden of the negative advertising that is poisoning our airwaves more each year. The danger is that these techniques, while they work, are undermining the public's confidence in officeholders and institutions. Politics is becoming more a process of winning power than wielding it well. A candidate whose words are driven by the polls and shaped by the ad agencies may find himself elected with a hollow mandate.[7]

ABC's political director, Hal Bruno, concurred, pointing out that "it is the polls that tell a campaign where to go negative."[8]

Ken Bode, then of NBC News, saw polls as the "computer virus" of political reporting. "Far more than any other year I have been involved in covering politics, polls dominated the story. Every story you read or saw on television, and I mean almost without exception, was in one way or another framed by a poll or included reporting on polls. Everybody had a poll."[9]

The Dukakis campaign felt besieged. "We were constantly being asked about the polls," recalled Kirk O'Donnell, one of the governor's key lieutenants. "Tracking polls took over. 'What were your overnight numbers?' was always the first question I'd get on the plane every morning."[10]

Pollsters themselves were uneasy. Andrew Kohut, then president of the Gallup Organization, reflecting on 1988 relative to earlier elections, noted:

The biggest difference was the extent to which the polls were seen as intrusive. Not just because there were so many of them, but because people had become aware of the crucial role polling advisers were playing in the campaigns. People saw the campaigns as poll-driven. They didn't like the campaign; and, with polls playing a prominent role in both the coverage of the campaign and in the structuring of the campaign, the polls came under a lot of fire.[11]

The American people are clearly troubled. As we will discuss, recent studies have shown that the public shares the concern of many political observers about the quality of our politics.

A Time to Take Stock

Modern polling made its debut in the 1936 election by predicting FDR's election to a second term. In the more than fifty years since, public opinion research has seen three generations of practitioners. It has taken hold in the academic disciplines of political science, psychology, sociology, economics, statistics, and even history. It is routinely called upon by agencies of government. It is firmly established around the globe in countries at all levels of economic development and even in countries with closed political systems.

The half-century mark is reason enough to pause and take stock. But given the issues of credibility and legitimacy brought to the fore in the 1988 campaign, the need for an assessment takes on added urgency. Thus this book.

In the first chapter we review the purposes envisaged for their new craft by the founders of opinion research. We share their sense of promise at the prospect that the influence of well-connected and well-financed interests could be counterbalanced by the public's view of the issues facing government. We then turn to changes in the environment in which the polls have come of age since the 1930s: the evolving role of the political parties, the arrival of television, and the emergence of campaign consultants. We also reflect on how the polls have affected this environment as they have come to play new and larger roles.

Chapter 2 picks up on the questions asked about polling in the wake of the 1988 election. In particular, it looks at the effect the polls and the media have on each other: how media demands affect the kinds of polls that are conducted; how poll findings shape the news and the way it is covered; and what effect both the polls and media have on the election itself.

The purpose of Chapter 3 is to provide an overview of the essentials of reliable and valid polling. It is intended as a nontechnical recapitulation of the most important aspects of polling method that poll consumers may find useful in sizing up a poll for themselves.

Most polls appearing in the print and broadcast media have been conducted by or for news organizations. Steeped in a culture of rugged independence protected by the Bill of Rights, these organizations vigorously resist being told how to go about their business. However, when they sponsor, conduct, or report polls, they are using the methods of opinion research, a discipline which has its own traditions and criteria of competence. As a result, issues of standards and public accountability in polling are not easy to sort out. It is to this dilemma that Chapter 4 is addressed.

In conclusion, Chapter 5 attempts to reckon with the question put squarely on the table in the preceding chapters: how do public opinion polls contribute to the well-being of the body politic and the democratic process? It asks what the consequences of polling, intended or unintended, may be on the way the public's views are expressed in our system. Finally, it considers the effect of public opinion polls on the way interests compete in a democratic system of government.

Notes

1. Quoted in Barbara Matusow, "Are the Polls Out of Control?" *Washington Journalism Review* 10 (October 1988): 18.
2. Richard Morin, "Trying to Gauge the Pulse of Public Opinion: Polls Reflect Mood Shifts, Survey Quality," *Washington Post,* August 18, 1988, A25.
3. Jeff Alderman, quoted in Matusow, "Are the Polls Out of Control?" 18.
4. Alderman quoted in E. J. Dionne, Jr., "In the Confusing Land of Electoral Polls, Which Numbers Count the Most?" *New York Times,* August 17, 1988, A18.
5. Interview with Paul K. Perry, retired president of the Gallup Organization, in Irving Crespi, *Public Opinion, Polls, and Democracy* (Boulder, Colo.: Westview Press, 1989), 15, 136n.
6. These were two of the principal findings of the post-mortem conducted by a panel of the Social Science Research Council. See, Frederick Mosteller,

Herbert Hyman, Philip J. McCarthy, Eli S. Marks, and David B. Truman, *The Pre-Election Polls of 1948* (New York: Social Science Research Council, 1948).
7. The Compton Report, KING TV-5, Seattle, October 28, 1988.
8. Hal Bruno, interview with the author, Washington, D.C., July 28, 1989.
9. Ken Bode, telephone interview with the author, September 8, 1989.
10. Kirk O'Donnell, interview with the author, Washington, D.C., July 25, 1989.
11. Andrew Kohut, interview with the author, Princeton, N.J., June 29, 1989.

c h a p t e r   o n e

Polling and Its Changing Environment

The distinguishing characteristic of modern politics
is that it is based on conflicts about the public
interest rather than conflicts among special interests.

E. E. Schattschneider

Polling has both shaped and been shaped by the environment in which it has thrived. Facets of political life we take for granted today would not exist were it not for public opinion research. Presidential popularity ratings have become a staple in the business of governing. Special interests often compete for clout by citing poll-based indications of public support. The modern campaign for public office is now built around polling.

At the same time, the polls have been influenced by fundamental changes in the setting in which they operate. The political parties have redefined the way in which they mediate between the public and the nation's leadership. The smoke-filled rooms where decisions used to be made have given way to expanded popular participation. Meanwhile, the broadcast media have quickened the pace of political life, broadened public exposure to world events, and made the diversity of our population more visible.

A retrospective glance accentuates the transitions that have taken place. For example, the complaint that polls have become a substitute for good political reporting would have been implausible in the Truman, Eisenhower, or Kennedy years. And who would have thought even two decades ago that Congress would consider establishing uniform poll closing across the nation's time zones to adapt to modern means of tabulating the vote?

Some Founding Premises

A useful starting point for an inquiry into modern polling as an institution is to recall the philosophical underpinnings provided by its founders. As recovery from the Great Depression progressed, the 1930s were increasingly energized by a sense that the nation's problems were tractable. Social science historian Jean Converse writes of the prevailing mood: "Pollsters saw themselves as innovators who would defend a democratic faith with new methods of conveying the popular will. They saw their role as providing a continuous measurement of public opinion which would supplement and strengthen the normal operations of representative government and protect it from the domination of lobbyists and special interests." [1]

Archibald Crossley, who founded his own opinion research firm in 1928 after a decade's experience in market research, saw in the polls a vehicle to check the "false presentations of public opinion" made by the pressure groups. While Crossley left most polling on electoral politics to George Gallup and Elmo Roper, he was mindful of the power of the tool: "Scientific polling makes it possible within two or three days at moderate expense for the entire nation to work hand-in-hand with its legislative representatives, on laws which affect our daily lives. Here is the long-sought key to 'Government *by* the people.' " [2] Crossley also saw the public opinion poll as a vehicle "to discover the basis upon which conflict can be eased and good will advanced among peoples of the world." [3] In fact, in his retirement he engaged fellow octogenarians of his Princeton Class of 1917 in the project of underwriting case studies of how polls could reduce conflicts around the globe. [4]

George Gallup was the fiercest advocate of the polls as an instrument of democracy. In *The Pulse of Democracy* he and Saul Rae argued that the poll was a potent foil to entrenched interests, a way to ensure that discourse in the corridors of power had an appropriate respect for the majority view. [5] Gallup's upbringing in rural Iowa nurtured a distinctly populist political philosophy. His son, George Gallup, Jr., remembers his father as a reformer: "He was always very change-oriented, always challenging the status quo. Very early on he saw polling as a great instrument of change." [6]

Gallup's faith in the ability of the public to fend off manipulators was unbending. In fact, Converse faults his view of democracy for not anticipating "that corrupt leaders or aggressive pressure groups might effect their will by manipulating public opinion or capitalizing on public confusion or ignorance." [7] But Gallup was not inattentive to the changing ways the political game was played. In his later years, he railed against the influence of money in the political process, calling for government to be the only source of funding for election campaigns. [8] He was also alert to the emerging technologies of communication and warned that they would further empower the powerful.

Gallup persisted in the view that the public opinion poll could be likened to a referendum placed before the voters. He did not accept the notion that the public could be manipulated easily through contrived appeals in the mass media. It was not easy, he contended, to subvert the public's capacity to size up the relative appeals made by contending sides on an issue. Gallup's view is worth noting in some detail:

> Most citizens at that early time [the founding of the nation] lived in isolated rural communities with little information regarding either domestic or foreign affairs. Today, the media make such information available in a matter of minutes or hours to virtually the entire population. The typical citizen, therefore, is likely to have access to the same sources of information as a member of Congress.
>
> Highly technical issues cannot be decided by those who are not knowledgeable in such matters, but certainly on nearly all major issues of the day the people collectively are competent to make wise judgments, and the mountain of polling data collected during the last 44 years is proof of this. [9]

It must be remembered that in the early years of polling the clouds of war were gathering over Europe. Those too young to have lived through the period have trouble appreciating how palpable concern was for the vitality of democracy. In fact, the ominous portents of German bombing of Great Britain in 1941 heightened the resolve that led to the founding of the National Opinion Research Center (NORC), one of the early university-based institutes for polling. [10]

The war effort brought the commercial polling enterprises of Crossley, Gallup, Roper, and others into contact with academics for the first time.[11] But academic acceptance of polling did not come easily. Contemporary students of politics and public opinion would have difficulty envisioning a world of empirical social science that did not give credence to poll findings. Today professional journals are filled with secondary analyses of poll data, time series are plotted with elegance, and many universities have their own survey research centers. Such was not the case before World War II.

Academic social scientists were wary of opinion polling in part because of its origins in market research. As Elmo Roper noted in 1968, three years before his death, "published public opinion research came out of marketing research—absolutely directly." [12] Suspicions abounded in academic circles that commercial agendas would subvert the independence of research and redefine norms of intellectual and methodological rigor. Early practitioners of market research rebutted their academic critics.[13]

Academic social science stuck to its ways. Don Cahalan recalls:

> Among sociologists in those days, many who considered themselves methodologically sophisticated thought that it was alright to study the interrelationships between variables in nonrepresentative samples with the assumption that the relationships would be similar to those found in truly representative samples.[14]

One academic, Hadley Cantril, recalled the frustration of having academic social science so reluctant to embrace survey and opinion research:

> While the survey technique in all its forms is now relatively old hat and part and parcel of the information kit of social scientists, of government at all levels, of aspiring politicians, and, of course, the market researchers, in the late 1930s there were practically no social scientists who gave any serious consideration to these methods. Most of my social science colleagues at the time either were ignorant about them or tended to belittle them because none of the men doing the pioneer work in the field were members of the academic fraternity.[15]

At the end of World War II, the occasional collaboration between academic and commercial research was enlivened by a renewed conviction that opinion measurement could make important contributions to the nation's well-being. Reflecting on the optimism of the period, Don Cahalan recalls that one objective of the 1946 conference that led to the formation of the American Association for Public Opinion Research (AAPOR) was to find a venue in which academic and commercial researchers might explore common ground.

Subsequent steps in the establishment of AAPOR involved intense discussion about how—even whether—to formalize terms of reference for the young field. A strong voice in these deliberations was that of Julian L. Woodward, a partner of Elmo Roper. Woodward saw the polls as "a public utility" and warned that the marketplace was inadequate to ensure that the public's interest would be served. "Polls must conduct themselves in such a way as to justify the responsibilities which will increasingly be theirs and to deserve the respect with which the public will regard them." [16]

AAPOR was formally established in 1947. Among its purposes was "to promote the proper utilization of public opinion research in democratic policy formulation." [17]

The Parties, Interest Groups, and the Public

Just a year after AAPOR's founding came the polling debacle of the 1948 presidential election, which fixed the attention of pollsters on the adequacy of their new craft. Today, the events of 1948 serve as a reminder of how far removed the polls were from the rough and tumble of the campaign. At the time polls did not overwhelm news reports of primaries or preconvention jockeying among the candidates; tracking-poll data did not flow to candidates on a daily basis; and there was no exit poll of voters on election day to explain why Truman had won.

In the early years of polling, political parties were the key mediating institution between the public and the nation's leaders. Party networks provided political intelligence on the public's view of issues large and small. Party activists made the important choices about who would run for office and what the issues would be.

As the two major political parties have attempted to adjust to changing circumstances, they have instituted new modes of operation that have recast their role in the political process. These changes in party politics, and accompanying changes in the political role of interest groups, have fundamentally altered the environment in which public opinion polls operate. We will consider each development in turn.

Mass-Based Nomination Politics

In 1968 frustrations fueled by the Tet Offensive in Vietnam, the assassinations of Martin Luther King, Jr., and Robert F. Kennedy, and the decision of Lyndon Johnson not to seek reelection to the presidency erupted into political turmoil. The Democratic National Convention became the focal point of this pent-up tension. Images of machine politicians collided with those of protesters accosted by Chicago Mayor Daley's police officers, and the Democrats nominated Hubert Humphrey, an ebullient liberal alienated from the liberals in his own party. Amid the turmoil, Humphrey assented to convention resolutions that would fundamentally reform the Democratic party and would have important consequences for the Republican party as well.[18]

The reforms brought broader public involvement in the nominating process, resulted in an increased number of primaries, and eliminated "winner-take-all" contests, in which the candidate earning a plurality of the primary vote would capture the entire state delegation to the national party convention. In 1968 only fifteen states held primary elections; by 1988 thirty-nine states did so. No longer would it be possible for a candidate to capture the party nomination, as Adlai Stevenson had done in 1952, without entering a single primary.

The first of two consequences of this transformation was that political reporters turned their attention away from the party insiders who struck the deals of the past to the public opinion polls that monitored how the race was unfolding.

The second consequence was that few incentives remained for candidates to campaign for the presidential nomination through their party. Nelson Polsby notes of these reforms:

> Rather than depending upon alliances with and commitments from state party organizations or interest groups allied to factions within state party organizations, candidates for the Presidency are increasingly obliged to mount their search for delegates by building their own personal organizations, state by state. This is necessary because frequently state party organizations wish to maintain neutrality toward all primary contestants in the hope of developing a decent working relationship with . . . the eventual winner of the nomination.[19]

Evidence in support of Polsby's view is the dwindling mention of a candidate's party in news stories over the years. Martin Wattenberg and his colleagues coded more than 10,000 election-related news stories appearing in the last two months of the eight presidential elections from 1952 through 1980. They computed the ratio of mentions of the candidate to mentions of the candidate's party and found that it rose from about two-to-one in the 1950s to five-to-one by 1980.[20]

Candidates are now better able to reach voters directly through the media rather than through the party. This critical element of direct access to the electorate emboldens candidates to enter the fray regardless of their standing with party regulars.[21]

Since self-starting campaigns have become feasible, Polsby notes "the balance of initiatives, and of responsibilities for the overall organization of the effort, has definitely shifted" to a new class of campaign operatives who "work not for the party but directly for candidates."[22] This has ushered into campaigns, and into the political process generally, a brigade-for-hire of media advisers, campaign organizers, fundraisers, and pollsters.

Parties as Vendors

Just as the Democrats were writing their party out of its traditional role in presidential politics, Republicans were beginning to craft an expanded role for their party, which soon became a major supplier of campaign services to its candidates, especially at the congressional level. Using a kind of institutional judo, the Republicans turned technologies that were diminishing the significance of the party into one of its principal assets.[23]

Today the party provides an imposing repertoire of services through three committees: the Republican National Committee, the National Republican Congressional Committee, and the National Republican Senatorial Committee. A combined staff of more than one hundred works at the Republican headquarters in Washington, D.C., with many being dispersed to key congressional districts as an election approaches. Campaigns get help in canvassing voters and in producing and placing television advertisements. Candidates have access to computerized data bases containing lists of possible contributors, basic demographic and political information, and voting and attendance records of opposing candidates. Candidates can even turn to the national headquarters for software to handle their financial accounting, statistical analysis of poll data, and word processing.[24]

The interparty imbalance of capabilities has prodded the Democratic party to catch up. Although it still lags far behind the Republicans in resources, it too has moved to provide direct assistance to candidates in media, issues research, campaign management—and polling.

Among the most valued services provided by both parties are political polls. Candidates and their campaign staffs have access to polls conducted by nationally known firms at greatly reduced rates. When the information needs of candidates overlap, the Senate and House committees of each party can make use of a common poll by distributing portions of the poll relevant to each of the candidates. Day-by-day tracking polls in the final days of a campaign are frequently conducted for candidates by the committees.

Using a schedule for the depreciation of the value of a poll drawn up by the Federal Election Commission, the national committees charge candidates just half the cost of the poll if the results are not shared with the candidates for fifteen days. If the candidates wait for sixty days, they are charged *only 5 percent* of the cost of the poll. A campaign can benefit from a poll at *no* cost whatsoever under two conditions: if the poll results are withheld from the campaign for 180 days or if the committee makes strategic recommendations based upon a poll but never shares the actual poll results with the campaign.[25]

Empirical evidence of the value candidates attach to these polling services is found in Paul Herrnson's survey of campaign officials in 1984 and 1986, in which public opinion information was consistently rated as one of the two most important services received. The finding obtained for campaigns in both parties, for both the House and the Senate, and among those running as incumbents, challengers, or for open seats. Republicans tended to be more enthusiastic about polling services than Democrats, reflecting the Republican committees' longer record of delivering polls.[26]

The renaissance of the national parties has contributed to the burgeoning campaign consulting industry. Half of the political consulting firms now operating have been founded since 1980. Fewer than 10 percent of them were in business prior to the 1964 election.[27] Another indicator of the growth of the industry is the expanding membership of the American Association of Political Consultants (AAPC). At its founding in 1967, AAPC had fewer than forty members. Today it has more than 800 members representing 400 firms.[28]

However, numbers alone do not account for the influence of political consultants. Their influence derives from the central roles they play in modern campaigns. In one study, most consultants reported that the candidates for whom they worked tended not to be involved in setting campaign strategy or in guiding day-to-day operations of the campaign.[29] In Chapter 4 we will return to these consultants in connection with their accountability to the public. Suffice it to say here that much consulting has been integrated into the operations of the national parties.

Interest Group Politics

The life of the pollster has also been dramatically affected by the proliferation of organizations representing assorted interests in Washington, in statehouses, and in the give-and-take of debates over policies and procedures.

The interest group politics that have evolved over the last two decades mirror the changes that have taken place in the parties. As opportunities for public participation in national-level nomination politics have increased, group loyalties have become more important as a basis for political behavior. Arthur Miller and his colleagues at the University of Iowa have demonstrated that group consciousness among women, blacks, and the elderly became an increasingly important variable in explaining voting behavior between 1972 and 1984.[30] Kay Schlozman and John Tierney have also shown that, even though corporations and trade associations still outnumber other types of interest groups having representation in Washington, the offices established most recently reflect racial, gender, social service, and "public interest" groupings.[31]

The burgeoning of interest groups in the nation's capital has brought about expanded use of public relations consultants, fundraising experts, and, yes, pollsters. Schlozman and Tierney found that more than three-quarters of Washington interest groups use the services of public relations consultants, either on staff or by contract, and more than a third have turned to a pollster. The sheer number of organizations involved (more than 2,700) conveys the magnitude of activity represented by the third seeking the expertise of a pollster.[32]

Television, Politics, and the Public

As television has transformed our politics it has reinforced the importance of polls about politics and redefined the role they play both before and after elections. Polls have much to do with the way politics is covered by television: they become news as leads in breaking stories and provide a leitmotif for news that would otherwise not come together in quite the same way without insights from a poll.

Since news organizations sponsor virtually all election-related public polls, it is in the media arena where the promises and perils of polling are most on display. But, before turning to a discussion of how polling fits into the modern environment of media and politics, we pause for a brief look at the intersection of television and politics. An understanding of how television has affected politics is essential to our consideration of the role of polling and of the pressures under which pollsters often have to operate.

The Television Transaction

More Americans get their news from television than from any other source. (See box.) Television is also the most credible news source for the public at large, a status it has held for at least two decades.[33] The only sphere in which television does not dominate is in the coverage of local politics. There the newspapers narrowly edge out television as the principal news source.

Television's dominance as the medium of news communication also derives from the way people transact with it. The viewer's involvement with television is far from passive: it is not simply a matter of information being passed from news organization to viewer. What is going on is far more subtle, involving the mix of assumptions viewers bring to the television set—the assorted cues, hopes, fears, and antipathies that animate human perception. The concept of *transaction* implies that the individual and the environment are inseparable, that we would not see things as we do except for the assumptions we bring to a situation or event, the intentions we have about possible future courses of action, and any larger meanings we might share with others as to the significance of what is happening around us.[34]

Tony Schwartz, a pioneer in radio and television advertising, grounds this concept by noting that the challenge of good television production is not "to get stimuli across, or even to package . . . stimuli so they can be absorbed." The challenge is to "evoke stored information . . . in a patterned way." [35] The subtlety of Schwartz's observation is that the body of "stored information" results from the viewer's prior engagement

Evolution of Public Opinion on Most Believable News Source

The question asked: "If you got conflicting or different reports of the same news story from radio, television, magazines and newspapers, which of the four versions would you be most inclined to believe—the one on radio, or television, or magazines, or newspapers?"

	12/59	11/68	12/78	11/88
Television	29%	44%	47%	49%
Newspapers	32	21	23	26
Radio	12	8	9	7
Magazines	10	11	9	5
Don't know	17	16	12	13
	100	100	100	100

Public Views of Best Source for Information about Candidates (November 1988)

The question asked: "During the last campaign, from what source did you become best acquainted with the candidates running in [local elections, like mayor, members of the state legislature]; [for the U.S. House from this district]; [in statewide elections, like U.S. senator and governor]; [for president and vice president] from the newspapers, or radio, or television, or magazines, or talking to people or where?"

	President and vice president	House of Representatives	Senator and governor	Local elections
Television	70%	43%	50%	36%
Newspapers	20	35	31	40
Radio	4	3	5	5
Other people	3	5	6	11
Magazines	3	1	1	1
Other source	2	5	4	5
	102	92	97	98

SOURCE: *America's Watching: The 1989 TIO/Roper Report*, The Roper Organization for the Television Information Office (two thousand personal interviews).

NOTE: Totals may not add to 100% due to multiple answers and "no opinion" responses.

in the pacing and portrayals of television just as it evolves out of an individual's direct experience in everyday dealings.[36]

The research community has reached no consensus as to the nature of the impact of television on political behavior. One line of argument contends that a large part of the public is *inadvertently* exposed to political information by television and may get more information about politics than it wants.[37] It is true that there is a downside tilt to the television audience in socioeconomic terms. (See box.) But the implication that the public is overwhelmed with information does not follow. There is compelling empirical evidence that the public as a whole is amply agile in sorting its way through the flood of information it confronts. People ignore that which is not relevant and build up a cumulative understanding of events if not specific knowledge.[38]

This "understanding-without-recall" aspect of the public's consumption of television is at the heart of the paradox of mass politics described by W. Russell Neuman. If the media are so all-powerful, asks Neuman, why does the American public remain so woefully ignorant? Have the effects of the media been exaggerated?[39]

Neuman's analysis has shown that the conception of the "two-step flow" of mass communications, according to which political information is passed from elites to the public through "opinion leaders" (who provide cues as to what is important), is no longer adequate to describe how the public gets its information about politics. "There is only weak evidence of a trickle-down flow of political information. Those who are interested in political information follow the media and talk with each other. Those at the lower levels of the sophistication continuum neither attend to the media nor discuss politics very much."[40]

The vast majority of the public (Neuman suggests about 75 percent) are "marginally attentive" to politics.[41] It is this broad spectrum of society that receives much of its information about political matters directly from the broadcast media, unmediated by opinion leaders in the community. To the extent public opinion polls become part of this political information, the media assume responsibility for characterizing the division of public opinion on the issues and the public's disposition toward the candidates.

Polls and Media Reality

Much has been written about the grid through which events must pass to be judged newsworthy. It is beyond the scope of this book to at-

Principal News Source of Americans by Education and Income

The question asked: "Which one of these do you rely on most for information on national affairs: your daily newspaper, television, magazines, or radio?"

	TV	Newspaper	Magazines	Radio	None and don't know
National	56%	28%	2%	9%	5%
By education					
Less than HS	70	17	*	6	8
HS graduate	59	26	2	9	4
Some college	48	35	3	8	5
College graduate	37	41	5	13	5
By household income					
Under $10,000	70	15	1	7	7
$10,000-$19,999	59	24	2	9	6
$20,000-$29,999	56	28	3	9	5
$30,000-$39,999	50	34	2	9	5
$40,000-$49,999	48	33	3	12	3
$50,000 and over	41	42	4	10	3

SOURCE: The Gallup Organization for Times Mirror Center for the People and the Press. Personal interviews with 4,244 adults, April 25-May 10, 1987.

NOTE: Totals may not add to 100% due to rounding.

* Designates less than one-half percent.

tempt a recapitulation of the vast literature on the subject of what becomes news.[42] We can, however, highlight those aspects of the news process that affect the political and media environment in which the polls operate.

Criteria of newsworthiness have been summarized colorfully by Roger Ailes, media consultant to George Bush's 1988 presidential campaign, in his "orchestra pit theory of politics." Speaking at a post-mortem on the 1988 election held by Harvard University's Institute of Politics in December 1988, Ailes asked: "If you have two guys on stage and one guy says, 'I have a solution to the Middle East problem,' and the other guy falls in the orchestra pit, who do you think is going to be on the evening news?" [43]

In gross terms, Ailes may have it right. An empirically derived sense of what is "news" is found in the study by Robert Clyde and James Buckalew of the way news editors determine which events to cover among a vast array of potential stories. A sample of television and newspaper editors was presented with sixty-four fictitious news stories. The editors were asked which stories they would use and why. The three criteria employed most frequently in making these judgments were the presence of conflict, the public's familiarity with the actors or situations portrayed, and the timeliness of the story. [44]

Critics and students of the media see such research as confirming the tendency of the media to substitute the trivial for the significant in political coverage. Doris Graber notes that "the overriding consideration in choosing issues, as in other political coverage, is newsworthiness rather than intrinsic importance. . . . Even when ample time is available to explore serious issues in depth, as happens when presidential nominating conventions are covered in full, the emphasis is on brief, rapidly paced, fresh-breaking events." [45]

For their part, candidates often do little to dispel such a formulation. Ed Rollins, who had directed the campaign of Jack Kemp, candidly admitted: "In America we don't stand out there and have great debates on great issues. And every time you start talking about issues, you lose some of the 18 points that swing back and forth. It's unfortunate, but that's the reality of the game." [46] Even an idealistic Democrat, presidential candidate Jimmy Carter, when asked by newspaper editors early in the 1976 campaign why he had not prepared white papers and made specific proposals on key issues, was quoted as saying the only presidents who had done so were "Presidents Dewey, Humphrey, and McGovern." [47]

A sprawling diversity of visual images is used in television news to convey the gist of an event or issue being covered. Gladys Engel Lang and Kurt Lang describe this as a process that enriches the viewer's perspective by opening new vistas while simultaneously impoverishing that perspective by leaving out so much. The impression imparted is, to a large extent, a one-way process:

> Information flows from the professional producers of content to audiences, most of whom can do little more than accept or ignore

Issues in Presidential Campaigns: A Colloquy

Roger Ailes: One thing you don't want to do is get your head up too far on some new vision for America because the next thing that happens is the media runs over to the [other] side and says, "Tell me why you think this is an idiotic idea."

Judy Woodruff: So you're saying the notion of the candidate saying, "I want to run for President because I want to do something for this country," is crazy.

Ailes: Suicide!

SOURCE: Remarks made at conference of campaign managers held by the Institute of Politics at Harvard University, December 2-4, 1988. See *Campaign for President: The Managers Look at '88,* ed. David R. Runkel (Dover, Mass.: Auburn House, 1989), 136.

what is transmitted. Not only do these professional mass communicators talk far more to their audience than they listen but they also listen more to one another than they do to their audience.[48]

This consensual quality of news judgment has been noted by Bernard Roshco, who brings both the journalist's and the sociologist's perspective to the study of news. Roshco stresses that judgments about newsworthiness derive from professional values built into the incentive structure of news organizations and transmitted to cub reporters early in their careers. Obviously, differences of view about the importance of a story occur daily, but these "are thrashed out within a largely shared frame of reference, acquired by common exposure to prevailing norms."[49]

This aspect of the psychology of news judgment plays to the best and the worst in the relationship between journalism and polling. When they do their job well, the polls help news organizations second-guess the terms of reference to which Roshco refers. On such occasions the reporting of opinion data truly informs us about the breadth and depth of trends crisscrossing society.

Yet at the same time polls can reinforce the worst consensual tendencies of news organizations: the preoccupation with the horse-race aspect of elections, simplistic characterizations of the public's view on a complex issue, or specious implications of volatility among the electorate. Ben Bagdikian observes that polls, having the aura of objectivity and being attributable to an independent source, often relieve reporters of the burden of forming their own judgments on the implications of a story.[50]

The best and worst of the symbiosis of polling and journalism are also highlighted by the immediacy of television as a medium of communication. The "as it happens" quality of television has reinforced the presumption among news organizations and political operatives that the attention span of the American public is contracting. The assumption was an explicit part of the strategy of the Bush campaign in 1988.[51] On network television the average sound bite shortens with each election cycle, and is now down to just under ten seconds.[52] Whereas many correspondents' reports on television evening newscasts frequently exceeded two minutes in length a decade ago, today they seldom extend to a full two minutes.[53] Few types of news stories are as amenable as polls to telegraphic reporting without seeming to lose their authenticity or authority.

The Process Becomes News

In today's political campaigns, especially for the presidency, the competition is as much between the media and the candidates as among the candidates themselves. Each has assets that meet the needs of the other: candidates need exposure that only the media can provide, the media need inside information that only sources in the campaigns have, and each strives to control the conditions under which the candidates are presented to the electorate. Although adversarial, the relationship is one of mutual dependence.

In the battle between news organizations and campaigns for control of the political agenda, the reciprocal vulnerabilities of the two institutions become apparent. The news media are vulnerable to manipulation by the campaigns. The campaigns are vulnerable to control by the media. Being second-guessed, judged peremptorily, or given short shrift by a television reporter can threaten a candidate's lifeline to the public.

Attempts by campaigns to manage news, not new to the politics of the 1980s, have become a high-stakes political game.[54] The frustration of a competent political reporter facing a staged news event comes through in Ken Bode's recollection of a day late in September 1988:

> We were in Ohio at a county courthouse, a beautiful little county courthouse with local cheerleaders and high school band about 7:30 in the morning and the rally began. These poor people hadn't even had time for coffee. And [vice-presidential candidate] Dan Quayle treated them to the most detailed and vivid rendition of Willie Horton's adventures on his furlough that I have ever heard. When it was over with, he said virtually nothing else.
>
> Unfortunately we had nothing else to use for the *NBC Nightly News* that night than Quayle talking about crime. It turned out that it matched very nicely with what George Bush was doing that day. He was in New York City receiving the badge of a policeman slain in a drug incident. He was pictured against a sea of blue uniforms in the background as the slain officer's father presented Bush with his son's gold badge. They got what they wanted: a crime story that would play for a full day.[55]

Yet the media need to be where the news might be. And the appetite of television for compelling pictures seems insatiable. The structure of the relationship between news organizations and campaigns for high office thus makes it difficult for reporters not to cover a candidate's doings, no matter how contrived.

The candidates are also vulnerable: news coverage of their doings may no longer be just a matter of what was said, where, and when. Reporters increasingly ask why an event was staged or why an issue was framed as it was. In the last week of the 1988 campaign, for example, more than two-thirds of the political stories in the *New York Times* dealt principally with the strategies of the Bush and Dukakis campaigns rather than with substantive issues or policy differences between the candidates.[56] Thus the campaign process itself has become news.

News organizations have been taken to task for not being more aggressive in second-guessing the tactics employed in the 1988 election campaign, and particularly for failing to check the veracity of claims made in negative television advertisements.[57] However, news organizations face the dilemma of evaluating the information they report without appearing judgmental. Meanwhile, the media consultants will push as hard as they can. Larry McCarthy, who works for Republican candidates, is frank:

The media are really trapped whatever they do. If they become more judgmental in terms of the accuracy of the TV spots, they'll get hammered by the campaigns for no longer being neutral observers. If the media sit back and let the candidates take great liberties regarding the accuracy of what they say in their commercials, ad-makers like me will go as far as we can. We want to win. I am going to make an ad which I think will have the most impact. Just like any lawyer, I want to present my side of the facts as vigorously as I can.[58]

McCarthy's credibility on this score was established by his hard-hitting television commercial about Willie Horton, a black man who raped a Maryland woman while he was on furlough from a Massachusetts prison. While its ostensible purpose was to portray Dukakis as soft on crime, inclusion of a picture of Horton sent nonverbal messages on other issues.

While media consultants will fight hard for their candidates, McCarthy does note that media scrutiny of television advertisements can be quite chastening. "Media attention to the minutiae of an ad and a willingness to cry foul are strong checks against ads that play loose with the facts."

David Broder has noted that the incentives for journalists and the needs of the public are increasingly out of sync toward the end of a campaign. While repetition of its message is the essence of any electoral campaign, the reporter's instinct is to search out what is new. Thus, in the final days of a campaign, many voters may be focusing seriously on the election for the first time. They need basic information about the candidates, the same information that has become old hat to the reporters who have been living with it for months.[59]

Behind the competition between the media and the campaigns lie shared motivations. The media, especially television, and the campaigns are basically doing the same thing: trying to capture the imagination and loyalty of as much of the American public as possible. Just as the candidates joust for advantage with the electorate, the television networks seek a competitive edge to lure and hold the attention of viewers.

The polls have become a hard currency in American politics. It is to the polls that news organizations and the campaigns turn for a sense of what is going on in the minds of "real voters." Much of the thrust and parry between campaigns and the news media takes place in terms of what the latest polls show. What is not well understood are the implications. It is to those we turn in the next chapter.

Notes

1. Jean M. Converse, *Survey Research in the United States: Roots and Emergence 1890-1960* (Berkeley: University of California Press, 1987), 121-122.
2. Archibald M. Crossley, "Straw Polls in 1936," *Public Opinion Quarterly* 1 (1937): 38; cited in Converse, *Survey Research in the United States,* 122.
3. Archibald M. Crossley, Presidential Address, American Association for Public Opinion Research, 1953; cited in W. Phillips Davison, "In Memoriam: Archibald Maddock Crossley, 1896-1985," *Public Opinion Quarterly* 49 (Fall 1985): 396-397.
4. The project resulted in a book: *Resolving Nationality Conflicts,* ed. W. Phillips Davison (New York: Praeger, 1980).
5. George H. Gallup and Saul Rae, *The Pulse of Democracy* (New York: Simon and Schuster, 1940).
6. George Gallup, Jr., interview with the author, Princeton, N.J., July 31, 1989.
7. Converse, *Survey Research in the United States,* 123.
8. See George H. Gallup, "Preserving Majority Rule," in *Polling on the Issues,* ed. Albert H. Cantril (Cabin John, Md.: Seven Locks Press, 1980), 172-173.
9. Ibid., 170.
10. As recounted by Don Cahalan, NORC founding director. Harry Field's concern about the vitality of democratic institutions was brought into focus by the German attacks on Great Britain in 1941 and was a significant element of the motivation to establish the National Opinion Research Center at the University of Denver. (It was later moved to the University of Chicago.) Don Cahalan, "Origins: The Central City Conference," in *The History of the American Association for Public Opinion Research,* ed. Paul B. Sheatsley, unpublished.
11. The earliest academic-commercial collaboration was between the Office of Public Opinion Research, established by Hadley Cantril at Princeton University, and the Gallup Poll in regular soundings of the American public's perception of the growing threat of war in Europe. See Hadley Cantril, *The Human Dimension: Experiences in Policy Research* (New Brunswick, N.J.: Rutgers University Press, 1967), chaps. 4, 6-8.
12. Elmo Roper in an interview with Robert O. Carlson on August 14, 1968, as part of the AAPOR archive at the University of Chicago; cited in Converse, *Survey Research in the United States,* 113.
13. Henry C. Link of the Psychological Corporation lamented in 1948 that "surveys like the Barometer [a national survey of consumer buying habits developed by the Psychological Corporation in 1932], the Gallup, Crossley,

Roper and other polls are not more widely recognized as the peculiar instruments of psychological research." See Link, "The Ninety-Fourth Issue of the Psychological Barometer and a Note on its Fifteenth Anniversary," *Journal of Applied Psychology* 32 (1942): 106; cited in Converse, *Survey Research in the United States,* 111; and Link, "Some Milestones in Public Opinion Research," *International Journal of Opinion and Attitude Research* 1 (March 1947): 36-46.

14. Cahalan, "Origins: The Central City Conference."
15. Cantril, *The Human Dimension,* 23. Cantril's frustration with his academic peers was evident three decades earlier. Prodding social scientists to get out into the "real world," he wrote in 1934:

> Instead of selecting full-bodied problems from everyday life and attempting to create new techniques or to adjust existing ones which would elucidate the problems with the least amount of distortion, investigators have tended to reverse the order and have adapted their problems to fit standardized laboratory methods. The choice lies between thorough studies on authentic problems, conducted with the best techniques that can be devised, and controlled laboratory experiments on problems which have no relation to life itself.

   Hadley Cantril, "The Social Psychology of Everyday Life," *Psychological Bulletin* (May 1934): 298.
16. From remarks by Woodward at the 1946 conference in Central City, Colorado. A comprehensive account of this period is found in Paul B. Sheatsley, "The Founding of AAPOR," in *The History of the American Association for Public Opinion Research,* ed. Sheatsley.
17. Ibid.
18. For an account of this period, see Nelson W. Polsby, *Consequences of Party Reform* (New York: Oxford University Press, 1983), 9-52, esp. 33.
19. Ibid., 72.
20. Martin P. Wattenberg, *The Decline of American Political Parties: 1952-1980* (Cambridge, Mass.: Harvard University Press, 1984), 93-94.
21. For a discussion of this point, see Doris A. Graber, *Mass Media and American Politics,* 3d ed. (Washington, D.C.: CQ Press, 1989), 197.
22. Polsby, *Consequences of Party Reform,* 73.
23. For an elaboration of this point, see Larry J. Sabato, "Where Party Works at the Local Level," Stephen E. Frantzick, "The Rise of the Service-Vendor Party," and Paul S. Herrnson, "Prospects for the Parties," in *Media Technology and the Vote: A Source Book,* ed. Joel L. Swerdlow (Washington, D.C.: The Annenberg Washington Program, 1988), 164-176.
24. For an excellent description of these services and the rejuvenation of the national parties, see Larry J. Sabato, *The Party's Just Begun: Shaping*

Political Parties for America's Future (Glenview, Ill.: Scott, Foresman, 1988), 77-81.

25. See *Title 11—Federal Elections,* 2 *U.S.C.* 106.4. A discussion of these provisions is also found in Sabato, *The Party's Just Begun,* 78; and Paul S. Herrnson, *Party Campaigning in the 1980s* (Cambridge, Mass.: Harvard University Press, 1988), 78-79.

26. See Herrnson, *Party Campaigning in the 1980s,* 84-119.

27. Mark P. Petracca, "Political Consultants and Democratic Governance," *PS: Political Science and Politics* 22 (March 1989): 12.

28. See Walter De Vries, "American Campaign Consulting: Trends and Concerns," *PS: Political Science and Politics* 22 (March 1989): 21.

29. Petracca found that 44 percent of the consultants surveyed reported that "when it comes to setting issue priorities, candidates are neither very involved nor very influential." Marginal involvement by the candidates rose to 60 percent regarding "the day-to-day tactical operation of the campaign." Petracca, "Political Consultants and Democratic Governance," 13.

30. See Arthur H. Miller, Grace L. Simmons, and Anne Hildreth, "Group Influence, Solidarity and Electoral Outcomes" (Paper delivered at the annual meeting of the American Political Science Association, Washington, D.C., August 27-30, 1986).

31. Of 2,721 special interests with their own offices in Washington, D.C. in 1980, Schlozman and Tierney found that "seventy-six percent of the citizens' groups, 56 percent of the civil rights groups, and 79 percent of the social welfare and poor people's organizations" had been established since 1960. The comparable figure for trade associations was 38 percent and for corporations, 14 percent. See Kay Lehman Schlozman and John T. Tierney, *Organized Interests and American Democracy* (New York: Harper and Row, 1986), 75.

32. Schlozman and Tierney conducted their "Washington Representative Survey" in 1981. Of 200 organizations sampled, 36 percent had some access to a pollster, either on staff or through a contractual relationship. Forty percent of trade unions responding in the survey indicated access to a pollster compared to 38 percent of citizens groups, 31 percent of corporations, and 30 percent of trade associations. Twelve percent of all organizations indicated having a pollster on staff with the percentages being higher for trade unions (16 percent) and corporations (11 percent) than for citizen groups (8 percent) or trade associations (3 percent). Ibid., 101.

33. These data are corroborated by findings of the Gallup Organization for Times Mirror in September 1987: 56 percent of a national sample indicated they relied most on television for "information on national affairs," 28 percent relied most on the daily newspaper, 9 percent on radio, and 2 percent on magazines. The Gallup/Times Mirror study also found 71

percent of respondents indicating that they regularly watch one of the network evening news programs.

34. This concept of perception was developed by Hadley Cantril in *The "Why" of Man's Experience* (New York: Macmillan, 1950). See also F. P. Kilpatrick, *Explorations in Transactional Psychology* (New York: New York University Press, 1961); and *Psychology, Humanism and Scientific Inquiry: The Selected Essays of Hadley Cantril,* ed. Albert H. Cantril (New Brunswick, N.J.: Transaction Books, 1989), esp. chaps. 3 and 13.

35. Tony Schwartz, *The Responsive Chord* (Garden City: Anchor Press, 1974), 25; quoted in Graber, *Mass Media and American Politics,* 174.

36. It is far from clear, however, how real the distinction is between what one might call the "synthetic participation" of viewers accumulating images and impressions solely from television and direct involvement with the outside world. On the one hand, it might be hypothesized that impressions from television would not be cumulative unless they touched in some plausible fashion on things people have experienced first-hand. On the other hand, it might be argued that ceaseless exposure to situations far outside personal experience is sufficient to create in viewers a sense of vivid reality.

37. This general point has been made by Michael Robinson in "American Political Legitimacy in an Era of Electronic Journalism: Reflections on the Evening News," in *Television as a Social Force: New Approaches to TV Criticism,* ed. Douglass Cater and Richard Alter (New York: Praeger, 1975), 110-119. Its implications have been discussed in Austin Ranney, *Channels of Power: The Impact of Television on American Politics* (New York: Basic Books, 1983), 11.

38. Doris Graber followed a panel of 200 individuals from all walks of life through the 1976 election cycle to assess their ways of coping with the information onslaught. Her sanguine conclusions of the sample's general ability to cope are reported in her book, *Processing the News: How People Tame the Information Tide* (New York: Longman, 1984), chap. 10, esp. 201-205.

39. W. Russell Neuman, *The Paradox of Mass Politics: Knowledge and Opinion in the American Electorate* (Cambridge, Mass.: Harvard University Press, 1986), esp. chap. 6.

40. Ibid., 147-148.

41. Ibid., 171.

42. See Herbert J. Gans, *Deciding What's News* (New York: Pantheon Books, 1979); Bernard Roshco, *Newsmaking* (Chicago: University of Chicago Press, 1975); W. Lance Bennett, *News: The Politics of Illusion* (New York: Longman, 1988); Michael Parenti, *Inventing Reality: The Politics of the Mass Media* (New York: St. Martin's, 1986); and Shanto Iyengar and Donald Kinder, *News That Matters: Television and American Public*

Opinion (Chicago: University of Chicago Press, 1987).

43. Ailes made these remarks at the quadrennial conference of presidential campaign managers held by the Institute of Politics at Harvard University, December 2-4, 1988. See *Campaign for President: The Managers Look at '88*, ed. David R. Runkel (Dover, Mass.: Auburn House Publishing Co., 1989), 136.

44. Robert W. Clyde and James K. Buckalew, "Inter-Media Standardization: A Q-Analysis of News Editors," *Journalism Quarterly* 46 (Summer 1969): 349-351; cited in Graber, *Mass Media and American Politics*, 84-86.

45. Graber, *Mass Media and American Politics*, 215.

46. *Campaign for President*, ed. Runkel, 217.

47. The April interview with Governor Carter is recounted by Robert Chandler, then vice president for administration of CBS News, in "TV and the 1976 Election: A Dialogue," *Wilson Quarterly* (Spring 1977): 85-86.

48. Gladys Engel Lang and Kurt Lang, *Politics and Television Reviewed* (Beverly Hills, Calif.: Sage, 1984), 201.

49. Roshco, *Newsmaking*, chap. 7, esp. 105-106.

50. Ben Bagdikian, former managing editor of the *Washington Post*, is now professor emeritus of journalism at the University of California at Berkeley. This point was made during an interview with the author, Berkeley, February 9, 1990.

51. Lee Atwater, architect and manager of the Bush campaign, has noted that the campaign planned its strategy around the assumption that "there would be a very short attention span not only in the primaries but in the general election." See *Campaign for President*, ed. Runkel, 34.

52. Kiku Adatto has examined the duration of "sound bites" (uninterrupted speech) from the candidates aired in TV newscasts. Whereas sound bites were an average of 42.3 seconds in 1968, they were only 9.8 seconds in 1988. Kiku Adatto, "The Incredible Shrinking Sound Bite," *New Republic*, May 28, 1990, 20.

53. Roger Mudd, then of NBC News, made this observation in *Television and the Presidential Campaigns*, ed. Martin Linsky (Lexington, Mass.: Lexington Books, 1983), 83.

54. Jack Germond and Jules Witcover date "issue-a-day" news management to the Nixon White House; see their *Whose Broad Stripes and White Stars: The Trivial Pursuit of the Presidency 1988* (New York: Warner Books, 1989), 55.

55. Ken Bode, interview by telephone with the author, September 8, 1989. In the course of the interview, Bode also expressed his irritation at the Dukakis campaign's daily effort to tell NBC what the angle should be on the day's anticipated events. Sam Donaldson has similar recollections of 1984 when he criticized ABC for going too often with what it was fed by

the White House rather than doing "wider pieces" that would put the candidates in the context of issues such as the federal deficit. See Martin Schram, *The Great American Video Game: Presidential Politics in the Television Age* (New York: William Morrow, 1987), 305.

56. Marjorie Randon Hershey did a content analysis of two dailies, the *New York Times* and the *Indianapolis Star*. In both cases, strategy and tactics dominated news coverage in the last weeks of the campaign. Seventy-one percent of stories in the *New York Times* and 66 percent of those in the *Indianapolis Star* dealt primarily with campaign strategy, which Hershey defined as pertaining to "the choice of locations for campaign stops, style and atmosphere of the campaign, staff activities, relative standings of the candidates, fund-raising activities, endorsements, efforts to attract support of groups, political benefits and costs." See her "The Campaign and the Media," in *The Election of 1988: Reports and Interpretations,* ed. Gerald M. Pomper (Chatham, N.J.: Chatham House, 1989), 97.

57. R. W. Apple, Jr., was one of the first to call attention to the failure of news organizations and political analysts to point out that the Massachusetts furlough program, the issue dramatized by the Willie Horton commercial, was originally a Republican idea. ("Will the Networks Succeed in Getting the Candidates to Talk Substance in 1992?" the *New York Times,* May 10, 1989.) And, a week after the election, *Newsweek* magazine's cover story headlined "How the Media Blew It."

58. Larry McCarthy, interview with the author, Washington, D.C., July 28, 1989.

59. See David S. Broder, *Behind the Front Page: A Candid Look at How the News Is Made* (New York: Simon and Schuster, 1987), 262-263.

c h a p t e r   t w o

Polls, Politics, and the Press: Reciprocal Effects

> If in dealing with events we concentrate on what and
> how, and ignore the why, then we are not really
> searching for anything.
>
> *Edward R. Murrow, May 5, 1957*

No election has so clearly demonstrated the mutual dependence of polls and press as did the presidential campaign of 1988. Although this relationship has been the subject of countless articles and discussions, its dimensions became a more explicit and persistent part of the drama of the campaign in 1988 than ever before.

It is instructive, therefore, to look back at 1988. The task is complicated because much of the dynamic of the campaign resulted from a structure and schedule for the nominating process that was defined not by the press or the pollsters but by the political parties. Cause is thus not easy to separate from effect.

There is much in the relationship between polling and journalism that benefits both enterprises. But polling and journalism also play to one another's vulnerabilities. This chapter explores these reciprocal influences by asking: (1) What effect do polls have on the reporting of politics by news organizations and, to the extent the effect can be identified, how is the public affected? (2) How do journalistic criteria of what is newsworthy influence the way polls are conducted and reported? (3) What steps can be taken to ensure a better working relationship between polling and the news organizations that sponsor and report polls?

The Ubiquity of the Polls

"This was the Year of the Poll," declared Stephen Isaacs in a 1973 article entitled "Were Polls Overemphasized?" Four years later Philip Meyer wrote that "the proliferation of polls created a new competitive atmosphere" for the 1976 electoral contests. And in 1980 E. J. Dionne, Jr., then of the *New York Times,* asked: "How many times do you have to count something to know if you've counted enough? Judging from the proliferation of polls of public opinion, there appears no limit on the number of times attitudes can be numbered, sorted and analyzed." [1]

But it was 1988 in which the polls seemed truly ubiquitous. Unfortunately the impression of heightened polling activity cannot be documented definitively. Records of the number of polls and polling organizations have been ad hoc and provide no reliable information on trends in polling. Research showed a blossoming of polling activity in the 1970s, but records have not been kept systematically since then. [2]

Most of the major public pollsters report conducting no more polls in 1988 than in 1984. [3] But the major news organizations form only part of the picture. At least three initiatives in 1988 added polling numbers from new sources:

- The Gallup Organization greatly expanded its activities by conducting preprimary and general election polls for CONUS, an association of local television stations. The outreach of reports from these polls was immense, as 24 television stations and 110 newspaper outlets released polls that were "exclusive" in their local markets. This syndication arrangement gave the local stations more polls for the same amount of money spent in earlier elections. [4]
- Regional polls, such as those conducted by the Roper Organization for the *Atlanta Constitution-Journal,* by Scripps-Howard, and by the *Miami Herald,* were more visible in the early months.
- From Labor Day until the election, KRC Communications, Inc., in tandem with the American Political Network, released daily poll results tracking the presidential race. The results were based on a rolling average of the last three days' interviews.

The impression that an avalanche of poll information descended on the political process in 1988 stems not only from the level of activity among pollsters but also from the frequency with which polls were picked up by the media and the prominence they were given. Polls have been receiving higher billing in network newscasts during successive presidential elections: whereas only 8 percent of the poll stories broadcast in 1972 led evening newscasts, more than a third were at the top of the program in 1984.[5]

The year 1988 also saw a mushrooming of multiple reports of the same poll. We have already noted how a single Gallup study for CONUS would be offered as an exclusive story by many local television stations covering different markets. However, it was the arrival on the scene of *Hotline* that swamped the news with reports of polls. Billed as "the daily briefing on American politics," *Hotline* was available by midmorning Monday through Friday. Subscribers would access a data base by computer and print their own copy of the 15-25 page report containing abstracts of political stories carried in newspapers nationwide and on the prior evening's network news programs, interviews with campaign insiders, and highlights of key Senate races.

Hotline also featured a "poll update" and a "50-state report." The former summarized key findings from national polls released within the preceding 24 hours; the latter highlighted state and local polls coming to the attention of *Hotline's* stringers. *Hotline* urged pollsters to fax their latest results for inclusion in the next day's issue.

The impact of *Hotline* on political reporting in 1988 is difficult to underestimate. Because no news organization, not even the television networks, could cover all the bases in the early stages of the campaign, *Hotline* became a big asset in keeping far-flung correspondents abreast of what the candidates were doing. In the words of one television producer:

> It is a great time-saver. I became totally dependent upon it. It saved us hours and hours we used to spend going through the news clips we could get, which were late and voluminous. You had to read *Hotline* because it told you things you couldn't learn otherwise.

Or, as a political consultant put it: "You knew for sure that virtually every person you would talk to in that day was taking their points, their information for the day, largely from *Hotline*."

Douglas Bailey, one of the founders of *Hotline,* reports that the service had 120 regular subscribers during the 1988 campaign. However, this number understates the outreach: one television network, counted as a single subscriber, would circulate more than 100 copies internally.[6] Additionally, the campaigns, consultants, academics and those who follow politics closely received copies. Extrapolating from conservative estimates of circulation within subscribing organizations, it is not unreasonable to estimate that at least 2,500 copies of *Hotline* had been read by noon on each day of the campaign.

Why should a single medium such as *Hotline* make such a difference in the way polls were reported? Interviews with news editors and reporters suggest at least five reasons:

- State and local polls that otherwise would not have received national media exposure were picked up by major news outlets and their correspondents.
- The news value of many polls was lost in earlier years because they did not come to the attention of reporters on a timely basis. *Hotline* changed that with its twenty-four-hour news cycle. The polls reported were always fresh. They had news value, whether or not they were reliable or contained insights into the campaign that were new or significant.
- CBS and the *New York Times* enjoyed a competitive advantage in earlier election years because of the national outreach of the *New York Times*. By comparison, the *Washington Post* and the *Los Angeles Times* are not "national" papers. The *Wall Street Journal*, while a national paper, was not active in a joint polling venture prior to 1988. With *Hotline* all of the print-broadcast polling teams became visible: CBS News/*New York Times*, ABC News/*Washington Post*, NBC News/*Wall Street Journal*, CNN/*USA Today*. So, too, did the *Los Angeles Times* and its polls.
- In politics, current information is essential for survival. Thus it was understandable that *Hotline* caught on quickly in the political community. However, it came at a cost: dependence on a single source of information nurtured shared terms of reference as to what was going on. Thus the "pack journalism" of 1988 arose not so much from reporters comparing notes on the campaign bus as from easy access to the "electronic bus" that became a single, common source of reporters' cues for the day.[7] Use of the common source added momentum to whatever consensus was emerging about the race. As Ken Bode, former political correspondent for NBC News, put it: "At the end with the daily fifty-state report and tracking numbers, there was an aura of

hopelessness to the Dukakis campaign and an atmosphere of inevitability to the outcome. What reporter was going to look so foolish as to give the sense that the election was anything but over?" [8]

- Polls were reported by *Hotline* as they were published in local newspapers across the country. Major elements of the stories were taken just as they appeared locally; *no* attempt was made to verify the accuracy of the newspaper accounts. When information on sample sizes, populations, and sampling error was available, *Hotline* would reprint it. In general, however, the reader was left to assess the quality of the poll. Sophisticated poll consumers usually found that too little information was presented to enable them to assess the reliability of the polls reported. To other poll consumers, all of the polls appeared equal. In this sense, *Hotline* became the great poll leveler, giving equal attention and standing to all polls it reported. The problem was compounded when, toward the end of the campaign, *Hotline* maintained tallies of the probable electoral vote count by relying heavily on the latest polling numbers, regardless of their reliability.

The last point deserves some elaboration. As we will discuss in Chapter 3, there are many reasons all polls are not equal. Samples vary greatly in quality depending on the degree of attention paid to the probabilities with which people become eligible for inclusion in a poll and the amount of effort interviewers make to contact them. But, even assuming no differences in ways questions are framed, polling cannot be likened to a financial accounting that will yield a bottom line on which auditors will agree.

Opinion research is inexact in two senses. First, public opinion is multifaceted and dynamic. People hold opinions with varying levels of intensity, base those opinions on varying amounts of information, and are affected in varying degrees by sentiments that are in conflict with each other. Second, like the empirically based natural and social sciences, polling is a process of estimation. It relies on samples to estimate the probable characteristics of the entire population.

Of Variability, Volatility, and Validity

The consequences of the proliferation in the number of reported polls are twofold. First, differences among contemporaneous polls show up more often. Second, apparent shifts in public opinion are detected at shorter intervals of time.

Both consequences have the effect of keeping polls in the news and often leave the erroneous impression that the views of the electorate are inherently unstable. When contemporaneous polls differ, the news story tends to be that the polls have differed, rather than why they have differed. When polls fluctuate, reporters and analysts tend to choose "volatility" as the explanation, claiming that voters are given to unexpected swings in their preferences among the candidates.

Polls taken prior to a major election may vary for many reasons. To determine the factors that might explain poll differences one must take into account the phase of the campaign in which the polls have been conducted. For this reason, we will examine the 1988 election cycle and attempt to identify the sources of differences in the polls as the campaign progressed.

Before the Primary Phase

Measures of the standing of candidates in the Democratic and Republican fields began to appear in January 1987. As a sign of how unformed opinions were at this stage, four of every five persons registered to vote and considered likely voters either had no preference among contenders for their party's nomination or expressed a preference with the proviso that it was "still too early to say for sure." This finding of the CBS News/*New York Times* poll obtained among both Democrats and Republicans.[9]

During 1987, the candidates were formally declaring for their party's nomination, positioning themselves in the early battlefields of Iowa and New Hampshire, raising money, building an organization, and receiving increased attention from the media. But from the public's standpoint, the political temperatures had not risen much. Likely Democratic and Republican voters remained overwhelmingly uncommitted to a candidate. The proportions observed in the January 1987 CBS News/*New York Times* poll held relatively steady. Even a year later, in January 1988, 79 percent of likely Democratic voters and 71 percent of likely Republican voters were either undecided or expressed only a tentative preference.

Polls reporting the standing of candidates can appear erratic in this kind of setting because polling organizations often use different approaches to measure public preferences. And because most people are only beginning to form their impressions of the candidates at this early stage, slight differences in polling methodology can have a sizeable effect on results. The point is made well by Andrew Kohut, president of the Gallup Organization during the 1988 election: "Small differences in methodology would not make a big difference if you are measuring a stable property, but they can when you are trying to measure an unstable property." [10]

Concurrent polls will produce different results if they have not used the same base in computing percentages of candidate support. For example, two polls in March 1987 had widely disparate measures of strength for George Bush among the Republican candidates. ABC/*Washington Post* reported that he had the support of 47 percent of those polled; NBC/*Wall Street Journal* reported only 28 percent support. The polls were conducted less than a week apart. No important intervening event could account for the difference. Instead the difference was explained in part by the fact that ABC/*Washington Post* reported the views of self-described Republicans and independents who "leaned" Republican. No effort was made to determine how likely these registered voters were to vote in their states' primary or caucus. In contrast, NBC/*Wall Street Journal* attempted to screen out of the sample respondents not likely to cast a primary or caucus ballot. The net effect was that the better-known Bush name was more likely to be volunteered by the less politically involved respondents who were included in the ABC/*Washington Post* sample but excluded from the NBC/*Wall Street Journal* sample.

Inclusion or exclusion of high-profile names on lists of candidates presented to respondents can affect poll results in another way. For example, the CBS News/*New York Times* poll presented two lists of candidates to registered Democrats in mid-May 1987. The first list included only announced candidates. The second list included the names of prominent individuals about whom there was speculation but who had not indicated an intention of running: Gov. Mario Cuomo (N.Y.), Sen. Bill Bradley (N.J.), and Sen. Sam Nunn (Ga.). As can be seen in Table 2-1, the percentages for Jesse Jackson and Michael Dukakis were particularly affected: each was five percentage points "stronger" without the inclusion of Cuomo, Bradley, or Nunn.

Another example shows how poll numbers can lead to a misreading of what is at work in the public mind. When former senator Gary Hart (D-Colo.) dropped out of the race in May 1987, Governor Dukakis appeared to be the major beneficiary as the percentage of those supporting him doubled. But when the better-known Hart reentered the race

TABLE 2-1   Preference for Democratic Nomination

	List A	List B
Cuomo	—	25%
Jackson	17%	12
Bradley	—	6
Dukakis	11	6
Simon	6	5
Nunn	—	4
Gore	5	4
Gephardt	4	3
Babbitt	2	3
Clinton	2	2
Biden	2	1

SOURCE: CBS News/*New York Times* poll; 453 telephone interviews (May 11-14, 1987) with Democrats intending to vote in a primary or caucus.

seven months later, he immediately took the lead in all major polls.

The December results could *not* be interpreted as confirming Hart's underlying strength with the electorate. The percentages reported for Hart in the December polls were *reliable* in the sense that all polls picked up about the same degree of impact of his reentry on the standing of the Democratic candidates. However, the conclusion that Hart was the strongest candidate, based on the poll reports of the candidate standing question, was not *valid*. Gary Langer of the Associated Press quite correctly noted at the time that the story was not that Hart had topped the charts, but that he faced the daunting challenge of gaining the confidence of the almost half of all Democrats who held him in very low regard.[11]

Not all pollsters believe that the public is well served by these early soundings. They argue that the public can be misled into thinking that the polls are measuring the actual strength of the candidates rather than name recognition, dislike for another candidate in the race, or the impact of recent events.[12] We will return to this question in Chapter 3 in connection with our consideration of how public opinion crystallizes.

Primary Season

From the pollster's standpoint the political environment prior to a primary or caucus presents the most difficult set of circumstances in which to measure public opinion. By definition an election among candidates within a political party eliminates the stabilizing effect partisanship tends to exert in a general election. In a presidential race, the battle in the general election is over only about one-fifth of the electorate, the remaining four-fifths being reasonably committed to the candidate of their party. In primaries and caucuses, however, it is open season.[13]

Even more telling is the repeated finding that a notable portion of the electorate remains undecided until the closing days of a presidential primary. Even with the flurry of the primary campaigns to which voters have been exposed, one-quarter to one-third of the primary voters indicate that they decide on a candidate *in the three days* before the primary.

In the 1988 New Hampshire primary, for example, 39 percent of Democratic voters interviewed by CBS News as they left polling places indicated that they had made up their minds over the weekend. For Republican primary voters, a comparable 34 percent reported deciding three days before voting. In the South Dakota primary a week later, the percentage of voters deciding in the last three days was 36 among Democrats and 25 among Republicans. Although the proportion of Republicans waiting to decide until the end declined to a relatively steady 20 percent thereafter, preprimary uncertainty among the Democrats persisted until early April, by which time the battle lines had been drawn and candidates were reasonably well known. (Data on time of voter decision in forty-one primaries appear in Appendix A, Table A-1.)

The late-deciding segment of the electorate is very impressionable and is especially attuned to developments in the campaign that might help them size up the candidates. Again, taking the CBS exit poll of New Hampshire primary voters, it can be seen that Rep. Richard Gephardt's (D-Mo.) win in Iowa was a significant factor in his second-place showing in the Granite State: 76 percent of the people who voted for him in New Hampshire came to a decision *after* Iowa. Sixty-two percent of Paul Simon's support in New Hampshire also came to him after his second-place finish in the Iowa caucuses.

Polling up to the last minute usually picks up these late decisions, provided first that the poll has accurately assessed which respondents contacted in the course of its interviewing are truly likely to cast a ballot, and second that the poll has measured the intensity of commitment to a candidate.

Problems pollsters encountered in the 1988 New Hampshire Republican primary offer a dramatic illustration of the need to interview up to the very end of a campaign and to look closely at strength of support.

Two days before the 1988 New Hampshire primary, the *Washington Post* led a story with the following observation: "Senator Robert J. Dole, R-Kan., is at one of those rare personal moments in politics when every instinct of a veteran campaigner tells him that he is going to win. . . . Dole's instincts are supported by public opinion polls." [14] The day of the primary the *Post* ran another story quoting Dole's campaign manager as saying of Bush's apparent decline, "to have the campaign fall out from under you like that says something devastating." [15] Dole's pollster, Richard Wirthlin, was even calling the senator "Mr. President." [16]

When the votes were counted, Vice President Bush had defeated Dole by more than nine points and the polls came in for scrutiny. The Gallup Poll received the most attention because its final poll before the primary was farthest off: it had overestimated Dole's expected vote by six points and underestimated Bush's strength by eleven points.

The main cause of the Gallup Poll's error was that it had stopped interviewing on Sunday afternoon, before a televised League of Women Voters debate, before Dole refused to sign former Delaware governor Pierre DuPont's pledge not to raise taxes, and before Dole quipped "get back in your cage" to a heckler he encountered the morning of the primary.[17]

Three other polls picked up the gains Bush was making over the weekend. CBS and the *New York Times* did foresee the Bush victory. The *Washington Post* reported Bush rising but did not anticipate his victory. The *Boston Globe* decided not to report the results of its poll after the percent of Republicans who said they were undecided doubled over the weekend.

Warren Mitofksy, then head of CBS News's election unit, draws the following moral from the New Hampshire experience: "You can't stop interviewing early in races that are changing. When you stop early, you are bound to have conflict among the polls. And when you have conflict, the critics will eat you alive." [18]

The harrowing uncertainties of precaucus and preprimary polling kept the Gallup Organization from getting involved for years. The *New York Times* still does not engage in preprimary polling, although its television polling partner, CBS News, does conduct periodic preprimary polls.

The Choice Emerges

Now that nominations for the presidency are primary-driven, the choice the nation will face in November usually begins to emerge well before the national party conventions. Before the conventions formalize the party nominations, media attention understandably turns to trial-heat polls that pit the prospective candidates of the two parties against each other. But there is a kind of time warp in that the attention of most voters does not shift so quickly.

Although the electorate has weathered four to five months of the preliminaries, it is not in an "if the election were being held today" frame of mind with respect to a choice between nominees of the two parties. Nonetheless, poll questions are cast in such terms even before the earliest primaries and caucuses.

Figure 2-1 displays the variation among the polls in each phase of the 1988 campaign. The measure of variation is the standard deviation of the percentages favoring each candidate.

The standard deviation of Dukakis's percentages in seven polls conducted in February and March was dramatically larger than that of Bush's percentages. It is not surprising that the percentages for Dukakis should bob up and down in early trial-heat questions because Dukakis was a virtual unknown in the early months of 1988. By April only 14 percent of Democrats and Democratic-leaning independents told Gallup Poll interviewers they knew something about him. By contrast, 89 percent of Republicans and Republican-leaning independents said they knew something about George Bush.

Dukakis began to do better against Bush in trial heats as he demonstrated strength in the primaries. As it became increasingly clear that Dukakis would be the nominee of his party, his poll standings against Bush tended to become more stable. By early June, the polls converged in measuring a 12- to 15-point margin over Bush. But what were these polls really saying? Was Dukakis really that much stronger than Bush?

As events were soon to prove, the Dukakis advantage over Bush in mid-June trial heats was short-lived. By the time delegates began to gather for the Democratic convention in mid-July, Dukakis's lead over Bush had receded to single-digit proportions; one poll even had him three points behind.[19]

The mid-June Dukakis lead over Bush turned out to be synthetic in two respects:

FIGURE 2-1 Standard Deviations of Percentages Supporting Bush and Dukakis at Specified Intervals During 1988

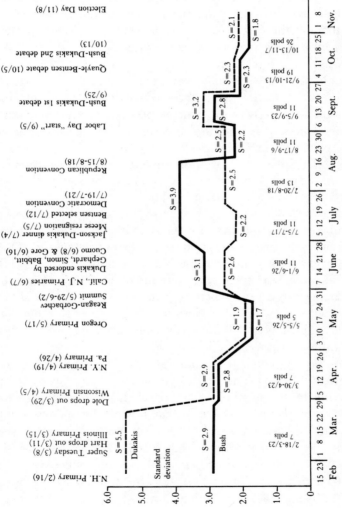

NOTE: S=Standard deviation. Excluded from these calculations are the tracking polls done by KRC between the national party conventions and from Labor Day to the election, a total of 68 sets of trial-heat numbers. This is more than half the total number of trial-heat numbers released by *all* other polls from the New Hampshire primary to election day (125). Inclusion of the KRC trial heats in the standard deviation would have washed out any significant variation evident among the other polls because its tracking polls seldom varied significantly from day to day. (For an elaboration of this point see p. 50.)

- In spite of the impressive trial-heat numbers, Dukakis was still little known to most voters. The percentage of Democrats and Democratic-leaning independents who said they knew something about him in July had only grown to 26 percent in the Gallup Poll.
- During the first week of July, a CBS News/*New York Times* poll found that less than a third of those who chose Dukakis in a trial-heat question strongly favored him. About the same proportion said they supported him primarily because they did not like Bush.[20]

What the mid-June trial heats were picking up was the general impression that Dukakis might be a viable alternative to the better-known Bush. They did *not* indicate that the roots of Dukakis's support ran deep. The temptation of journalists and politicians, however, was to seize on the margin of one candidate over another and to magnify its significance, suggesting an advantage that would carry over into the general election campaign. Ed Rollins, then of the Kemp campaign, believes that the heady poll lead induced in the Dukakis campaign a disdain for George Bush and resulted in its underestimation of his potential as an adversary.[21] It has also been suggested that the Dukakis trial-heat margin over Bush precipitated the decision of the Bush campaign to "go negative" as a strategy.[22]

The Convention Poll Roller Coaster

The weeks preceding conventions of the two major parties usually produce the least stable polling numbers, in part because a candidate usually gets a boost—or, in the political vernacular, a "bump"—in support after being nominated.[23] This is a time of peak media exposure for both candidates. However, it must be remembered that many voters remain tentative in their support for the candidates; as much as a third of each candidate's support must be considered "soft." [24]

High media visibility and tentative voter preferences form a mix that is bound to yield unstable poll results. At each party's convention politically significant events, such as the designation of the vice-presidential nominee, are reported in the media. However, the fluidity of the political situation means that differences in polling methodology again become important factors in accounting for discrepancies in the polls.

Figure 2-1 underscores the degree of fluctuation in what the polls were reporting between July 4 and mid-August 1988. What were poll consumers to make of the mixed signals the polls were sending? Two impressions became widespread, although neither was very accurate. The first was that disarray among the polls ought to cast doubt on their reliability. The second was that the electorate was increasingly volatile.

The issue of poll reliability, to be addressed in some detail in the next chapter, involves the differing approaches polling organizations take to the measurement of candidate preference. These questions include: How rigorously should likely nonvoters be screened out (eliminated) from the sample and what screening approach should be used? When can the inference be made that respondents "leaning" toward a candidate will vote for that candidate on election day? Should trial-heat questions be placed early or late in the poll questionnaire?

Before and between the conventions there are many reasons for poll findings to vary other than fundamental changes in public opinion. Even so, fluctuation in the polls is often tossed off as reflecting "volatility" among the electorate. This characterization usually sells the public short. It conveys a mercurial or fickle quality to public opinion that does not do justice to the exercise the American people are engaged in as they assimilate events and search for cues to the qualities of those who might lead the nation.

To characterize movement in trial-heat figures as a postconvention "bump" for a candidate explains little about what the electorate took away from its exposure to the convention. A trial-heat result provides insight only inferentially into the public's reaction to the convention itself.

Some dispute this view and see nothing wrong with trial-heat polls between and immediately after the conventions. Indeed, Warren Mitofsky argues that it would be a mistake not to conduct them because "we owe the public the information." [25] The problem with this argument is that the information the public receives is usually provided without much explanation or interpretation. There is a good deal of sense to Andrew Kohut's argument that trial-heat questions are inappropriate to measure the public's reaction to the conventions. As he puts it: "There is nothing improper about these polls; the measurements are not biased or inaccurate. The problem is that they are meaningless; they don't tell us much about what is really going on in public opinion." Kohut suggests that favorability ratings of the candidates before and after the conventions would be adequately sensitive to changes in public perception and would be more faithful to what is actually being measured.[26]

Pundits promulgating the volatility thesis would be well advised to sit in for an evening's work alongside the interviewing staff of a polling organization. They would learn, as pollster Burns Roper points out: "It's not volatility on the part of the voter. It's that many people don't know who they are going to vote for; all the while they are doing their level best to answer the questions we pollsters are putting to them." [27]

Instant Polls: The Debates

Twenty minutes after the second 1988 presidential debate between George Bush and Michael Dukakis, Peter Jennings broke into postdebate commentary to report the results of an ABC poll: Bush was the winner in the eyes of 49 percent, Dukakis the winner for 33 percent.

Conducting 639 interviews, analyzing the results, and broadcasting them in so short a period of time is no mean logistical feat. Reflecting on the "accomplishment," ABC News president Roone Arledge recalled the scramble to put together a quick poll after the debate between vice-presidential candidates Lloyd Bentsen and Dan Quayle: "That first night we weren't sure we were going to be able to put together that poll in half an hour. This time we were and we told our people ahead of time." [28]

But is such an "instant" poll good opinion research? Is the public well served?

It is exceedingly difficult to achieve a good sample if interviewing is confined to a few hours' time because callbacks to hard-to-reach respondents are normally impossible. In addition, quick measures are notoriously perishable. ABC's own experience after the first Bush-Dukakis debate illustrates the point. Interviews a day after the debate suggested that 20 percent of those polled thought the debate was a draw or had no opinion about it; a day later, the proportion holding this opinion had more than doubled to 43 percent.

Four years earlier, CBS News/*New York Times* showed a shift in opinion of similar magnitude within two days. A poll taken immediately following the first debate in 1984 reported that 43 percent believed Walter Mondale had won; two days later another poll had Mondale's victory percentage at 66.

The classic example of the perishability of quick postdebate polls occurred in 1976 after the second debate between President Gerald Ford and Jimmy Carter, as the public awakened to the magnitude of Ford's blunder in referring to the freedoms enjoyed by the peoples of Eastern Europe. Fifty-three percent of respondents interviewed within 12 hours of the debate claimed that President Ford had won, against just 35 percent for Governor Carter. Respondents interviewed up to three days later completely reversed the conclusion: Carter had won according to 58 percent and Ford according to 29 percent.[29]

No predictable pattern emerges from instant postevent measures. In the first of the examples presented above the percentage saying that the debate was a draw doubled; in the second example, the percentage saying that one candidate was the clear winner increased substantially. Does this mean that instant polls have no inherent validity? Pollster Peter Hart finds polling on the heels of an event dangerously misleading: "When you measure opinion at the most turbulent time you are going to get the least accurate measurements. These polls are not truly reflective of what is going on."[30] NBC News decided not to conduct quick postdebate polls in 1988 because, in the words of Mary Klette, the network's polling director, "we didn't know what it was that we would be measuring."[31]

The methodological problems with instant polls are addressed in the next chapter.

The Final Push: The General Election Campaign

A blip of greater variation in the polls occurred in the two weeks after Labor Day (Figure 2-1). This is probably explained by the staggered intervals at which polling organizations shifted from samples of registered voters to more narrowly defined samples of "likely voters" or the "probable electorate."[32] (As will be discussed in Chapter 3, excluding registered voters who are unlikely to vote often has the effect of making the sample more upscale in socioeconomic terms, and thus sometimes more Republican.)

Variation among the twenty-six polls conducted in the last three weeks of the campaign was among the lowest of the entire campaign. There are several reasons for this. First, the public had gotten to know the candidates and the preferences of most voters had a strength and coherence such that events were not likely to have much impact. Second, during this period polling organizations tended to conform in reporting the preferences of "likely voters." Third, most polls explored the disposition of respondents who indicated they were still undecided. Those leaning toward a candidate were usually counted as supporters, thus contributing to stability in measurements of candidate support.

The experience of 1980 haunts most pollsters. Virtually all the major polling organizations failed to anticipate the magnitude of Ronald Reagan's defeat of Jimmy Carter.[33] Two hypotheses have been offered.

The "big burst" theory has been advanced by the Gallup Organization, CBS News, and the candidates' two pollsters, Richard Wirthlin and Patrick Caddell. It holds that events in the last days of the campaign—Reagan's outperforming Carter in the Cleveland debate and the breakdown of negotiations for the release of the U.S. hostages held in Iran—were decisive.

One of several pieces of empirical support for the theory came from reinterviews conducted by CBS News/*New York Times* with people contacted prior to the election. The CBS News/*New York Times* study found Jimmy Carter's support six percentage points lower in the post-election study than before the election. Those who had said they would vote for Carter but did not do so divided about one-to-two between voting for Reagan or staying home election day.[34]

The Gallup Organization found that Reagan's support against Carter rose from 42 to 46 percent in the last week of the campaign. Had Gallup not stopped its interviewing on the Saturday before the election, it is probable the Reagan victory margin could have been anticipated.[35]

Everett Ladd and Donald Ferree concur that the debate between Carter and Reagan was an "event producing an extraordinary shift in the public's perceptions, shifts favoring the Republican nominee." They note that both campaigns regarded the debate as a high-risk venture.[36]

An alternative hypothesis, the "closet Reagan voter" theory, has been suggested by Burns Roper. "I think what happened was that there were a lot of closet Reagan Democrats who were not about to admit they were going to vote for a Republican, especially such a conservative one. I'd bet they kept their true sentiments from their spouses, their co-workers, and certainly from the pollsters." [37] Roper supports the theory by noting that respondents in his 1980 final preelection survey who made up their minds at the last moment tended to favor Carter over Reagan. Thus while not arguing that there was a last-minute trend for Carter, Roper does question whether a shift took place of the magnitude of the "big burst" theory.

Regardless of which theory was believed to be at work in 1980, pollsters knew they wanted to keep their eyes on last-minute swings in

1988. Thus, there was greater reliance than ever before on "tracking polls" designed to gather a limited amount of information that could be reported quickly, usually day-by-day. The most conspicuous of these tracking polls were conducted daily from Labor Day to the election by KRC for the American Political Network. With droning steadiness the numbers were reported. The small standard deviation (s) of the percentages for George Bush in these tracking polls demonstrates how flat the trend line was, especially because the statistic is measuring variation in polls that used exactly the same methodology day after day:

Labor Day to first debate (20 polls)	$s = 1.9$
Between debates (18 polls)	$s = 0.7$
Second debate to election (24 polls)	$s = 1.3$

Although reservations have been expressed by media consultants as well as pollsters, tracking polls have become accepted as a staple of modern campaigns. However, because of their small sample sizes and other limitations discussed in the next chapter, their use by news organizations as a means of keeping the public informed has not become generally accepted.

The pertinent point here is that, although news organizations may think they need tracking polls in the last few days of a campaign, many journalists and reporters view tracking as early as Labor Day as polling overkill. The implication imparted to the general public was that daily release of new poll numbers was necessary because voter sentiment was so volatile. The trend line produced by KRC's tracking polls in 1988 would seem to show the fallacy of that notion.

Volatility and Validity

The task of ferreting out the true meaning of disparate poll findings throughout the election cycle is greatly eased by understanding two concepts in social research: *reliability* and *validity*. Reliability has to do with the consistency with which repeated applications of the same measure yield the same result. In the case of Gary Hart's reentry into the race, for example, virtually all the polls showed him ahead of the other Democratic candidates. The consistency in results from similar measures suggests that these polls were reliable.

Validity is quite another matter. It pertains to the use made of a measure. Accordingly, a measure may be reliable, but the conclusions drawn from it may not be valid. That is, independent polls may yield consistent results to the same questions, but the inferences drawn from them may go beyond what the questions actually reveal about public opinion.

The validity of an inference from a measure of public opinion can be established in a number of ways.

• One way is to assess the plausibility of the measure. Does it make intrinsic sense? This approach presupposes general agreement on the exact dimensions a measure is trying to capture and that the measure itself is straightforward and unencumbered by assumptions or elaborate procedures.

• A second way to establish the validity of a conclusion is to seek external confirmation of the conclusion at the same point in time or to track its predictive accuracy down the road.

• A third check can help when no external confirmation is possible. This approach consists of finding another measure that relates to the concept under study that can be used at the same time.[38]

The first approach is not particularly helpful, as it leaves much room for argument as to the plausibility of a conclusion. Simply arguing that Gary Hart was indeed the strongest of the candidates when he returned to the race in December 1987 does not help much without other checks on validity.

The second approach—that of obtaining external confirmation—is often difficult to implement. The acid test of preelection polls, of course, is an election. However, most polls during a presidential campaign are conducted far in advance of a tally of ballots. So much can happen during a campaign that few would judge the validity of a poll by how well it predicts the outcome of an election weeks or months away.

The only consistently realistic means of assessing the validity of inferences from a poll is the third approach: to seek out related measures in the same poll or in a contemporaneous poll. Applying this approach to variation in polls at different phases of the election cycle, we note the following:

• In the case of Hart's dominance of the standings after reentering the 1988 race, we have already seen that analysts played down his strength because of the high negative ratings he received from Democrats in the same polls

- In the case of postconvention bumps, the validity of inferring electoral strength from trial-heat gains can be checked by looking at how much people know about the candidate and how strongly, and why, they support the candidate
- In the case of an instant postdebate poll, the validity of the conclusion that one candidate picked up strength can be tested by seeing whether the "who won" question correlates with any change in the trial-heat standing of the candidates, whether respondents had heard any commentary about the debate or talked with others about it, whether certain aspects of each candidate's performance were seen as most or least impressive, and whether the opinions of viewers differed from nonviewers

In short, validity of a poll is established in the discussion and explanation that accompany reported findings. This is why, for example, the *Los Angeles Times* has a policy of not putting a poll number in a headline or story lead. In the words of its polling director, the late I. A. Lewis: "A number isn't a lead. What the number means is the lead." [39]

Political analysts, reporters, and sometimes pollsters have difficulty resisting the snappy, one-line summary of what a poll says. If they succumb to the temptation and discuss a poll's implications without adequate attention to the limitations of the data, they risk falling into one of several kinds of "validity traps."

We have already touched on one such validity trap, that of conveying the impression that a candidate's standing within a party or against the candidate of another party can be taken directly as a measure of political strength. The "if the election were held today" context of poll questions simply does not reflect the way many people are thinking about the campaign, especially early on. [40] Indeed, the very reason for this question wording is to get respondents to express a preference when they may not have focused on the choice they may have election day. Thus trial heats and other measurements of candidate support need to be accompanied by other measures, for example, of knowledge about the candidates and intensity of support.

Stated more generally, this validity trap involves drawing inferences about the state of public opinion when the questions that have been asked do not tap effectively the dimensions of opinion about which the conclusions are being drawn. As was observed earlier, trial-heat questions may register a gain for one candidate after a party convention. What is being picked up, however, is not an actual shift in support between the candidates, but the public's intensive exposure to one of the candidates.

A similar validity trap occurs when the results of an instant poll are released by a news organization without the audience being reminded that opinions can change as events are mediated by opinion leaders and by general discussion in the community. The problem is compounded if the news organization does not repeat the measure using identical questions in the next survey and report the results. This is why the *Washington Post* has a policy of including questions asked in its overnight polls in its next regularly scheduled poll.

Related to the foregoing validity traps is the penchant of political reporters to note the "spread" between one candidate and another. Changes in the spread imply more movement in public opinion than has been measured. For example, suppose a poll showed Candidate A leading Candidate B by 52 percent to 40 percent. The spread would be twelve percentage points.[41] Suppose further that a subsequent poll with the same sample size and methodology reported Candidate A having 49 percent and Candidate B having 43 percent. The margin between the candidates in the second poll would be only six percentage points, compared to twelve points earlier. To some, this would seem like a tremendous comeback for Candidate B when in fact there was an improvement of just three percentage points. This is particularly pertinent in tracking polls where movement is what people are looking for.

Winnowing of the Candidates: What Role Do the Polls Play?

News organizations have been harshly criticized for meddling in the process by which candidates are winnowed during the presidential primaries and caucuses. They are accused of imposing themselves by setting "expectations" for how well candidates must do in one primary or another, of passing judgment too quickly on the implications of primary outcomes, and even of determining in advance of the entire process which candidates merit coverage and which can be slighted.[42] The polls are usually implicated in these criticisms for fueling a cycle that can distort news coverage: poll standings affect the amount and kind of attention the news media give to a candidate, which in turn affects that candidate's standing in the polls.

To ascribe to the media and, in lesser degree, the polls such a determining role in the outcome of the nominating process is to minimize the impact of two aspects of the structural reforms of the 1970s: a front-loaded election calendar and the shift from elite- to mass-based selection of the candidates. Put another way, for the "media determines outcome" argument to hold up, it must be shown that the impact of the timetable imposed by the reforms of the 1970s is of less significance than media content in creating momentum for one candidate or in freezing out another.

In the three subsections that follow, we look at some recent cases, review what has been established empirically about the electorate's reaction to events, and finally assess the degree to which news organizations impose themselves, and polls, on the process.

Three Cases

As noted at the outset of this chapter, it is difficult to disentangle cause from effect when there are as many variables at work as in the interactions of politics, polling, and the press. One of the best ways of dealing with the problem is to examine concrete cases and to identify which factors best explain the way events unfolded. To that end we look at three cases: Gary Hart's sudden emergence in 1984, Richard Gephardt's early withdrawal from the 1988 race after months of intensive campaigning, and the collapse of Bob Dole's campaign after the 1988 New Hampshire primary in spite of the fact that he was well known and well liked among Republicans when he entered the race in 1987.

Hart in '84.   "No polls meant no press" is how Michael Robinson describes Hart's predicament going into the 1984 primaries. Drawing upon his analysis of CBS coverage of the 1980 election, Robinson argues that "polls drive press." His account of 1984 states that public attention to Hart's surprise victory in New Hampshire drove up his poll standings, which led to coverage by the national media. The polls are further implicated, according to Robinson, because the support they showed for Hart nationwide induced major correspondents to file tough if not hostile reports on the Colorado senator.[43]

Such inferences of causality between poll standings and the amount and kind of news coverage the candidates received grossly oversimplify what was taking place in the 1984 race.

In fact, quite contrary to the "polls lead to press attention" theory, the *Washington Post,* having picked up Hart's impending victory in its poll, was so dubious of its own finding that it led its story on the day of the primary with the conclusion that the race was a dead heat. The magnitude of Hart's victory was all the more stunning against the backdrop of a CBS News/*New York Times* poll released just before the primary showing Mondale the favorite of half of the Democrats polled.

What accelerated the pace of Hart's popularity and his coverage by the press was a mix of the calendar and the underlying weakness of the Mondale candidacy. With respect to the calendar, good national press about New Hampshire fed Hart victories a week later in neighboring Vermont and two weeks later in other neighboring states (Massachusetts and Rhode Island) and in Florida.

With respect to the Mondale candidacy, dissatisfaction with the former vice president was creating a void that would become the major dynamic of the 1984 Democratic race. Hart, it turned out, had far greater appeal to those dissatisfied with Mondale than did any other candidate. This was not an unmitigated boon for Hart because it meant that much of his popularity resulted not from enthusiastic support for him but from antipathy to Mondale.[44] Larry Bartels has shown that Hart's momentum picked up most in the three weeks between the Iowa caucuses and Super Tuesday as he came to be seen as a viable alternative to Mondale. However, because Hart lacked a solid base of support, his momentum began to dissipate after Super Tuesday even among anti-Mondale Democrats and even though Hart remained the only realistic alternative to Mondale.[45]

Press scrutiny of Hart was to be expected in light of the news he made in New Hampshire. His poll standings, which did rise nationally after the New Hampshire primary, need not be invoked to explain why news organizations attempted to catch up with events. After all, a potential president had sprung from the pack and the American people knew very little about him.

Gephardt in '88. The rise and fall of Rep. Richard Gephardt (D-Mo.) are explained principally by two vagaries of the 1988 campaign that threw his strategy off stride: the withdrawal of Gary Hart from the race in early May 1987 and the withdrawal of Sen. Joseph Biden in late September 1987.

A key premise of the Gephardt strategy was playing David to the Goliath from Colorado who had held an overwhelming lead in the early 1987 Iowa polls. Gephardt crisscrossed Iowa for months, doggedly determined to finish an impressive second. But when Hart succumbed to the political weight of his indiscretions, this strategy lost its bite. William Carrick, a key staffer to Gephardt, recalls the campaign's reaction: "Instead of being an impressive challenger hustling away at the front-runner, we were suddenly the front-runner . . . a premature front-runner. From that day on, there were no subtleties. . . . The media and the politicians had one view: 'Gephardt has got to win in Iowa.' " [46]

The conclusion that Iowa was a "must win" for Gephardt resulted from a logic driven in considerable degree by the way Gephardt had positioned his campaign. More than any other candidate, Gephardt had adopted a one-state strategy. Moreover, just as New Hampshire was deemed a must for Massachusetts governor Dukakis, neighboring Iowa was key for the Missouri representative.

After the Hart withdrawal, Gephardt's campaign took another hit: speculation about the campaign's complicity in the release of a videotape showing similarities between speeches of fellow-candidate Joseph Biden and Neil Kinnock, the rhetorically adroit leader of Britain's Labour party. When Biden dropped out of the race in late September 1987, Gephardt slipped in the polls; not long after, one of the television networks withdrew the crew it had assigned to Gephardt.[47]

There was little in the polls to feed journalistic expectations against which Gephardt's showing in the caucuses could be gauged. The *Des Moines Register and Tribune*'s Iowa Poll showed that, before Hart's withdrawal, Gephardt was stronger than other challengers to Hart, but not by much and in meager single-digit numbers relative to Hart's support by more than half of likely caucus-goers. Gephardt's support jumped from 9 to 24 percent when Hart pulled out but dipped again as 1987 wore on. Instead, it was Sen. Paul Simon of Illinois who made impressive gains as the year drew to an end. And, when Hart reentered the race in mid-December 1987, Gephardt had fallen behind both Simon and Dukakis.[48]

Gephardt's success in Iowa brought revived interest in his campaign and much scrutiny. Although he subsequently placed second in the New Hampshire primary, the rigors of the ensuing "Super Tuesday" primaries proved overwhelming. The gauntlet of sixteen primaries and one caucus on the same day was forbidding to a campaign that had put its energies in a sole state and could not count on existing roots or organizational muscle in the South.

Dole in '88. The demise of the Dole candidacy had much in common with the experience of Gephardt: the candidate was propelled to an early lead that he was not able to capitalize on or to sustain. Like Gephardt, Dole won in the Iowa caucuses. But unlike Gephardt, Dole had gone into the caucuses a nationally known figure holding a sturdy second place in the polls among the Republican hopefuls. It was thus reasonable to presume that Dole might be able to start a snowball rolling in New Hampshire if he could show that Bush was vulnerable.

The undoing of Dole took not more than a week, although the drama played on for five weeks before he withdrew. The crucial week fell between the Iowa caucuses and the New Hampshire primary, where a win was the necessary condition for Dole to continue. Bush's strength in the South was daunting, and the Dole campaign was well aware that anything other than a clear victory in New Hampshire would fall short of the mark.[49]

The urgency of a New Hampshire victory was heightened by Dole's narrow margin of victory in Iowa and by the fact that evangelist Pat Robertson had nudged Bush from second place there. New Hampshire Republicans had ample opportunity to watch all of this as the nearby Boston television stations were providing extensive coverage of developments in Iowa that were considered to be key to the fortunes of the Massachusetts governor. Dole's campaign polls picked up a spurt of support for the senator in New Hampshire after the Iowa results. In fact, *Newsweek* magazine approached the Dole staff on the Saturday before the New Hampshire primary about putting Dole on the cover of its next issue, which was due out on Monday. Dole's pollster, Richard Wirthlin, did not discourage the magazine's initiative.[50] Things seemed to be going well.

But rough sledding over the next two days altered the prognosis dramatically. On Sunday afternoon at the League of Women Voters debate, candidate Pete DuPont, the former governor of Delaware, challenged his counterparts to pledge not to raise taxes. Dole declined. Then, the morning of the primary, the senator encountered a heckler and, unable to check his quick tongue, uttered, "Get back in your cage!" The clip played on newscasts throughout the Granite State. Meanwhile, the well-organized Bush forces had been active: hundreds of foot soldiers under the command of the state's governor, John Sununu, were zealously getting out the vote for Tuesday. The result was that Bush trounced Dole in New Hampshire by a margin almost large enough to subsume Pat Robertson's portion of the vote.

Larry McCarthy, Dole's media adviser, recalls that Iowa "propelled us to a status we were not ready for. Suddenly we became the front runner and that was something for which we never had a strategy." As evidence of his point, McCarthy adds that the campaign had been seduced by the alluring, but invalid, premise that the wide acceptance of Dole's message in Iowa would be replicated as he took his campaign to other states. "Dole could deliver the same message in Iowa and later that day in New Hampshire and it would be like night and day. The tragedy is that we had only one message." [51]

Dole's New Hampshire coordinator suggested afterward that the polls had much to do with the outcome of the primary. He argued that the flood of tracking polls sustained the enthusiasm of political reporters for a Bush-on-the-ropes story. This, in turn, energized Bush partisans to get out the vote.[52] However, even though the public polls did not anticipate the magnitude of Dole's defeat in New Hampshire, most of them did detect that his support was soft.[53] Meanwhile the Bush campaign knew from its own polling that three-quarters of those favoring Bush did so enthusiastically.[54]

The polls picked up Dole's attractiveness as a possible Republican nominee prior to the primary/caucus season. But the circumstances of his surge to prominence after Iowa, the failure to do more than repeat his Iowa message in New Hampshire, weak organization in the Granite State, and bad press at the last minute surely outweighed the effect of reported polls in explaining the primary's outcome.

Having failed to demonstrate the vincibility of the Bush candidacy in New Hampshire, Dole had few assets to sustain him on Super Tuesday. In fact, the Kansas senator was eclipsed by Bush in every Super Tuesday state, even in neighboring Missouri. Three weeks later he withdrew from the race.

These cases underscore the structural factors at work in the rise and fall of candidates. The undoing of both Gephardt and Dole was the immediacy of the challenge of the New Hampshire primary following victory in Iowa and the preparation for the gauntlet of Super Tuesday. The emergence and demise of Gary Hart had less to do with his intrinsic appeal to the electorate than with the strengths and weaknesses of the

Mondale candidacy. Little in these cases suggests that the polls contributed much to the rhythm of events.

Expectations, Preferences, and Momentum

While George Bush may have coined the phrase "Big Mo" in 1980, it was Jimmy Carter's lieutenant, Hamilton Jordan, who saw that big momentum could be created without a big political base. Jordan's prescience might better be termed "procedural judo" for he realized that the obstacle course defined by reforms of the Democratic party had to be turned from a liability into an asset. The nomination would be captured not through the coalition-building congenial to traditional Democrats, nor by striving for a broad base of popular support. Instead, the calendar could be turned to the candidate's advantage by concentrating on the earliest caucuses and primaries and anticipating how the press would cover these events. The object was to parlay early gains into favorable media attention, expanded fund raising, and strength in subsequent primaries.

Although political scientists have not yet pinpointed the psychology of voters that builds momentum behind a candidate, they have demonstrated that voters' perceptions of the viability of a candidate (a) are affected dramatically by events and (b) can affect their willingness to support that candidate.

As to the impact of events, James Beniger has shown that from 1936 to 1972, national poll standings of the candidates during the presidential primaries were affected by the outcomes of those primaries. However, he was not able to show the reverse: that primary outcomes were influenced by poll standings.[55]

In 1984, Henry Brady and Richard Johnston followed the perceived strength of the candidates through the campaign. Their analysis of a "rolling cross section" from the National Election Study (NES), in which interviews were conducted on a weekly basis from the first of the year well into the primary cycle, picked up the public's reaction to events. Mondale's perceived viability as a candidate dipped dramatically after New Hampshire as Hart bounded onto the scene. Not long after Super Tuesday, Mondale's perceived viability picked up and Hart went into decline. Meanwhile, the view that incumbent Ronald Reagan was decidedly electable in November held steady throughout the primaries.[56]

The question of whether assessments of viability affect voter preferences is far more complex. Larry Bartels has shown that in 1980 voters' impressions of the likelihood that a candidate would win the nomination were more highly correlated with their preference for that candidate than were their views of the candidate's position on issues, ideology, or personal qualities.[57]

But the direction of causality must be established. Are people drawn to a candidate because of his or her perceived viability (reflecting a desire to get on the bandwagon) or are people inclined to project viability onto a candidate they particularly like (wish fulfillment)? Three explorations of this question—two by Bartels and one by Brady and Johnston—warrant review.

1. Larry Bartels drew upon two 1,000-case surveys of the 1980 NES, one conducted between Iowa and New Hampshire and the other in April after several important primaries had been decided. Using statistical modeling, he was able to examine the simultaneous and reciprocal influences of the bandwagon effect and the projection effect (wishful thinking). He found that both effects were at work.[58]

In the case of Jimmy Carter's standing relative to the other Democratic candidates in the 1980 primaries and caucuses, the projection effect was stronger than the bandwagon effect in both surveys. That is, people were more likely to think Carter would win if they liked him than they were to prefer him if they thought he would win. In the case of Bush, people were more likely to support him before the 1980 New Hampshire primary if they thought he would win than they were to think he would win if they preferred him. However, by April, the scene had changed. Reagan had won primaries in New Hampshire, Alabama, Florida, Georgia, Illinois, and South Carolina. There was little doubt he would be the Republican nominee. Bartels's model showed that people were more likely to think Reagan was a winner because they liked him rather than the other way around.[59] These findings led Bartels to conclude:

> The bandwagon effect is most important in settings where the nomination is perceived to be very much in doubt, and least important in settings where one candidate has established a clear predominance. . . . By contrast, it is clear . . . that the magnitude of the projection effect is much less variable.

Moreover, while "most of the formal models of the dynamics of the nominating process suggest that expectations and preferences should drive each other in a continuing upward spiral," Bartels notes that "the three most notable bandwagons in recent nominating campaigns—Carter's in 1976, Bush's in 1980, and Hart's in 1984—all appeared to slow during the course of the primary season." [60]

2. The model developed by Brady and Johnston in connection with the 1984 primary cycle also dealt with voters' preferences and perceptions of candidate viability. It took into account an individual's position on various issues, knowledge of the candidates' positions on those issues, and perceptions of the traits of the candidates. While voters' preferences affected their views of the viability of the four major Democratic candidates, the study revealed that there was no significant bandwagon effect. [61] Brady and Johnston conclude that "[perceived] viability does reflect people's preferences to some degree, but it is not entirely determined by preferences."

3. Bartels's approach to the 1984 election was different from Brady and Johnston's and was different from his own approach to the 1980 election. Bartels differentiated between two kinds of expectations: "internalized" expectations in which the perceived chances of a candidate affect an individual's evaluation of that candidate; and "direct" expectations in which the perceived chances of a candidate affect an individual's choice at the ballot box but do not affect the individual's evaluation of the candidate. This distinction was important because in 1984, as in earlier elections, survey respondents gave a candidate high ratings on a "feeling thermometer" but still did not vote for that candidate. [62]

Bartels developed a two-staged model to take into account this discrepancy between evaluation and choice as each evolved week by week throughout the campaign. For our purposes, two conclusions are important:

- The lower the level of information about the candidate, the more expectations of a candidate's chances affected preferences for that candidate
- The more certain the outcome became, the less susceptible respondents were to having their preferences affected by their expectations

Bartels concluded that the impact of momentum in nomination politics "is a contingent impact," one dependent "upon a particular set of political circumstances—a relatively unknown challenger, a newsworthy early surprise, a favorable primary calendar." [63]

The Media in the Momentum

The problem of sorting out how much momentum is due to the flywheel of the mass media is complicated by the paucity of good data and the complexity of interactions between events and news coverage of those events.

Events frequently turn conventional wisdom within news organizations upside down. One need only recall the "winners" of the past: Edmund Muskie in 1972, John Glenn in 1976, Edward Kennedy in 1980.

Nonetheless, news organizations do have to make decisions regarding allocation of their resources. Contrary to popular belief, news organizations, including the television networks, cannot afford to cover all candidates at the beginning of a primary cycle. By mid-1987, for example, there were 14 announced candidates from the two major parties. As Ed Fouhy, former director of NBC's election coverage, put it:

> One of the things that critics of the networks don't figure into their calculations is the economics of how much it costs to cover an election. They attribute a motive to a network covering or not covering a story when, in fact, the reasons are economic. It is very expensive to have a producer, correspondent, two-person crew, and an editor all in the field at one time, to say nothing of all the equipment. [64]

As Doris Graber has documented, coverage in the first six months of an election year tilts dramatically toward first-tier candidates. Seventy-four percent of news coverage during the preconvention phase in 1976 went to Gerald Ford, Ronald Reagan, and Jimmy Carter. The figure was comparable in 1980: 71 percent of coverage from January through July went to Carter, Reagan, and Kennedy. Adding coverage of John Anderson, the figure reached 81 percent, meaning that only 19 percent of media coverage was devoted to the six other contenders (George Bush, Howard Baker, Jerry Brown, John Connally, Philip Crane, and Robert Dole). [65]

It is not easy to implicate the polls in this tilt in coverage toward apparent strong contenders. Although United Press International (UPI) cannot be taken as representative of all print and broadcast journalism, an examination of its stories on the potential success of candidates found that polls made up only a small proportion of its political coverage. Brady and Johnston analyzed the content of UPI's coverage of the primary candidates in the first seven months of 1984. Of more than 5,000 lines of copy devoted to the potential success of the candidates, only 11.6 percent explicitly invoked a public opinion poll.[66]

From the candidate's standpoint, sparse early coverage can be frustrating. Ed Rollins recalled the early days of the 1988 Kemp campaign:

> Without reporters you had film crews and producers making news judgments. . . . You were very dependent on the *Washington Post,* the *New York Times* . . . to follow the stories. I think the networks basically went more into the mode of just looking at the fancy pictures as opposed to really covering stories of the campaign. They did themselves a great injustice. Whether they did the campaigns a great injustice, I don't know.[67]

Some critics suspect that polls have an undue influence early on as news organizations make decisions about deployment of their resources. This is said to be particularly true of the networks, where the costs are so much greater.[68] Second-guessing these decisions is difficult, but concerns that news organizations rely too heavily on early polls are mitigated by several considerations.

News organizations learn from their own experience. Seared by the embarrassment of missing George McGovern as the dark horse of 1972, they were especially attentive in 1976 to the stirrings of the possibly viable Carter candidacy.[69] Similarly, the dwindling momentum of Bush's candidacy in 1980 no doubt led to caution in interpreting Hart's boom after the 1984 New Hampshire primary.

Additionally, public funding of presidential elections has provided journalists with an "objective device" by which to assess a campaign's vitality.[70] Most observers would concur that those candidates unable to obtain matching funds in timely fashion stand little chance of remaining viable. Financial strength is usually accompanied by a campaign infrastructure of sufficient depth to indicate that a campaign has some staying power.

The thought process of news organizations is well summarized by

ABC's Brit Hume: "What seems to happen in the early stages of a political campaign is that the coverage tends to go to the candidates *who have accomplished things* in the preliminary phases: they've built the organization, raised the money, lined up the endorsements. They've done all those unofficial things before a vote has been cast, which gives political reporters reason to believe they have a credible campaign candidate." [71] In short, the primaries are real tests.

David Broder argues that the cumulative effect of the procedural reforms of the 1970s has been to reduce the power of the press in screening the candidates. [72] There are more primaries today than there were in the 1960s, so that the electorate plays a larger role in deciding which candidates are nominated and has more exposure to the candidates.

It is not self-evident that the polls propel news organizations to limit coverage of a candidate. Jeffrey Gralnick, vice president and executive producer at ABC News, notes that the polls are clearly a factor in allocating network resources. But even were a candidate to linger at two or three percent in the polls, coverage would not be slighted if there was evidence the candidate was putting together an organization and raising substantial funds. [73]

Images of Jimmy Carter's minuscule, but muscular, "peanut brigade" landing in snowy New Hampshire are all that is needed to keep the shrewd news director attentive to those low in the polls. In this regard, Richard Morin, polling director for the *Washington Post,* points out that early polls can help give new faces a chance. Indeed, Sabato even argues that the polls can help keep alive a campaign that might otherwise fold. He cites the case of 1972 when poll results provided an incentive for Sen. Edmund Muskie and former vice president Hubert Humphrey not to withdraw in favor of George McGovern. [74]

Three conclusions can be drawn from this analysis. First, momentum for a candidate results more from the structure of the nominating process than it does from the way news media cover that process. That is, the calendar of primaries and caucuses stipulated by the parties lays down real challenges for candidates to bring their message to the electorate and for the electorate to respond. Second, pollsters can no longer be quite so sanguine in dismissing the bandwagon effects of their polls. Third, momentum and possible bandwagon effects dissipate as the electorate has a chance to size up the candidates.

The Horse Race: Reporting or Creating the News?

The principal obligation of news organizations is to gather and present the information that they believe should be brought to the attention of the American people. Against such a criterion, what is to be gained by treating the campaign as a horse race, and keeping track of who is ahead? How well is the public served? The issue of horse-race journalism has been with us for decades, but the frequency of polls in 1988, and especially of tracking polls intended for public release, prompts a fresh look.

Few would argue that the horse race is not a legitimate news story. News executives, editors, and reporters interviewed for this book were unanimous in their belief that the principal justification for focusing on the horse race is to answer the question foremost in the public mind: "Who's ahead?"

There are other arguments for reporting on the horse race. For one thing, poll standings, which are often in flux, provide something new to report. Another reason trial-heat polls are taken seriously is that reporters covering candidates are often so close to a given campaign that poll results can help them compensate for their lack of a comparative basis for judging how things are going.[75]

At times, trial-heat figures form the very essence of the story. Consider the drubbing Walter Mondale was taking in the polls after Gary Hart's win in New Hampshire in 1984. Brit Hume did a tough piece on ABC's "World News Tonight" noting that Mondale's "own polls, too, show he's in serious trouble, but Mondale, as always, managed a good morning smile for the cameras as he left his hotel. . . . Later he talked to ABC News about the unprecedented political reverses that began with his stunning loss in the New Hampshire primary."

Too poll-driven a story? Not in the eyes of Mondale's press secretary, Maxine Isaacs, who recounts, "I have to tell you we believed the end was near. After New Hampshire, Gary Hart gained twenty points in every state where we were supposed to be strong. . . . I think Brit's portrayal was completely accurate." [76]

Nonetheless, nagging doubts persist within news organizations about how well the public is served by the reporting of trial-heat polls. During the 1976 presidential primaries, for example, NBC News conducted polls in many states but, not wanting to influence voters, did not broadcast the results.[77] CBS and its polling partner, the *New York*

Times, did not publish the results of trial heats on the theory that the purpose of polling was not to find out who was ahead but to gauge the issues of concern to the electorate. Neither news organization adhered to this policy in 1980.

For a period during the 1978 campaign, the *Boston Globe* discontinued its own polling because of the concern of then editor Thomas Winship about its possible impact on the electorate. Competitive pressures soon forced the paper to revive its surveys, but Winship insisted that no poll reports appear on the front page.[78]

Even stronger actions have been contemplated. After the 1980 election CBS anchor Dan Rather recommended closing down the network's polling operation entirely, despite his regard for it.[79] More recently, Ken Bode recommended that NBC not release any polls during the last month of the 1988 campaign. Although he agreed polls might be necessary to understand some aspects of the race, he urged that they be used only internally within the network.[80]

As a matter of current editorial policy, the *Los Angeles Times* does no polling two weeks before an election. According to the paper's polling director, the late I. A. Lewis, "the function of the poll is to help us understand what the voters are thinking, not to predict the election." [81]

The misgivings that impel thoughtful journalists to such recommendations must be addressed. They cluster around six issues: whether polls are "news"; whether polls encourage pack journalism; how often poll findings take on a reality of their own; whether polls encourage or inhibit journalists from using their best judgment about the dynamic of a campaign; whether a drumbeat of trial-heat results impairs a campaign's ability to get its message out to the electorate; and whether tracking polls are polling overkill.

Are Polls "News" ?

Bode's recommendation that NBC not broadcast the results of polls touches on the first issue. Network executives rebuffed his suggestion, contending that NBC was obligated to report any news that it had. Bode's response was that "polls aren't news; they only exist because we paid for them. If they were so good and were really newsworthy, why didn't everybody else report them. I believe they are a form of corporate advertising." Bode argues further that the teaming up of television networks and newspapers has made matters worse by heightening the perceived legitimacy of jointly sponsored polls and thereby increasing their potential audience.[82]

Media critic Bagdikian concurs, noting that by sponsoring polls a news organization is able to promote itself as an authoritative source to which people must turn to know what is going on in an election.[83] From a reporter's vantage point, Paul Taylor of the *Washington Post* is frank to admit a news organization's interest in its own poll: "I tell you there is institutional pressure. You spend a lot of money on polls." [84]

Concern along these lines is not new. Burns Roper raised the issue a decade ago, noting that news media that have their own polling operations "have a natural inclination to push their own polls." Larry Sabato is even tougher: "The news media are creating their own conflict of interest: they *make,* not just report, news by commissioning polls, and they have a vested interest in promoting their pollster and purchases of surveys." [85]

The incidence of polls in 1988 rekindled the debate. In their account of the campaign, Jack Germond and Jules Witcover had qualms about whether the criterion of newsworthiness drove the use of trial heats. They saw stories shaped increasingly by polls, not because the results were intrinsically newsworthy but because "more news organizations have become more deeply involved—in terms of money and their corporate psyches—in the polling business." [86]

As compelling as these arguments may be, news organizations had little choice but to begin conducting their own polls: it was the only way they could get information they trusted. For years political reporters have been cornered by campaign staffers peddling "inside" poll information. Occasionally, campaigns have knowingly distributed bogus data.[87] More often, however, the numbers leaked to the media are accurate but are released without sufficient detail to enable a reporter to make much sense of them.[88]

It should also be noted that collaboration between print and broadcast news organizations can improve the quality of a poll. Adam Clymer, political editor of 1988 election coverage for the *New York Times,* notes that, in addition to making greater resources available, friendly competition between the polling partners can sharpen the analytic edge. Additionally, he suggests that the combined cachet of two organizations increases the willingness of people to be interviewed and thus improves the quality of the samples.[89]

To the charge that polls frame news coverage, Sheldon Gawiser, former director of polling at NBC News, recalls: "My most successful polls included ideas from field reporters as well as questions from our senior correspondents. In most cases, it was the reporters driving the polls rather than vice versa." [90]

Ben Bradlee, executive editor of the *Washington Post,* is alert to the problem, but he thinks it is the paper's readers who benefit most. "We pay attention to our own poll, because it is our constant: we have control over it, we have one person making the judgments and doing the analyses. If we have a poll that says something, we will play it on page one. The CBS News/*New York Times* poll? We will note it. Are we giving undue importance to our own poll? Absolutely, but we know it is something we can stand behind." [91]

Do Polls Spur Pack Journalism?

There is merit to the notion that pack journalism survives less as an artifact of the physical proximity of reporters "on the bus" than as a by-product of shared terms of reference defined in large part by the latest polls. Today's journalists are especially susceptible to the psychology of the pack when they find their news sources reinforcing conclusions suggested by the polls. Richard Morin of the *Washington Post* is especially troubled on this score. In his experience, reporters are least critical in their reporting of polls when this mix is present. In spite of the caveats he writes into a poll story, he finds that "once it goes out on the wire and is picked up by newspapers around the country, the paragraphs that are cut first are those with the monitions in them." [92] The Gallup Poll has the same experience as local editors rewrite its releases with varying degrees of attention to important details.

At the same time, just as the polls can reinforce tendencies toward pack journalism, they can also counteract them. Consider the following from the 1988 campaign:

- News stories about the "invisible army" that evangelist Pat Robertson would mobilize were neither substantiated by the polls nor borne out by events.
- Speculation in the press about the enduring popularity of Lt. Col. Oliver North was shown to be overblown by polls taken not long after his emotionally charged testimony before Congress in connection with the Iran-Contra scandal.

- Many a pundit—loyal Republican and eager Democrat alike—was stunned at the selection of Sen. Dan Quayle as George Bush's running mate. It was assumed that the choice foredoomed the ticket in November. Polls quickly revealed the public's lack of concern about the specifics of Quayle's qualifications and its negative reaction to the media's treatment of Quayle.
- Most members of the press traveling with Michael Dukakis were convinced that his fortunes could only decline after the second debate with Bush. However, even though Dukakis did not make the gains needed for a comeback, his national percentage against Bush did not decline; in some states he even moved up a point or two.[93]

Do Polls Take on a Reality of Their Own?

Poll percentages can acquire a reality of their own, borne of their apparent ability to cut through the ambiguities of politics with precision and objectivity. But, as we noted earlier, a poll result is only as good as the conclusions drawn from it. Thus, trial heats can be among the most misleading of poll numbers. Did the fact that Dukakis led Bush by 17 percentage points right after the Democratic convention really mean the electorate was on the verge of rejecting George Bush? Clearly not, but Bush's campaign was plagued at the time by news stories about his seeming inability to do anything right and the poll numbers fed right into the story line. Was Gary Hart really as strong upon entering the race for a second time, as suggested by poll numbers that were two to three times larger than those of Dukakis, Simon, Gore, or Gephardt? Obviously not, but news organizations headlined Hart's poll standings.[94]

Do Polls Stifle the Journalist's Own News Judgment?

Trial heats can pose the subtlest of dilemmas for political reporters. Many a reporter assigned to cover a political event has been in the position of drawing conclusions about how well the event went for the candidate while knowing that the dynamics of the campaign being picked up in the polls are moving in a contrary direction. The late Dennis Kauff of Boston's WBZ-TV described the predicament: "No matter how well a candidate's appearance seemed to go . . . [it] doesn't change the fact the polls show that he is falling behind." [95] Richard Morin recalls the confusion of one of the *Post's* national correspondents who had witnessed the electric response of a predominantly white audience to Jesse Jackson but remained aware that Jackson's poll support among white Democrats was very narrow.[96]

The question of whether polls complement or displace sound political judgment on the part of news organizations warrants greater attention by news editors and executives. As tracking polls incessantly generate candidate standings, there is much to the concern that the daily fare of numbers reinforces the pack instinct and may make reporters more cautious and reactive.

Do Polls Crowd Out the Message Campaigns Are Trying to Get Across?

In the daily struggle between campaigns and news organizations for control of the news agenda, broadcast seconds and column inches are lifeblood. Media preoccupation with the latest poll numbers often frustrates campaigns attempting to get their message out to the public. When asked to comment on the polls, campaigns are often put on the defensive. The Dukakis campaign was quite explicit on this score.[97] However, campaigns tend to complain about polls bearing bad tidings while proclaiming those bringing more congenial news.

Are Tracking Polls Polling Overkill?

Taken together, tracking polls and journalistic competition for news have had the effect of quickening the cycle within which the significance of an event is assessed. The impact of an event such as public response to a new stump speech or television commercial is now measured on a political stopwatch that is calibrated in twenty-four-hour intervals, even though the "natural" evolution of its impact might take a good deal longer.

There are occasions when the impact of an event is so devastating that tracking polls will pick it up within a day. Such an event was President Reagan's quip about the rumored mental health problems of Governor Dukakis. The rumor was never substantiated and the issue receded, but for a few days its negative impact on Dukakis's standing against Bush in tracking polls was pronounced.[98]

More often, however, the political metabolism of the general public operates on a different time clock. For example, a new campaign advertisement seldom produces movement among the electorate in fewer than several days because repetition is the principal source of its effect. Not only do people see an advertisement several times, they hear about it and discuss it with others. Even were conditions optimal (such as excellent time placement and "roadblocking" of competing political advertisements at the same time on other channels), only the slightest effect should be expected in twenty-four hours.[99]

Some have argued that tracking polls so overloaded the system in 1988 that polls in general were devalued. Of 140 national trial heats reported from the conclusion of the convention phase to election day, 67 (or 47 percent) were conducted by KRC Communications Research for the American Political Network (APN), publishers of *Hotline*.

The sheer volume of these reports invites inquiry into the objectives presumably being served. The presumption of APN/KRC was that polling could best complement political reporting by providing the same kind of information upon which the campaigns were making daily strategic and tactical decisions.[100]

The assumption is not shared by many in news organizations. Virtually all reporters and news editors interviewed for this book said that if the APN/KRC tracking polls ceased to be available they would find it difficult to justify to their own organization the cost of starting tracking polls as early as Labor Day.

In addition, if news organizations wanted to replicate the important information campaigns get from tracking polls, they would conduct interviews in the swing states and not with a national sample such as APN/KRC used. They also would attempt to screen out unlikely voters and not rely on samples of respondents merely reporting they were registered to vote.

Polling and Journalism: Uneasy Allies

The challenge in the news business is to be both first and accurate; one without the other puts the news organization at a competitive disadvantage. For this reason it is impossible to separate the question of whether a poll is good research from the question of whether its reporting is good journalism.

If a poll does not stand up on methodological grounds, how can a story written or broadcast about it be good journalism? If a poll does stand up to scrutiny on methodological grounds, it may be the subject of differing news judgments but at least it has crossed a threshold of credibility.

In one sense, polls are no different from other types of information that come into the newsroom. News judgments must be made about their reliability and their pertinence to an emerging story line. But, as with other kinds of scientific or technical information, journalistic criteria alone are not sufficient to assess the adequacy of a poll. As we will point out in Chapter 4, the theory and method of public opinion research have their intellectual roots in the social sciences. In this sense, polling represents an uneasy alliance between journalism and the social sciences. Each field has its own criteria of professional competence. More often than not, it is when these criteria come into conflict that controversies about the polls flare up.

Criteria in Conflict: News Versus Research

Consider two cases from the 1988 election.

ABC's report of a Dukakis surge the weekend before the 1988 Republican convention. At the outset of this book, we quoted the puzzlement of ABC anchor Peter Jennings when in two days Dukakis bolted from a position three points behind Bush in one poll to fifteen points ahead of him in another. The sequence of events was as follows.

ABC and its polling partner, the *Washington Post,* were conducting one of their regular national surveys the week before the Republican convention. Interviewing was to take place as usual over three evenings, in this case, Wednesday, Thursday, and Friday. Extending interviewing for three days permits attempts to reach people who are not at home when interviewers first call. Four attempts were to be made to reach each designated respondent: the first call and three "callbacks."

The polling environment at the time of the Republican convention was one in which national tracking polls conducted by KRC Communications for the *New Orleans Times-Picayune* showed support for Dukakis dropping from 45 percent on the basis of interviews Friday and Saturday (August 12 and 13) to 40 percent on Thursday (August 18).

ABC, planning its scheduled opening broadcast Friday, August 12, before the convention in New Orleans, wanted to make use of its own poll results. Evidence of a Bush recovery after his poor showing against Dukakis in the afterglow of the Democratic convention, if borne out by the poll, would be an important part of the preconvention story from New Orleans.

The decision was to include in the Friday program the partial results of the poll, based on the 384 interviews that had been completed—about a third of the intended sample. Jennings reported that "Republicans will arrive in New Orleans with some modestly encouraging news about their candidate in the latest ABC News poll." The reported results: Bush leading Dukakis, 49 to 46 percent. The *Washington Post* wanted no part of the early release and insisted its name not be used on the air.

The sample upon which the Friday release was based consisted of first attempts and some second attempts to reach respondents in some regions of the country. However, certain parts of the country had not been contacted at all. In this sense, it was a poorer sample than is achieved on risky one-night polls in which at least all regions of the country are interviewed. (The *Post* was judicious in choosing its words later when describing the sample: "It could not be determined with confidence that the 384-interview partial sample was representative of the probable electorate." [101] Then, as the Republican convention opened, ABC further confused the situation by reporting on its Monday broadcast the results of its overnight poll, conducted Sunday night, that showed Dukakis had jumped ahead of Bush and now held a fifteen-point lead (55 to 40 percent).

In fact, when all 1,119 interviews in the poll ABC had started with the *Post* were reported, Dukakis indeed came out ahead of Bush, but by 49 percent to 46 percent. The issue presented in stark terms in this case is the clash between editorial interests in staying on top of a story and methodological considerations about the quality of survey data.

ABC cannot be faulted for wanting to include opinion data in its Friday broadcast. This was to be the kickoff of the network's convention coverage. The network had an additional incentive to get the poll on the air Friday night: audiences for network newscasts are substantially greater on weeknights than weekends.

ABC can be faulted for insensitivity to the limitations of the data upon which its release was made. Some effort was made to weight the sample to ensure proper balance by sex. However, even more elaborate weighting of the incomplete sample probably would not have overcome its inadequacies.

Both polling and editorial staff at ABC insist there was nothing intrinsically wrong with the Friday story. Polling director Jeff Alderman is quoted as saying that "it was an honest job." [102] Executive producer and ABC News vice president Jeffrey Gralnick stands behind the release, noting that "the sample was not that small." [103]

The fifty-state poll on the eve of the second 1988 presidential debate. ABC's differences with the *Washington Post* sparked a second major polling controversy in the 1988 election. The evening before the second Bush-Dukakis debate ABC devoted almost half of its "World News Tonight" program to the results of a 10,000-case public opinion survey it had conducted with the *Post.* The idea was to sample opinion in each of the fifty states to assess the race in terms of probable electoral votes. The tally led ABC to give 400 electoral votes to Bush (220 votes from 21 states judged to be firmly in his column and 180 votes from another 15 states leaning toward Bush). To highlight the results, ABC used the map of the United States on which it registers projected outcomes on election night. Anchor Jennings talked of a landslide in the making.

The *Washington Post* was much more guarded in its report of the massive survey. The story lead read: "Republican presidential nominee George Bush is maintaining a modest nationwide lead over Democrat Michael S. Dukakis, but his advantage takes on lopsided proportions when the race is broken down on a state-by-state basis." In its write-up, the *Post* did not follow the poll's results lockstep as did ABC. It used other polling information to allocate several states differently than the poll's results suggested: California, Illinois, Michigan, New Jersey, Ohio, Pennsylvania, and Texas. The combined electoral clout of these seven states is equal to one-third of the votes of the Electoral College.[104]

For the Dukakis campaign, the impact of the ABC broadcast was devastating, coming just as the Massachusetts governor was preparing for his make-or-break debate with Bush. Campaign chairman Paul Brountas recalls that "it said to the voters that Dukakis had to hit two grand slam home runs in that debate in order to come out even." [105]

ABC was roundly criticized for devoting as much airtime to the poll as it did. It was also rebuked for invoking the legitimacy of its election night map in reporting a poll more than three weeks in advance of the election.[106]

On technical grounds, the fifty-state poll had significant flaws. First, interviewing for it extended over three weeks. During this interval a number of politically significant events occurred, among them the first

Bush-Dukakis debate in Winston-Salem and the debate between vice-presidential candidates Quayle and Bentsen, which included Bentsen's famous "You're no Jack Kennedy" riposte.

Second, the sampling plan of the survey did not yield a sufficient number of cases in some states for anything but the crudest measure of voter preferences. While 10,018 interviews with likely voters across the nation sounds significant, it would have taken an aggregate number of interviews several times as large to have accommodated within sampling error the actual state-by-state election results. Moreover, the estimates for some states rested on as few as 135 interviews, a perilously small sample for most purposes, and certainly for a national television broadcast. Such small samples might suffice were the network using the polls only for rough internal guidance. But when they are used to inform the viewing audience, a higher standard of reliability is in order.[107]

To evaluate the use of the poll, two questions must be answered: Was it good research? Was it good journalism? The first question is easier than the second to answer. The unknown impact of events transpiring during the three-week period of interviewing and the inadequate sample are deficiencies of sufficient import to undermine confidence in the survey's findings. Generally accepted standards in the polling field make this assessment fairly straightforward.

The second question is a bit more problematic. Assessments of the state of the race in Electoral College terms are not new to journalism, nor were ABC and the *Washington Post* the only news organizations attempting such tallies.[108] The fifty-state poll story was really nothing more than another story about the possible outcome in the Electoral College. What was troublesome was that ABC imputed to the Electoral College projection more authority than it warranted by invoking data of dubious quality from what was described as a massive survey and arraying them on the red and blue map most viewers had seen only on the election night broadcast.

A story about possible Electoral College outcomes is certainly legitimate journalism. However, since the thrust of the story was to report the results of a massive poll, the methodological deficiencies of the poll undermined the validity of the story. In the process the public was not well served.

These two cases illustrate what can happen when methodological concerns about reliability and validity are subordinated to journalistic criteria of what is newsworthy. They also make the point that the quality of a news story is only as good as the quality of the information on which it is based.

Bringing in the Polling Professionals: Organizing the Polling Operation

The deadline-driven environment of a news organization is not always congenial to nuanced discussions about the extent to which data from a poll can be generalized. Nonetheless reporters, news editors, and news executives need to be attentive to the issue of what can and cannot be said about a set of poll numbers. As Ben Bradlee puts it: "Even the best editors there are have no expertise in polling. They know that once the professional pollsters take over, you've got to go with their rules." [109]

Whether a news organization maintains a polling operation of its own, contracts for polls with an outside organization, or just reports on polls that come to its attention, it falls to the management of the news organization to think through the question of how polls should be handled. Only management can formulate guidelines for making the most effective use of polling information. It is management that must spell out the responsibilities of the polling professionals, with particular reference to the degree of their authority for framing, writing, and reviewing a poll story before it is published or broadcast.

The quality of poll reporting in both print and broadcast news organizations is contingent primarily on the degree to which the polling professional is integral to the conception, production, *and final editing* of a news story. The late I. A. Lewis, director of polls for the *Los Angeles Times,* spoke to the problem: "The hardest thing in my job isn't writing questionnaires and analyzing the results. It is getting it right in the paper. It is more important for me to be the editor of a story than to write the story myself." Or, in the case of television, CBS's Warren Mitofsky: "While I can't tell them what should go on the air, I can tell them what shouldn't." [110]

It is more difficult for polling professionals to have clout with news organizations that do not have their own polling operations. The *Boston Globe,* for example, contracted with KRC Communications for polls during most of the 1988 election. KRC's director was frank to admit that the questionnaire he drafts "the *Globe* can amend in any way it sees fit." Once interviews and tabulations have been completed, he briefs editors and reporters on highlights of computer printouts.

However, when it comes to the final story, "I have nothing to do with writing the story." [111]

While news organizations pay varying degrees of attention to the professional polling expertise available to them, the trend is generally in a favorable direction. News organizations not having their own polling operation turn increasingly to survey professionals for counsel in connection with the ad hoc polls they do conduct. Surveys of newspapers by Rippey and Demers have shown a marked increase in the use of consultants, commercial firms, and academic polling centers. In 1978, two-thirds of the newspapers that had conducted polls relied primarily on their own staffs for the design and analysis. Eight years later, the proportion was less than a half. Interviewing was contracted out by a fifth of the newspapers in 1978 and by over a half in 1986. The full data appear in Appendix A, Table A-2. [112]

Only a handful of news organizations have a polling unit of their own; a slightly larger number have assigned a reporter to the polling beat. Most news organizations deal with poll reporting on an ad hoc basis, assigning poll stories to political reporters not otherwise committed or to reporters covering the topic with which the poll deals.

Will the number of polls conducted and reported continue to rise? Very likely. However, the composition of the polls will change. Given the financial squeeze confronting the news divisions of the television networks, it is probable that the networks will reduce their investment in polling. NBC, for example, now contracts with independent firms for the polls it conducts, rather than maintaining a full survey capability of its own. This reduction is likely to be offset, however, by syndications of the type introduced by the Gallup Organization to the members of CONUS.

It may also be balanced by an increase in polling activity by local news organizations. With the advent of telephone interviewing, much of polling has become "modularized." News organizations and independent polling practitioners can purchase samples of phone numbers and interviewing services from vendors and do their own data analysis using a personal computer. The easy availability of polling services places all the greater burden on local news organizations to become more discriminating about the polls they buy and those they report.

In the long run the conduct and reporting of polls by news organizations will improve to the extent reporters, managing editors, producers, and news executives learn enough about polling to know what they do not know. They must ask the sort of questions about poll methodology that will enable them to assess the limitations of a given poll and to gauge how far its results can be generalized. It is to these issues that the next chapter is directed.

Notes

1. Stephen Isaacs, "Were Polls Overemphasized?" *Columbia Journalism Review* (January/February 1973): 29-30, 39-42. Philip Meyer, "Learning to Live with the Numbers," *Columbia Journalism Review* (January/February 1977): 29. E. J. Dionne, Jr., "1980 Brings More Pollsters Than Ever," *New York Times,* February 16, 1980, A10.
2. Of 437 daily newspapers surveyed in 1978, 162 conducted polls; of those, more than half became involved after 1970. Survey by John Rippey, "Use of Opinion Polls as a Reporting Tool," *Journalism Quarterly* 57 (Winter 1980): 642-646, 721.
3. Adam Clymer of the *New York Times,* interview with the author, July 31, 1989; Jeffrey Gralnick of ABC News, interview with the author, July 20, 1989; Mary Klette of NBC News, interview with the author, July 20, 1989; Richard Morin of the *Washington Post,* interview with the author, July 24, 1989; Burns W. Roper, interview with the author, July 20, 1989; and Humphrey Taylor of Louis Harris and Associates, interview with the author, July 21, 1989.
4. Phil Balboni, former news director of Boston's WCVB-TV, spent half as much on polls in 1988 as in 1984 and purchased over twice as many polls. See Barbara Matusow, "Are the Polls Out of Control?" *Washington Journalism Review* 10 (October 1988): 17.
5. See Kevin Keenan, "Polls in Network Newscasts in 1984 Race," *Journalism Quarterly* 63 (Autumn 1986): 616-618; and C. Anthony Broh, "Horse-Race Journalism: Reporting the Polls in the 1976 Presidential Election," *Public Opinion Quarterly* 44 (Winter 1980): 514-529.
6. Douglas Bailey, interview with the author, Falls Church, Va., July 26, 1989.
7. We borrow the phrase from Timothy Crouse's classic, *The Boys on the Bus* (New York: Ballantine Books, 1972), which recounts the way the press covered the 1972 presidential campaign.
8. Ken Bode, telephone interview with the author, August 30, 1989.
9. The percentages below are from two questions: "Who do you want the Democrats/Republicans to nominate for President in 1988—[LIST OF NAMES]?" Respondents naming a preferred candidate were then asked:

"Is your mind made up, or is it still too early to say for sure?"

Interviewing dates	Democrats			Republicans		
	No preference	Too early	Total	No preference	Too early	Total
1/18-21/87	31%	49%	80%	24%	58%	82%
3/28-29/87	38	48	86	26	56	82
5/11-14/87	44	37	81	23	61	84
7/21-22/87	49	27	76	16	67	83
10/18-22/87	45	38	83	13	52	65
11/20-24/87	26	34	70	12	51	63
1/17-21/88	32	46	78	20	58	78
2/17-21/88	27	47	74	21	49	70
3/19-22/88	20	48	68	9	39	48

10. Andrew Kohut, interview with the author, Princeton, N.J., June 29, 1989.

11. Gary Langer, "Pollsters: Hart Faces Task of Restoring Voter Confidence," Associated Press wire story, December 15, 1987.

12. Burns W. Roper has stated, "I don't think polling prior to the start of an election year does either the candidates for office or the public at large a service. Early polling does not reflect real preferences." Address entitled "Political Polls: Some Things That Concern Me," delivered to the American Association for the Advancement of Science, New York, May 25, 1984.

13. For a good discussion of this aspect of volatility, see Irving Crespi, *Public Opinion, Polls, and Democracy* (Boulder, Colo.: Westview Press, 1989), 58-61.

14. Edward Walsh and James R. Dickenson, "Confidence Surging in the Dole Camp: Tracking Polls Show Senator Edging Past Bush in N. H.," *Washington Post*, February 14, 1988.

15. William E. Brock, quoted in Edward Walsh and David Hoffman, "Bush-Dole Contest a Toss-up in Polls," *Washington Post*, February 16, 1988.

16. William Lacy of the Dole Campaign so reported at the Campaign Managers Conference at Harvard's Institute of Politics; see *Campaign for President: The Managers Look at '88*, ed. David R. Runkel (Dover, Mass.: Auburn House, 1989), 139-140.

17. Further evidence of Bush's strength at the end came from an exit poll Gallup conducted for WCVB-TV in Boston. It showed that 19 percent of Republican primary voters had made up their minds in the last 48 hours of the campaign. Of this group, Bush was favored over Dole by nearly two-to-one.

18. Warren J. Mitofsky, interview with the author, New York, June 29, 1989.
19. Gordon Black, polling for *USA Today* and CNN from July 6 to 10, had Bush with 47 percent among registered voters and Dukakis with 44 percent.
20. A follow-up question was asked to those having a preference between Dukakis and Bush: "Would you describe your support for [Bush/Dukakis] as strongly favoring him, or do you like him but with reservations, or do you support him because you dislike the other candidate?" Among Dukakis supporters: 13 percent strongly favored, 19 percent liked with reservations, 12 percent disliked Bush. Among Bush supporters: 13 percent strongly favored, 16 percent liked with reservations, and 7 percent disliked Dukakis. Phone interviewing July 5-8, 1988; sample of 947 registered voters.
21. See the comments of Ed Rollins in *Campaign for President,* ed. Runkel, 256.
22. This argument is advanced, among other places, by Marjorie Randon Hershey in "The Campaign and the Media," in *The Election of 1988: Reports and Interpretations,* ed. Gerald M. Pomper (Chatham, N.J.: Chatham House Publishers, 1989), 82.
23. In 1976 Jimmy Carter opened up a lead over President Gerald Ford after the Democratic convention. The discord that emerged within the Republican party as Ronald Reagan challenged Gerald Ford had the effect of further expanding the Carter lead. Then within two weeks of the Republican convention, Ford regained lost ground, cutting dramatically into Carter's lead. The pattern does not always hold: after a made-for-television convention in 1984 Ronald Reagan received almost no boost against Walter Mondale.
24. After ascertaining the preference between Bush and Dukakis, the CBS News/*New York Times* poll asked those with a choice: "Is your mind made up, or do you think you might change your mind before the election?" The results for three surveys:

	July 5-8	July 31- August 3	September 8-11
Support Bush			
Mind made up	21%	23%	34%
Could change mind	18	11	13
Total support	39	34	47
Could change/Total	.46	.32	.28

Support Dukakis			
Mind made up	32%	32%	28%
Could change mind	16	18	11
Total support	48	50	39
Could change/Total	.33	.36	.28

25. Mitofsky, interview with the author, New York, June 29, 1989.
26. Kohut, interview with the author, Princeton, N.J., June 29, 1989.
27. Burns W. Roper, interview with the author, New York, July 20, 1989.
28. Quoted in Andrew Rosenthal, "After Third TV Debate, Networks' Policy Shifts," *New York Times,* October 15, 1988.
29. Thomas E. Patterson, *The Mass Media Election: How Americans Choose Their President* (New York: Praeger Publishers, 1980), 123. See also Gladys Engel Lang and Kurt Lang, "Immediate and Delayed Responses to a Ford-Carter Debate," *Public Opinion Quarterly* 42 (Fall 1978): 322-341.
30. Peter D. Hart, interview with the author, Washington, D.C., July 25, 1989.
31. Mary Klette, interview with the author, New York, July 20, 1989.
32. Shifts from samples of registered voters to some form of "likely voter" or "probable electorate" samples occurred among the major national polls as follows:

Organization	Interviewing dates for first "likely voter" sample
Harris	July 22-25
ABC News/*Washington Post*	August 31-September 6
Black/CNN	September 5-8
NBC News/*Wall Street Journal*	September 16-20
CBS News/*New York Times*	October 5
Gallup	October 7-9

Tracking polls by KRC for the American Political Network never shifted to likely voter samples before election day. The importance of the sample base is difficult to underestimate. According to the Federal Election Commission, 70.5 percent of the voting age population registered to vote in 1988. In contrast, only 50.15 percent actually voted. See *FEC Journal of Election Administration* 16 (Summer 1989): 4.
33. The Reagan margins over Carter reported in the final preelection measures of the major national polls were: ABC News/Harris, five percentage points; CBS News/*New York Times,* one point; and Gallup, three points. The candidates' polling organizations had wider margins: Decision Mak-

ing Information (for Reagan) showed Reagan winning by eleven points, and Cambridge Survey Research (for Carter) had Reagan ahead by ten points. Reagan's margin when the votes were counted was 9.8 percentage points.

34. For a review of the CBS News/*New York Times* postelection analyses for 1980 and 1984, see E. J. Dionne, Jr., "Yes, Late Voter Swings Do Happen, But Underdogs Can't Count on Them," *New York Times,* November 5, 1988. See also Warren J. Mitofsky, "The 1980 Pre-Election Polls: A Review of Disparate Methods and Results," in *Proceedings of the Section on Survey Research Methods,* American Statistical Association (1981): 47-51.

35. See Andrew Kohut, "A Review of the Gallup Pre-Election Methodology in 1980," in *Proceedings of the Section on Survey Research Methods,* American Statistical Association (1981): 41-46.

36. See Everett C. Ladd and G. Donald Ferree, "Were the Pollsters Really Wrong?" *Public Opinion* 3 (December/January 1981): 16.

37. Roper, interview with the author, New York, July 20, 1989. Evidence in the contrary direction emerges from a comparison of the responses of likely voters in the final Gallup survey who expressed their preference directly to interviewers and those who marked their preference on a "secret ballot." There was virtually no difference in the proportions for Reagan or Anderson between the two modes of questioning. However, the secret ballot approach yielded 4.5 percentage points more support for Carter than the nonsecret approach. See Kohut, "A Review of the Gallup Pre-Election Methodology in 1980," 44.

38. The names for these approaches are, respectively, face validity, criterion validity, and construct (or concept) validity. For discussions of reliability and validity, see William J. Goode and Paul K. Hatt, *Methods in Social Research* (New York: McGraw-Hill, 1952); Claire Selltiz, Lawrence J. Wrightsman, and Stuart W. Cook, *Research Methods in Social Relations* (New York: Holt, Rinehart, and Winston, 1976); Kenneth D. Bailey, *Methods of Social Research* (New York: The Free Press, 1978); and Edward G. Carmines and Richard A. Zeller, *Reliability and Validity Assessment* (Beverly Hills, Calif.: Sage Publications, 1979).

39. I. A. Lewis, interview with the author, Los Angeles, February 12, 1990.

40. See Roper, "Political Polls: Some Things That Concern Me."

41. A point of clarification: many political reporters refer to this margin as a 12 *percent* margin, when it is a 12 *percentage point* margin. In this example, if the weaker candidate had 40 percent support, a 12 percent increment above 40 would amount to 4.8 percent, putting the stronger candidate at 44.8 percent, not 52 percent!

42. This last point has been made, for example, by Patterson and Davis who

argue that "before the campaign officially begins, the news media essentially screen the contenders, deciding which ones are worthy of serious consideration by the electorate and which are also-rans." See Thomas E. Patterson and Richard Davis, "The Media Campaign: Struggle for the Agenda," in *The Elections of 1984*, ed. Michael Nelson (Washington, D.C.: CQ Press, 1985), 144.

43. Michael J. Robinson, "News Media Myths and Realities: What Network News Did and Didn't Do in the 1984 General Campaign," in *Elections in America*, ed. Kay Lehman Schlozman (Boston: Allen and Unwin, 1987), 156.

44. Kathleen Frankovic has shown that in many primary states the percent strongly supporting Hart was considerably less than the percent giving him qualified support or seeing him primarily as an alternative to another candidate. Furthermore, the proportion of his support resulting from dislike of the other candidates was higher than similar proportions of support for Mondale or Jackson. Her analysis is based on CBS News/*New York Times* exit polls. See "The Democratic Campaign: Voter Rationality and Instability in a Changing Environment," in *Elections in America*, ed. Schlozman, 266-273.

45. Bartels also notes that Hart's dwindling support among anti-Mondale Democrats casts some doubt on the theory that voters approach their electoral choices strategically: if Hart were still the only viable alternative to Mondale, the "strategic voting" hypothesis would suggest that their support for Hart should hold firm. See Larry M. Bartels, *Presidential Primaries and the Dynamics of Public Choice* (Princeton, N.J.: Princeton University Press, 1988), 116-118.

46. Recounted in *Campaign for President*, ed. Runkel, 3.

47. Recounted by Carrick in *Campaign for President*, ed. Runkel, 4.

48. The trend for the principal candidates in Iowa:

	1987							1988	
	Apr.	Early May	Mid-May	Aug.	Nov.	Early Dec.	Mid-Dec.	Jan.	Feb.
Hart	65	56	—	—	—	—	29	13	7
Gephardt	7	9	24	18	14	11	6	19	25
Dukakis	3	4	11	14	18	14	16	18	15
Simon	1	1	6	13	24	35	18	17	19

SOURCE: The Iowa Poll of the *Des Moines Register and Tribune*.

NOTE: Hart withdrew May 9; reentered December 15.

49. William Lacy of the Dole campaign stressed this point in reflecting on the campaign. See *Campaign for President,* ed. Runkel, 37.
50. Richard Wirthlin, interview with the author, McLean, Va., July 28, 1989.
51. Larry McCarthy, interview with the author, Washington, D.C., July 28, 1989.
52. This view of Thomas Rath's is found in Paul Taylor, "Did Pollsters Give Bush His N.H. Win?" *Washington Post,* February 28, 1988.
53. The Gallup Organization advised its CONUS clients after the primary that it had not reported enough information about the strength of support for the two candidates because, even though the Gallup Poll found Dole's lead over Bush holding steady before the primary, it did pick up softness in support for Dole. ABC News/*Washington Post* also noted the softness of support for Dole and in polls later in the year placed more reporting emphasis on the strength of voter preferences. For a discussion of this, see Kenneth E. John, "1980-1988 New Hampshire Presidential Primary Polls," *Public Opinion Quarterly* 53 (Winter 1989): 593-594.
54. Bush pollster Robert Teeter: "Our polls showed us at about a 40 percent support level for a year—and, of that, 30 percent was hard-core support. The Iowa loss stripped us right down to our hard-core. But we knew exactly who the 10 percent were, and we were able to go right back after them in a targeted way." Quoted in Taylor, "Did Pollsters Give Bush His N.H. Win?"
55. James R. Beniger, "Winning the Presidential Nomination: National Polls and State Primary Elections," *Public Opinion Quarterly* 40 (Spring 1976): 22-38.
56. See Henry E. Brady and Richard Johnston, "What's the Primary Message: Horse Race or Issue Journalism?" in *Media and Momentum: The New Hampshire Primary and Nomination Politics,* ed. Gary R. Orren and Nelson W. Polsby (Chatham, N.J.: Chatham House, 1987), 176-177.
57. Larry M. Bartels, "Expectations and Preferences in Presidential Nominating Campaigns," *American Political Science Review* 79 (September 1985): 805.
58. Variables in the model that were assumed to affect expectations included media exposure, education, sex, and race. Variables assumed to affect preferences were the state of the economy, taxes versus services, defense, Iran, and leadership. Since expectations about candidate viability and candidate preference were both dichotomous variables, Bartels used a nonlinear logit model.
59. Ibid., 808-811.
60. Ibid., 812, 814.
61. See Brady and Johnston, "What's the Primary Message?" 180.

62. For example, a Field poll of California Democrats in March 1976 produced a provocative inconsistency: a significant number of respondents chose one candidate when asked to select from an eleven-candidate field and another candidate when presented only two candidates. Specifically, 72 respondents in the sample selected Hubert Humphrey from the list of 11 candidates as their preference but opted for Morris Udall or Henry Jackson when they were paired with Humphrey one-on-one in another question. See Henry E. Brady and Larry M. Bartels, "An Agenda for Studying Presidential Primaries," SRC Working Paper No. 62 (Survey Research Center, University of California at Berkeley, 1982). Similar discrepancies between general evaluations and choices were noted by J. Merrill Shanks, Warren E. Miller, Henry E. Brady, and Bradley L. Palmquist, "Viability, Electability, and Presidential 'Preference': Initial Results from the 1984 NES Continuous Monitoring Design" (Paper delivered at the annual meeting of the Midwest Political Science Association, Chicago, 1985). Both are cited in Bartels, *Presidential Primaries,* 132.

63. The first part of the Bartels model took into account a respondent's predisposition toward a candidate, level of information about that candidate, and subjective estimate of the chances the candidate would win. The second part of the model dealt with the divergence between evaluations of the candidates and actual preference for them. See Bartels, *Presidential Primaries,* 125-130, 269, 331-333. The model has been criticized for failing to take into account the unexpected, such as Walter Mondale's "Where's the beef?" jibe at Hart. See James W. Davis's review of Bartels's book in *Presidential Studies Quarterly* 19 (Summer 1989): 653-656. However, in one analysis Bartels does deal with the impact of events by looking at the actual amount of support for the candidates week by week. He then estimates the "net effect" of expectations by subtracting from Hart's overall level of support the proportion of his support that can be attributed to the expectation that he would get the nomination.

64. Ed Fouhy, interview with the author, Washington, D.C., July 25, 1989.

65. Data for 1980 in Doris A. Graber, *Mass Media and American Politics* (Washington, D.C.: CQ Press, 1989), 220; data for 1976 in communication from Graber to the author, July 14, 1989.

66. Brady and Johnston coded 5,044 lines of UPI text pertaining to the potential success of the candidates. See Brady and Johnston, "What's the Primary Message," 136-137.

67. Quoted in *Campaign for President,* ed. Runkel, 148.

68. Schram, for example, contends: "The two-man race coverage occurs because political journalists take their campaign catechism from the public opinion polls. They tell us who the front runner is and who the number-

one challenger is—no matter if, at this early stage, it is only a measure of name recognition at the starting gate and does not reflect what the voters will be thinking once they finally focus on the campaign and take the true measure of the candidates." See Martin Schram, *The Great American Video Game: Presidential Politics in the Television Age* (New York: William Morrow and Co., 1987), 131.

69. See F. Christopher Arterton, *Media Politics: The News Strategies of Presidential Campaigns* (Lexington, Mass.: Lexington Books, 1984), 200.

70. Nelson W. Polsby makes this point in his *Consequences of Party Reform* (New York: Oxford University Press, 1983), 59.

71. Comments made at the First William Benton National Conference, March 1-2, 1985; see John D. Callaway, Judith A. Mayotte, and Elizabeth Altick-McCarthy, *Campaigning on Cue* (Chicago: The William Benton Fellowships Program in Broadcast Journalism, University of Chicago, 1988), 12. Emphasis added.

72. David S. Broder, *Behind the Front Page: A Candid Look At How The News Is Made* (New York: Simon and Schuster, 1987), 278.

73. Jeffrey Gralnick, interview with the author, New York, July 20, 1989.

74. Richard Morin, "In Praise of Early Polls," *Washington Post,* August 23, 1987, B5. Larry Sabato, *The Rise of Political Consultants: New Ways of Winning Elections* (New York: Basic Books, 1981), 85.

75. Commenting on the polls at a Harvard conference on the media and politics, NBC's Tom Brokaw noted: "The horse race changes all the time, and that's one of the reasons it gets attention." See *Television and the Presidential Elections,* ed. Martin Linsky (Lexington, Mass.: Lexington Books, 1983), 34. David Broder writes: "The reporters on the candidates' planes are probably in the worst position to see how the race is going." See Broder, *Behind the Front Page,* 242.

76. Hume's report and Isaacs's reaction are recounted in *Campaigning on Cue,* ed. Callaway, Mayotte, and Altick-McCarthy, 34-36.

77. See William E. Bicker, "Network Television News and the 1976 Presidential Primaries: A Look from the Networks' Side of the Camera," in *Race for the Presidency: The Media and the Nominating Process,* ed. James David Barber (Englewood Cliffs, N.J.: Prentice-Hall, 1978), 101.

78. Bill Kovach, "A User's View of the Polls," *Public Opinion Quarterly* 44 (Winter 1980): 570.

79. Rather is quoted by Martin Schram: "I remember I had a meeting in Ed Joyce's [president of CBS News] office and Ed said, 'Well, are you serious about closing it down?' And I said, 'I'm absolutely serious about closing it down'.... In retrospect, we didn't have the guts to do it.... We said to ourselves time after time in early 1983, 'I'm not going to have our coverage dictated by polls. The tail is not going to wag the dog. Not this time.' Well,

lo and behold, the tail did wag the dog. . . . The problem with these polls is it comes out in black and white, and it all looks authoritative—and it isn't." See Schram, *Video Game*, 136-137.

80. Ken Bode, telephone interview with the author, August 30, 1989.

81. I. A. Lewis, interview with the author, Los Angeles, February 12, 1990.

82. Bode, telephone interview. Academically based polls also seek out media partners both as a source of financial support and for heightened visibility. This point was made by former Eagleton Institute (N.J.) poll director Cliff Zukin in an interview with the author, San Francisco, February 9, 1990.

83. Ben Bagdikian, interview with the author, Berkeley, Calif., February 9, 1990.

84. Taylor made these remarks at the Institute of Politics post-mortem on the 1988 election. See *Campaign for President*, ed. Runkel, 165.

85. Burns W. Roper, "The Impact of Journalism on Polling," in *Polling on the Issues*, ed. Albert H. Cantril (Cabin John, Md.: Seven Locks Press, 1980), 16. Sabato, *The Rise of Political Consultants*, 317-318.

86. Jack W. Germond and Jules Witcover, *Whose Broad Stripes and White Stars? The Trivial Pursuit of the Presidency*, 1988 (New York: Warner Books, 1989), 57.

87. One such episode involved a pollster who leaked numbers in a race for statewide office showing the client with a two-point lead. The leak came at a time when the campaign seemed dead in the water: funds were not coming in and media attention was meager. The reporter went with the story and the contributions picked up. But the client was defeated. After the election, the same reporter's post-mortem noted that the boomlet for the vanquished candidate had been entirely contrived; internal campaign polls at the time had showed the candidate behind.

88. Evans Witt of the Associated Press recounts Democratic pollster Alan Secrest's concern that "it is genuinely becoming 'pollster wars' out there. Too many people are playing fast and loose with polling data. . . . It is unconscionable, but understandable with so much at stake." See Witt, "Poll Wars: State Polls in the 1986 Election," *Public Opinion* 9 (January/February 1987): 43.

89. Adam Clymer, interview with the author, New York, July 31, 1989.

90. Sheldon Gawiser, interview with the author, New York, March 19, 1990.

91. Benjamin C. Bradlee, interview with the author, Washington, D.C., July 26, 1989.

92. Richard Morin, interview with the author, Washington, D.C., July 24, 1989.

93. Paul Taylor and T. R. Reid reported that the Dukakis campaign's internal polls showed the Massachusetts governor gaining in key states such as California and Ohio in response to the populist appeal he adopted in mid-

October. They also reported that the Bush campaign picked up the same movement toward Dukakis. See "Bush Lead Shrinks in Big States," *Washington Post,* October 29, 1988.

94. The December 17, 1987 edition of the *New York Times* carried the headline: "Gary Hart Has Joined the Rev. Jesse Jackson at the Front of the Democratic Presidential Field in the Latest *New York Times*/CBS Poll."

95. Quoted in Schram, *Video Game,* 185.

96. Morin, interview with the author, Washington, D.C., July 24, 1989.

97. Jack Corrigan, operations director of the Dukakis campaign, noted at the Institute of Politics campaign managers conference that the prominence of polls in news coverage "makes it much harder to get our message out." See *Campaign for President,* ed. Runkel, 168.

98. Susan Estrich, director of the Dukakis campaign, asserts that tracking polls by the campaign showed an eight-point drop for Dukakis against Bush in twenty-four hours. Ibid., 254.

99. Larry McCarthy, interview with the author, Washington, D.C., July 28, 1989. Focus groups are sometimes used to measure immediate reactions to an advertisement, but the usual expectation is that the advertisement needs to run for several days for its impact to be reliably assessed.

100. Republican political consultant Douglas Bailey, a founder of *Hotline,* recalls the years he has been on the campaign's side of phone conversations with the press. He found reporters hungry for information that would help them understand a campaign's strategy and tactics. Bailey thinks the media still do not understand their own need for this kind of "inside" information. Interview with the author, Falls Church, Va., July 26, 1989.

101. Richard Morin, "Trying to Gauge the Pulse of Public Opinion: Polls Reflect Mood Shifts, Survey Quality," *Washington Post,* August 18, 1988, A25.

102. Quoted in Matusow, "Are the Polls Out of Control?" 18.

103. Gralnick, interview with the author, New York, July 20, 1989.

104. Paul Taylor and Richard Morin, "Poll Indicates Bush Has Big Electoral-Vote Lead: Advantage in Popular Votes Narrower," *Washington Post,* October 13, 1988. The poll's outcome was also at variance with conclusions reached by the "reporting survey," an internal system used by ABC News to monitor the political situation state-by-state on a weekly basis.

105. Paul Brountas, quoted in *Campaign for President,* ed. Runkel, 167.

106. ABC political director Hal Bruno notes the irony in the fact that the amount of time devoted to the poll provoked criticism that ABC was hyping it, "when our purpose was to tone down the story with the needed caveats." Interview with the author, Washington, D.C., July 28, 1989.

107. In some states (for example, Illinois, Maryland, Pennsylvania, and Wash-

ington) the race was so close that samples in excess of 5,500 cases would have been required to estimate within sampling error the actual vote.

108. On October 27, 1988, the *Boston Globe* carried a story on page one by Walter V. Robinson with the headline, "Polls Show Bush on Verge of an Electoral Landslide," and the Electoral College map allocating state totals appeared inside the paper.

109. Bradlee, interview with the author, Washington, D.C., July 26, 1989.

110. I. A. Lewis, interview with the author, Los Angeles, February 12, 1990. Mitofsky, interview with the author, New York, June 29, 1989.

111. Gerry Chervinsky, president of KRC Communications Research, quoted in Robert L. Kierstead (The Ombudsman), "Using Polls with Caution," *Boston Globe,* June 26, 1989.

112. In 1986 Demers replicated a 1978 survey by John N. Rippey. Questionnaires were mailed to 786 daily newspapers; responses were received from 413 papers. See David Pearce Demers, "Use of Polls in Reporting Changes Slightly Since 1978," *Journalism Quarterly* 64 (1987): 839-842; and Rippey, "Use of Polls as a Reporting Tool," 642-646, 721. These findings are corroborated by Irving Crespi's survey of news organizations conducting preelection polls at the state level in 1980. He found that interviewing for 48 percent of the polls was conducted by a full-service survey firm or interviewing agency and that outside counsel was sought for design and analysis in 38 percent of the polls. See Crespi, *Pre-Election Polling: Sources of Accuracy and Error* (New York: Russell Sage Foundation, 1988), 155-160.

chapter three

Why All Polls Are Not Equal: A Guide to Polls of Quality

Polls pinpoint likelihoods and tendencies, not
certainties. They tap into fluidities, not stabilities.
And they measure approximately, not precisely.

Charles W. Roll, Jr.

Just as the strength of a chain depends on the strength of each of its links, the quality of a public opinion poll is only as good as the quality at each of its stages. Although there are trade-offs in the design, conduct, and analysis of a poll, shortcomings at any stage can jeopardize the entire poll.

Our purpose here is not to present a "how to" overview of polling methodology.[1] Rather we intend to highlight important methodological issues that will help poll consumers make better use of the information available to them in evaluating poll reliability and validity.

Popular awareness of polls centers on the notion that the sampling procedures employed create a microcosm of the population at large. Thus, it is often asked how a few hundred people can be representative of an entire nation. The centrality of sampling in public perception of polling is fed by the news media, which report with dogged insistence the size of poll samples and the accompanying "margin of error."

The characterization of polling as basically a matter of sample size and error obscures two fundamental points about opinion research.

First, it understates the complexities involved in achieving a good sample and estimating its limitations. That is, as we shall explore in this chapter, pollsters have to deal with the problems of households without telephones, people not at home when an interviewer calls, people refusing outright to participate in a poll, and those who refuse to answer key questions.

The second way a preoccupation with sample size and error obscures an understanding of opinion research is that it underestimates the myriad ways in which "nonsampling error" can affect the results obtained. As we also will consider in this chapter, the results of a poll can be dramatically affected by the way questions are phrased (particularly with reference to issues that are complex or about which people tend to be ill-informed), the order in which questions are asked, and the degree to which public opinion has crystallized.

In addition the chapter addresses special polling techniques such as tracking polls, exit polls, and focus groups. It concludes by warning about the dangers of pseudopolls that continue to attract undeserved attention.

Sample Quality and Control

A necessary condition for poll reliability is care in the design of the sample and control over its implementation.

The theoretical objective is to ensure that every individual in the population under study has a known chance of falling into the sample. Only rarely do conditions obtain where every individual in the population has an equal chance of being included; the real world imposes too many constraints for simple random sampling to take place. Not only do logistical difficulties make it prohibitively costly to reach respondents on a strictly random basis, but also not all potential respondents consent to an interview or, if they do consent, stay with an interview until its completion.

However, by imposing a structure on the sample that is consistent with probability theory, the pollster can compute the likelihood of a respondent's entering the sample at each step in the process. It is these "probabilities of selection" that bear on "sampling error," the margin above and below a reported result that must be allowed to accommodate the chance that the sample is unrepresentative.

Approaches to Sample Design: Cost-Effectiveness and Variance

The sampling plan for a poll involves a series of trade-offs between the goals of finding a cost-effective approach to the interviewing process and limiting variance in the sample. On the one hand, the cost of a survey rests primarily upon the number of interviews conducted and the difficulty of conducting them. For example, telephone surveys are usually less expensive than in-person interview surveys; surveys with only one attempt to reach a designated respondent cost less than those with "callbacks" to contact hard-to-find respondents; and surveys with long interviews cost more than those with short interviews.

On the other hand, "variance" refers to how spread out the results would be if an infinite number of polls were conducted at the same time using the same methods and asking the same questions. As a general rule, the smaller the variance, the greater the reliability of the data a sample produces. Such an infinite number of soundings on the president's popularity, for example, would produce a distribution of an infinite number of approval ratings arrayed in the familiar bell-shaped curve. The contour (steepness) of this curve can be estimated using statistical techniques, taking into account the size of the samples and the effect of components of the sample design on the probabilities of people falling into the sample at different steps in the sampling process.

Three commonly used elements of sample design deal with the competing objectives of reducing costs and minimizing variance: "stratification," "oversampling," and "clustering." A word on each is in order.

Stratification. This procedure can help reduce sample variance. It can be used when there are characteristics of the population that are related to what is being measured and about which objective information is available. The characteristics are used to divide the sample into strata, each of which is homogeneous on a particular characteristic. A common form of stratification is by geographic region. Thus, for example, pollsters can use the known distribution of the population to stratify a national sample by region (such as East, Midwest, South, and West) and by degree of urbanization (such as central city, suburban, rural).

Oversampling. This element of sample design refers to interviewing a subgroup of the population in excess of its proportion in the overall population. The purpose is to ensure that enough interviews with this subgroup will be conducted to narrow the margin of error of results from this subgroup or to explore differences within the subgroup.

Common forms of oversampling target racial and ethnic minorities and individuals identifying with a particular political party.

For example, NBC News/*Wall Street Journal* reported in March 1990 that the views of Jews differed from non-Jews on the question of German reunification. With Jewish persons constituting only 3 percent of the U.S. population, a national sample of one thousand would not yield enough cases for statistically meaningful comparisons of the views of Jews and non-Jews. An oversample of Jews was required.

All other things being equal, a 1,200-case simple random sample will have smaller variance than a sample of twelve hundred made up of a randomly selected cross section of one thousand and an added oversample of two hundred. But it will not support the same level of analysis of the views of the subgroup that could have been oversampled.

Clustering.   This concept requires the greatest elaboration for it is here that the trade-off between cost-effectiveness in field work and variance is most noticeable. In the effort to reduce interviewing costs in both personal and telephone surveys, pollsters often build into their sample designs procedures that target interviewing on clusters of potential respondents. While such clustering increases the cost-effectiveness with which interviewers can find respondents, it has the effect of increasing sample variance when the clusters tend to be homogeneous.

An illustration: Imagine that one wanted to conduct a national poll with a sample of fifteen hundred personal interviews. It would be possible to dispatch interviewers to fifteen hundred locations drawn at random to interview just one individual in each location. It would also be possible to dispatch a team of interviewers to one randomly selected location in which all fifteen hundred interviews would be conducted. Both schemes would meet the criterion of random selection of respondents.

The first sample design would be immensely complicated, and the costs of logistics and interviewer time would be substantial. The second sample design would be easy to implement and would economize on interviewer costs. It would do so, however, at great risk to the representativeness of the sample because it would fail to protect the sample against characteristics (and opinions) that were unevenly distributed throughout the population. For example, it would be possible for the second sample design to fulfill the criterion of random selection even if all fifteen hundred interviews were conducted in the Amish part of Pennsylvania.

Pollsters can avoid these extremes by employing clusters in their sample designs. In the case of personal-interview surveys, localities are selected by probability procedures, taking care to monitor the probability with which households are designated for inclusion at each step in the sample plan. Clusters of five to ten households are usually employed. This cluster size is generally accepted as offering a reasonable trade-off between the costs of interviewing and protecting against homogeneity within a cluster on an important variable such as race or income.

In the case of telephone polls, clustering helps deal with the low incidence of residential numbers among the thousands of phone numbers that an interviewing staff could call.

Sampling in Telephone Polls

Virtually all polls about politics reported by the media are conducted by telephone.[2] Therefore, we will elaborate on the trade-offs between cost-effectiveness in field work and sample variance as they apply to telephone polls.[3]

There are well over 150 million telephones in operation in the United States. These phones are assigned to 37,000 possible combinations of area codes and prefixes (or exchanges, which make up the first three digits of a local number), for a total of 370 million different phone numbers that might be assigned to a given residence. But only about one-fourth of these numbers are residential. The rest have been assigned by the telephone companies to businesses and institutions, or are not working numbers.

The need for some system to reduce the volume of unproductive calls (that is, calls to nonresidential or unassigned numbers) quickly becomes apparent where "random digit dialing" (RDD) is used in its pure form (lists of random numbers generated by a computer). Press reports of polls commonly refer to interviews being conducted from an RDD sample. While RDD samples have the important advantage of random selection of households (including those with unlisted numbers) from all working numbers, they require a large number of dialings to yield a single completed interview at a household.

On average, it takes three to five dialings to determine whether a randomly generated number belongs to a residence or nonresidence, is not a working number, or has not been assigned by the phone company. Once the status of the number has been ascertained, there is a 75 percent chance it will be nonresidential. Taking both factors into account, it can take from fifteen to twenty calls to make the initial contact with a household. There is then a one-fifth to one-third chance that the individual answering the phone will refuse to participate in the poll. Applying these proportions to a hypothetical case of literal random digit dialing, it can take more than seventeen thousand separate dialings to complete a phone poll of one thousand interviews.

The inefficiency of the pure RDD approach has led pollsters to seek alternatives that increase the probability that each dialing will yield an interview. Some of the approaches that have been taken over the years are discussed below.

- Simply selecting numbers from telephone directories is inadequate because households with unlisted numbers are excluded and directories become dated even before they are published. A remedy, called "plus one" telephone sampling, has been to add "one" to the last digit of numbers taken from directories (for example, 495-1360 would become 495-1361).[4] However, this method does not protect against the contingency of a local phone company assigning its unlisted phones to a particular bank of numbers.
- It is possible, but time consuming, expensive, and sometimes not reliable, to cross-check phone numbers with various directories, such as "reverse directories" that list numbers by the location of residences, or phone lists developed by commercial mailing-list firms. However, these directories are often outdated, sometimes incomplete, and usually do not include the numbers of persons wishing to be unlisted.
- Increasingly, pollsters are buying telephone samples from private companies that specialize in keeping up-to-date records of working phone numbers and in identifying groups of phone numbers that can be eliminated because they are likely to be assigned to institutions. Interviewing staffs using such samples have a 65 to 70 percent chance of reaching a residence, compared with a 25 percent chance with simple random digit dialing. Firms that provide these samples can also tailor a sample to the pollster's specific needs. This is an important feature, as the boundaries of area codes and exchanges seldom conform to political or civil boundaries. Thus, without a tailored list, the first question in a poll must deal with whether the household reached is within the appropriate jurisdiction. Such questioning can be perceived as intrusive by the respondent.

- An approach taken with increasing frequency is that of sampling phone numbers in two stages. The most common variant of this approach, developed by Warren Mitofsky and Joseph Waksberg, is to conceive of a ten-digit phone number as having two elements. The first element (or "prefix") consists of the area code (three digits), the exchange (three digits), and the first two digits of the remaining number. The second element (or "suffix") consists of the last two digits. In the first stage of sampling a predetermined number of prefixes is randomly selected. In the second stage, one suffix per prefix is randomly selected and called. If the number turns out to be residential, other suffixes to the prefix are called until a specified number of residential contacts has been made. If the number turns out to be nonworking or nonresidential, the prefix is dropped from the sample. This approach achieves about 60 percent efficiency in finding residences in its second stage.[5]

Respondent Selection at the Household

The next point at which the costs of field work and variance intersect in a sampling plan is in the instructions given to interviewers regarding which individual in a household to try to interview and what to do if that person is not at home at the time of the initial contact. The problem obtains whether the survey is being conducted in person or by telephone.

In order to be able to compute the overall variance of a sample, the procedures used to select respondents must permit an analysis of the probability with which the respondent approached for an interview was selected from among all individuals in the household eligible for inclusion in the sample (the criterion of eligibility usually being voting age). This means three things. First, interviewers need to ascertain the number of telephone numbers assigned to the household. (A household with two phone numbers would have twice the chance of falling into the sample as a household with one number.) Second, interviewers must obtain basic information about the number of eligible respondents in a household contacted. Third, the range of discretion available to interviewers in determining who in the household to interview should be reduced as much as possible.

Three techniques used at the respondent-selection stage ensure that each individual in the household has a known chance of being interviewed. These techniques vary in the degree to which they may be perceived as intrusive, a significant consideration since inquiries about the composition of the household are the largest source of refusal to participate in a survey interview.[6]

- The most direct approach, named after the well-known sampling statistician Leslie Kish, is for the interviewer to ascertain the sex and age composition of the household and randomly select a respondent from this list. Although this procedure has logical appeal, it can appear invasive to potential respondents.[7]
- Rather than conducting a census of the household, an alternative approach asks only how many adults and how many men live in the household. A number of grids (four to six) displaying varying respondent-selection criteria are alternated to determine whom to approach in a household for an interview. The cumulative effect of using the grids is to achieve an equal probability of selection by sex and age in most households (that is, those containing up to four adults).[8]
- A third approach is the "next birthday" method in which interviewers ask to speak with the adult in the household with the next or most recent birthday.[9] Although the simplicity of the technique is appealing, problems occur if inquiries about birthdays are seen as threatening, as they often are among persons receiving various kinds of public benefits, or if the birthdate information is not known by all adults in the household.

These methods are used in "probability" samples—that is, samples in which it is possible to determine the probability (or known chance) of an individual falling into the sample at each stage of the sampling process. "Modified probability" samples are those in which probability methods are used at one stage of the selection process and nonprobability procedures are used at another (usually at the respondent-selection stage).

In the most common approach to "modified probability" sampling, the interviewer is instructed to ask to speak with a generically specified respondent, such as the "youngest man" or "oldest woman." In a more controlled sampling design, the specification is rotated from household to household in a pattern that usually achieves a good representation of respondents by age and sex, although not of age within sex.[10] In less controlled designs, interviewers are instructed to speak with either the "youngest man" or "oldest woman," depending on the number of interviews with each sex that has been prescribed for the interviewer.

Sometimes interviewers are instructed to interview whoever answers the phone. At other times their only instruction is to fulfill quotas of a specified number of men and women. In these situations a poll's sample can become biased through exclusion of those least likely to be at home when the interviewer first calls and through overrepresentation of people eager to cooperate with the interviewer. This loose procedure is often followed in "volunteer" polling operations in support of candidates eager to save money. Money is saved, but at great cost to the quality of the data.

These approaches to respondent selection are less invasive than probability methods that ask about household composition, but this advantage comes at a cost: Without the use of probability procedures in selecting respondents within households, the pollster has no way of knowing what chance those interviewed had of ending up in the sample. As a result, probability theory cannot be used to estimate the chance that the sample is unrepresentative. Therefore, the variance of the sample, and thus its "sampling error," *cannot* be computed. This means that *no* assertions about the poll's possible margin of error can be made in reports about the poll—whether on television, in a newspaper, or in a confidential briefing to a client.

Refusals, Response Rates, and Callbacks

Many news reporters and poll consumers tend to assume that a kind of mechanical process undergirds the generation of reported results. They lose sight of the fact that polling is a distinctly human transaction between interviewer and respondent. Dramatic evidence of this point is the challenge interviewers often face in securing the cooperation of the person who answers the phone and of the individual ultimately selected for interviewing.

Refusals. From one-fifth to one-third of the households approached by interviewers, whether by telephone or in person, refuse to participate in a poll. Refusal rates have been creeping upward since the 1950s and tend to be most troublesome in urbanized areas.[11] Refusals usually occur before the interviewer has had a chance to begin asking questions.[12] For this reason, it is desirable to minimize the intrusiveness of the questions about household composition used in respondent selection. In addition to initial refusals, about 5 percent of respondents in phone surveys "terminate" the interview for one reason or another. (Terminations in personal-interview surveys occur much less frequently.)[13]

"Refusal conversion" is possible when interviewers are well trained and well supervised.[14] Most often the reason for refusals is the inconvenience or timing of the request for an interview.[15] For this reason it is desirable that the interviewing staff have the flexibility to call a designated respondent back at a more convenient time to complete an interview. In addition, the well-trained interviewer can often persuade a reluctant potential respondent to participate by allaying doubts about the legitimacy of the study and worries about how long the interview might take.[16] It has been shown that the proportion of individuals ultimately willing to consent to a telephone interview has more to do with attempts to convert refusals than with the way the survey is introduced to the respondent. Therefore, as a general rule, the sooner the interviewer can get to the questions the better.[17]

Who refuses?   The research literature on the frequency with which various demographic groups refuse to be interviewed by telephone is considerable. The principal findings are that older persons tend to decline participation in surveys more than other age groups in both personal and phone surveys (but the phone refusal rate is more pronounced), and that blacks, less-educated persons, and individuals with lower incomes are less willing to be interviewed by telephone.[18]

Response rates and callbacks.   Dealing with refusals is only part of the problem of achieving a good "response rate," a term that refers to the percent of the designated potential respondents with whom interviews are completed.[19] Without using probability procedures to select respondents at the household, one has no idea what the chance is that an individual in the household will be approached for an interview. Therefore, response rates cannot be computed for samples that do not follow probability procedures throughout.

Just as important as refusals in determining response rates is the completion of interviews with people who have been designated as intended respondents but who are not at home when the interviewer calls. A poll in which only one attempt is made to reach the designated respondent will show a distinct bias toward women and older persons because they are most likely to be at home when the interviewer contacts the household.

"Callbacks"—or subsequent attempts to reach the designated respondent, whether by phone or in person—are the principal means by
which response rates are increased. Bringing hard-to-reach respondents
into a sample rounds out its demographic profile, making the sample
more representative. In addition, if there is reason to believe that an
initially reluctant respondent may consent to an interview, a callback
provides the opportunity to convert an earlier refusal.

The efficacy of callbacks was demonstrated conclusively by Michael
Traugott in a telephone survey of the state of Michigan in August 1984
in which as many as 30 attempts were made to contact designated
respondents. Of all respondents in the survey, 39 percent were interviewed on the first or second attempt, 57 percent had been interviewed
after three calls, 68 percent after four calls, 92 percent after ten calls,
and 96 percent after 15 calls.[20]

With successive callbacks the representativeness of the sample improved. For example, individuals aged 30 years or younger made up 23
percent of the sample after the first call; their proportion increased to 30
percent in the full sample. The male proportion of the sample was 34
percent after the first call and 44 percent by the time all interviews had
been completed. (See Appendix A, Table A-3 for complete data.)

Traugott concluded from the study that "by four calls (three callbacks) the sample assumes characteristics that are very close to those
observed by contacting another one-third of the eventual sample using
five or more calls."[21] It is thus reasonable that when polling firms do
callbacks (usually on successive days) they seldom make more than four
attempts to contact a designated respondent.

The changing demographic composition of the sample resulting
from successive callbacks in the Michigan poll also affected the political
profile of the sample. Whereas 51 percent of respondents after the first
call described themselves as Democrats, only 46 percent of the ultimate
sample so described themselves. Ronald Reagan's approval rating as
president was 47 percent among those interviewed on the first call but
was 58 percent when the entire sample had been interviewed. Similarly,
Reagan led Mondale by 48 to 45 percent after one call but by 52 to 39
percent after all calls had been made. Thus, as the Michigan case
demonstrates, without at least three callbacks the sample may be biased
on party affiliation and candidate preference, obviously key variables in
a preelection survey.

The experience of both the Gallup and Harris Polls in 1988 further

TABLE 3-1   Percent for Bush and Dukakis after Successive Callbacks

	Bush	Dukakis	Undecided	Number of interviews
After 1 call	47.8%	44.8%	7.4%	793
After 2 calls	48.9	43.6	7.5	977
After 3 calls	49.1	43.4	7.5	1,000

SOURCE: The Gallup Organization, used with permission.

underscores the importance of callbacks. As Table 3-1 shows, a Gallup Poll of one thousand respondents in October yielded an increasingly Republican cast to results obtained with successive calls. Similarly, successive calls in the last wave of interviewing conducted by Harris before the 1988 election increased the Bush margin. Of the 581 people interviewed on the first call, 49.5 percent supported Bush. However, the Bush percentage grew to 50.9 when the 113 people not reached until the second, third, or fourth attempt were added to the sample.

The variation in patterns of political preference by successive calls is vivid demonstration of the dangers of overnight polls, which usually do not provide for callbacks and thus exclude from their samples people not interviewed on the first approach to a household. Generalizing from the Michigan study, this can be well over half of all eligible respondents.[22]

Sample Coverage: Telephone versus In-Person Surveys

In spite of the dominance of the telephone in public opinion surveys, there are attributes of the personal-interview survey that are impossible to replicate by telephone. Relative to telephone interviewing, the in-person interview can increase rapport between respondent and interviewer, increase the likelihood that older persons will consent to be interviewed, permit use of displays, and expand opportunities for questioning about more sensitive political and financial matters. Personal interviews also permit use of the "secret ballot" technique in which respondents can mark their candidate preference on a ballot which is then placed in a ballot box carried by the interviewer.[23]

A major drawback to telephone polls is the sizeable proportion of households in the United States having no telephone (7.2 percent in 1986).[24] More important, nonphone households are not evenly distrib-

Relative Merits of Phone and Personal Interviews

	Phone	Personal
Speed	Faster	Slower
Cost[a]	Cheaper	More expensive
Establishing rapport between interviewer and respondent	Usually harder	Usually easier
Supervising work of interviewing staff	Easier	Harder
Proportion of respondents not voicing an opinion on questions asked	Slightly higher	Slightly lower
Observation of respondent's living conditions and neighborhood	Impossible	Possible
Ease with which respondents (especially older persons) can comprehend intent of questions	More difficult	Less difficult
Use of cards and displays that help respondents understand questions and achieve efficiency in covering material (such as lists of problems)	Impossible	Possible
Responses to open-ended questions	Usually shorter	Usually longer
Interview length[b]	Shorter	Longer
Respondent ease in talking about financial and political matters	Sometimes reduced	Sometimes increased
Use of secret ballot	Impossible	Possible

[a] Although telephone interviews are generally less expensive to conduct, if the questionnaire requires more than a half-hour of interviewing time, telephone costs increase to the point that personal interviews can become quite competitive.

[b] Pollsters are generally of the view that respondents will cooperate longer in personal interviews than over the telephone. However, research on the respondent's perception of the "burden" of an interview shows that it is not just the length of the interview that is involved. The subject matter affects people's willingness to stay with an interview, as does the amount of effort required of the respondent in the conversation. See Laure M. Sharp and Joanne Frankel, "Respondent Burden: A Test of Some Assumptions," *Public Opinion Quarterly* 47 (Spring 1983): 36-53.

uted among various social, economic, and demographic subgroups within the population.

As might be expected, poorer households are more likely to be without a phone. As might not be expected, however, the proportion of such households can exceed one in three: in the South, for example, 35.1 percent of all households below the poverty line in 1986 had no phone. But factors other than household income may be at work. Older persons who may be socially isolated or hearing-impaired may decline phone service even though they can afford it; mobile younger people may also decide against a phone.[25]

The incidence of households without telephones remains striking among households with children under six years of age; blacks; Hispanics; separated persons; married persons with no spouse at home; those with less than a high school education; those in households with an income of less than $15,000 (1986 dollars); those below the poverty line, especially in the South; unemployed persons; and those under 25 living with other than both parents.[26] An expanded display of the demographic profile of nonphone households can be found in Appendix A, Table A-4.

More elaborate breakdowns of these same data show the severity of the bias that exclusion of nonphone households from the sample can cause. For example, the percent of nonphone households in the South containing a child under six years is strikingly high among lower-income households: 59.0 percent of households with an income of less than $5,000 and 41.1 percent of households with an income of between $5,000 and $9,999 do not have telephone service.[27]

Of those households without a telephone, approximately two-thirds have no access to a telephone. Most of the remaining one-third have to go to another building (usually not adjacent) to get to a phone.[28]

The importance of the distribution of nonphone households is accentuated when the distribution of response rates is also taken into account (Table 3-2). Phone coverage and response rates can interact in shaping the composition of a phone sample. For example, if 93 percent of households nationwide have telephones and a response rate of 77 percent can be achieved in those households, 72 percent of the pool of potential respondents will be interviewed. However, the interaction of phone coverage and response rates varies among subgroups. Specifically, older persons, blacks, and the less educated are the most likely to be underrepresented in phone polls, whereas middle-aged persons, whites,

TABLE 3-2   Estimated Percent of Target Population Interviewed by Telephone Taking into Account "Coverage" and "Overall Response Rate"

	Phone coverage[a]	Response rate[b]	Percent interviewed[c]
Total	93	77	72
By sex			
Male	92	76	70
Female	93	79	73
By age			
17-24 years	89	75	67
25-44 years	94	84	79
45-64 years	96	77	74
65 years and over	97	62	60
By race			
White	94	78	73
Black	84	73	61
By education			
Less than 12 years	87	65	56
12 years	94	76	71
13 years or more	97	91	88

SOURCE: Owen T. Thornberry, Jr., and James T. Massey, "Trends in United States Telephone Coverage Across Time and Subgroups," in *Telephone Survey Methodology*, ed. Robert M. Groves, Paul B. Biemer, Lars E. Lyberg, James T. Massey, William L. Nicholls II, and Joseph Waksberg (New York: John Wiley and Sons, 1988): 48.

[a] Percent of households having a telephone.

[b] Average for the three national random-digit dial telephone surveys conducted by the National Center for Health Statistics, the federal agency for which the National Health Interview Survey is conducted. The cumulative sample size for the three surveys was 6,265.

[c] Coverage multiplied by response rate.

and the better educated are the most likely to be overrepresented relative to their numbers in the population as a whole.

Note in Table 3-2 the similarity in the "percent interviewed" among blacks and among those 65 years of age and over. The low rates have different origins. In the case of blacks, the low rate is explained principally by relatively lower phone coverage. In the case of older persons, the lower rate is explained by a higher refusal rate or tendency to defer to younger respondents in the household. This underscores the point that *both* coverage and response rates must be taken into account in assessing the adequacy of a sample.

The problems of coverage in telephone surveys relative to personal-interview surveys should not be overstated. With the exception of the U.S. Bureau of the Census, survey organizations seldom achieve nearly complete coverage in door-to-door surveys. Moreover, the telephone can provide access to households otherwise unreachable because of controlled entries and security arrangements.

Nonetheless, factoring in both coverage and response rates, telephone surveys yield samples that can differ from personal-interview surveys in important respects. Groves and Kahn's systematic comparison of the two interview modes highlights the persistent problem of nonresponse in telephone surveys. Table 3-3 summarizes the Groves and Kahn data and portrays a telephone sample that tends to be younger, more affluent, better educated, and more white than the personal-interview sample.

Weighting

Judicious weighting of a poll's results can prove essential to its reliability. This has nothing to do with "cooking the data," as is sometimes alleged. Rather, the objective is two-fold: to take into account the probabilities with which individual respondents are selected to become part of the sample and to mitigate problems of both phone coverage and nonresponse.[29]

Probabilities of selection.   In almost all polls, whether by phone or in person, people become eligible with unequal probabilities for inclusion in the sample. Households with two phone numbers, for example, have twice the chance of being called as households with one. Persons living in a larger household have less chance of being interviewed than persons living in a smaller household, assuming the study design provides for probability selection of respondents within the household.

To compensate for these inequities, the careful pollster will have interviewers ascertain the number of telephone numbers assigned to the household and the number of adults living in the household. Appropriate weightings for number of phones and members of the household can then be applied. In addition, unequal probabilities of selection are often built into the design of a sample when it is stratified on one or more variables or when a particular subgroup is to be oversampled. In those cases, appropriate weightings also need to be introduced.

TABLE 3-3   Composition of Samples by Mode of Interviewing

	Telephone	Personal
By age		
18-29	30.2%	28.2%
30-39	20.6	17.7
40-49	17.3	16.7
50-59	15.0	15.2
60-69	10.8	12.5
70 and over	6.0	9.6
	99.9	99.9
By sex		
Male	46.8	43.7
Female	53.2	56.3
	100.0	100.0
By race		
White	87.1	85.6
Black	9.3	10.6
Hispanic	2.3	2.8
Other	1.3	1.0
	100.0	100.0
By education		
Less than high school	9.5	15.6
Some high school	14.2	15.8
High school diploma	21.6	21.4
More than high school but less than B.A.	38.0	33.4
B.A. level degree	11.9	10.1
Advanced degree	4.9	3.7
	100.1	100.0
By total family income		
Less than $7,500	19.6	26.5
$7,500-$15,000	30.3	30.6
More than $15,000	50.1	42.9
	100.0	100.0

SOURCE: Robert M. Groves and Robert L. Kahn, *Surveys by Telephone: A National Comparison with Personal Interviews* (New York: Academic Press, 1979): 91-97.

NOTE: Telephone and personal samples relied on random selection of respondents at household level and many callbacks.

Poststratification.   Compounding any unequal probabilities of selection that may be inherent in the sample design are the problems of bias arising from nonresponse (mostly refusals) in both phone and in-person surveys and, in the case of phone surveys, from the incidence of nonphone households. To compensate for such biases, pollsters often use "poststratification," a process that involves weighting an obtained sample according to known characteristics of the population.[30] This requires current and accurate information about the population, which is not always easy to obtain. For example, data on the distribution of the population by educational attainment and income are not as readily available as up-to-date information on distributions by sex, race, age, and geographic area.

Under most practical circumstances, weighting reduces the variance of estimates made from a sample. However, it should be done with great care.

Turnout

About 235,000 people took part in the Democratic and Republican caucuses in Iowa in 1988—just over 11 percent of the voting age population of the state. Pollsters interested in measuring the sentiments of likely caucus-goers faced the imposing task of identifying this narrow band of the population. Put another way, the challenge was to eliminate the 89 percent of the population eighteen years of age or older not likely to attend a caucus. This meant that the candidate preferences of about nine out of every ten people contacted in a randomly selected sample were not relevant for a precaucus measurement. The question for the pollster was *which* nine in ten respondents should be eliminated from the sample.

The importance of identifying likely participants in an early caucus or primary is heightened by the fact that the contest is within a political party, thereby eliminating the stabilizing effect party loyalty has on the choice of as much as two-thirds of the electorate. While apparent swings in voter preference in precaucus and preprimary polls can reflect genuine indecision on the part of likely voters, they can also result from including in reported poll results the preferences of people who have little probability of ever attending the caucus or casting a primary ballot.

Variable levels of turnout remain a thorny problem for pollsters in general elections. Voter participation can range widely from state to state. In the 1988 presidential election, for example, only 39 percent of the voting age population turned out in Georgia, South Carolina, and the District of Columbia, but over 62 percent did so in Minnesota, Montana, and Maine.[31]

In connection with his study of media-sponsored preelection polls in 1980 and 1984, Crespi interviewed the principals of more than two dozen polling organizations and found widespread agreement that "one of the weakest design features of most polls is their inability to identify correctly likely voters, especially in low turnout elections." [32] The quantitative phase of his study corroborated the pollsters' concern by showing that the higher the turnout in an election, the more accurate were polls conducted before it, and the better a poll differentiated between likely and unlikely voters, the closer it was to the election's outcome. [33]

Three approaches—screening, scaling, and weighting—are taken to deal with the problem of turnout.

Screening. The simplest approach is asking questions to determine whether a designated respondent should be interviewed further or be screened out of the sample. The first such question is usually whether the respondent is registered to vote. Subsequent questions vary in number and mix. Sometimes only one additional question is asked, such as a straightforward inquiry about how likely it is that the respondent will vote. At other times a series of questions is asked, exploring the likelihood of a respondent's actually voting, past voting behavior, and the degree of interest in the election. The only respondents retained for the full interview are those whose replies to such screening questions indicate the intention to vote.

There are two drawbacks to this approach. First, by not obtaining background information on all respondents—including those screened out—it is impossible to assess the quality of the sample against known characteristics of the population.

Second, it is well known that respondents tend to give socially desirable answers in poll questions. Thus the proportion of people who say they are registered usually exceeds the proportion actually registered. When Gallup interviewers went back to check precinct records after the 1984 presidential election, they found that about one-fifth of respondents in the preelection poll had indicated they were registered to vote when they were not. Eighty-five percent of respondents reported that they were registered; in fact the names of only 67 percent appeared in the precinct records. [34] This is one reason why Gallup uses the more reliable method of scaling.

Scaling. This approach also uses a series of questions regarding the likelihood of voting. However, rather than using the questions to determine when to terminate an interview with a respondent deemed unlikely to vote, the questions are used to develop a scale on which the likelihood of each respondent's voting can be scored. This approach was pioneered by Paul K. Perry for the Gallup Poll.

When the technique was first employed in 1950, five questions were asked. As many as nine questions would ultimately be employed. By going back to election records in precincts where respondents indicated they were registered, Gallup interviewers were able to determine which respondents interviewed prior to the election had actually voted.

Over the years this information helped Perry develop a measure of the efficiency of each of the nine questions in predicting that an individual respondent would vote.[35] The nine questions were then used in combination, through the statistical technique of Guttman scaling, to point to a single dimension: the chance that an individual respondent would vote on election day. With scores for each respondent's likelihood of voting in hand, the entire sample could then be arrayed from respondents most likely to vote to those least likely to vote.

The next problem was to estimate the probable proportion of the voting age population that would actually vote. Perry found that responses to two of the nine questions in the turnout scale, when compared with the responses in the previous election, were quite predictive of aggregate turnout for the country as a whole. (The two questions relate to voter interest in the election and past voting behavior.) The turnout percentage thus obtained was then applied to the overall sample. The Gallup Poll's final preelection percentages for the candidates would then be tabulated on the basis of only that portion of the sample corresponding to the expected turnout.[36]

Perry reports that Gallup's experience with the turnout scale was particularly helpful in off-year elections. Reviewing data for 14 national elections (1950-1976), Perry found that tabulations based on full samples tended to be four percentage points more Democratic in off-year elections than tabulations based only on likely voters. There was still a difference between total and likely voter samples in years when there were presidential elections, but it was only two percentage points.[37]

Weighting by attributes associated with voting.   The third approach to turnout is to weight each respondent in the sample using a coefficient resulting from a mix of personal characteristics that have been shown to be associated with voting: attributes (such as education and region of the country), attitudes (such as intensity of partisanship, interest in the election, and sense of civic duty), and reported past voting behavior. Postelection validation of whether respondents actually voted is used to determine how closely related each characteristic is to turnout. This approach has evolved out of the National Election Studies conducted by the University of Michigan.

CBS News has adopted a variant of this approach that incorporates some of the Perry scale questions. The advantage Warren Mitofsky sees over the Perry-Gallup turnout scaling is that weighting each respondent retains a larger sample base for making preelection estimates of voter preference.[38] That is, unlike the Perry-Gallup approach, which drops unlikely voters from the base on which preferences are computed, *every* individual in the sample is counted in the final tabulations, some being weighted more heavily and others less heavily. Rather than speaking of poll results based upon interviews with "likely voters," CBS News reports results for "the probable electorate," in which voting intentions are weighted for the probability that each respondent will vote.

Even the best plans can go awry. For all their efforts to devise ways of dealing with varying levels of turnout, pollsters can be confounded by the get-out-the-vote efforts of enthusiastic partisans and by the statistical uncertainties caused by excessively low voter turnout.

The stunning showing of television evangelist Pat Robertson in Iowa's 1988 Republican caucuses is a case in point. When the *Des Moines Register and Tribune* tabulated its last precaucus poll on the basis of those "likely" to go to a Republican caucus, Robertson was supported by 13 percent to Bush's 23 percent. When the screen was tightened, so that the tabulations reflected only those who would "definitely" go to a caucus, Robertson's percentage rose to 19, putting him about even with Bush's support of 20 percent.[39] The next day, Robertson topped Bush decisively (24.6 to 18.6 percent) and caused speculation about Bush's vulnerability in the primaries to follow.[40] The chances are that even had the Iowa poll used a tighter likely voter screen, it would not have picked up the magnitude of Robertson's margin over Bush, for when turnout is as low as 11 percent of the voting age population, it is almost impossible to screen reliably for the likely voter.

A final point about gauging turnout in election polling is in order. Since most schemes for dealing with likelihood of voting have the effect of reducing the size of the samples upon which candidate preferences are computed, pollsters and poll consumers need to be mindful of the number of interviews on which reported percentages are based. This can be quite problematic in elections for which turnout is very low, such as many presidential primaries, races below the state level, and primaries for statewide office. Unless the size of the sample before screening is substantial enough, the number of cases of likely voters upon which preferences are based can be too small to produce statistically valid conclusions.

One need only remember that the turnout in the 1988 New Hampshire primary was less than 40 percent of the voting age population. Forty percent of what started as a 750-case statewide sample is only 300 interviews; 40 percent of a 500-case sample is just 200 interviews. In the words of the polling coordinator for the *Atlanta Journal-Constitution* at the time of the 1988 Super Tuesday primaries: "In the last survey, we were down to about 200 voters in each primary whom we were convinced would vote. The margin of error was roughly plus or minus eight percentage points, so I did a lot of praying." [41]

Interviewing

A final, but critical, facet of control over a poll's sample is the oversight of the field operation. Now that most polls are conducted by telephone from central facilities, control over the interviewing process has been greatly simplified: supervisors now can patch in through a master console to monitor interviews underway. Problems can be spotted and addressed quickly.

Phone interviewing is not without its problems, however. Respondents tend to be more comfortable in personal interview situations than when interviewed by telephone. Groves and Kahn have shown that people are more reluctant to discuss financial, political, and socially sensitive matters by phone than they are in person.[42] They also report that the faster pace of the telephone interview can compromise the quality of the information collected. A tendency of respondents to give shorter answers by phone can result in information that is less complete than that obtained in slower-paced personal interviews.[43]

The race of interviewers can also have an effect on the replies of some respondents. In the 1989 gubernatorial election in Virginia and mayoral race in New York, preelection polls and exit polls reported percentages for the two victorious black candidates in excess of the vote they in fact received. In both cases, there was evidence that white respondents were more reluctant to express their opposition to the black

TABLE 3-4   Effect of Interviewer Race on Expressed Opinions about Jesse Jackson (1988 New York Presidential Primary)

	Opinion of Jesse Jackson		
	Favorable	Unfavorable	Don't know
Among white respondents			
With white interviewer	21%	50%	29%
With black interviewer	29	39	31
Among black respondents			
With white interviewer	79	4	17
With black interviewer	93	0	7

SOURCE: Murray Edelman and Warren J. Mitofsky, "The Effect of the Interviewer's Race in Political Surveys with Multiracial Candidates" (Paper delivered to the 45th Annual Conference of the American Association for Public Opinion Research, Lancaster, Pa., May 17-20, 1990).

candidate when they were being interviewed by a black than when responding to questions from a white interviewer.[44] As Table 3-4 indicates, CBS News found statistically significant differences in the ratings obtained by Jesse Jackson in the course of its polling prior to the 1988 New York Democratic primary.

One way to mitigate the effects of the interviewer's race in interracial elections is to assign interviewers to phone numbers or neighborhoods of known racial composition. As challenging as race-of-interviewer problems are becoming, they are amenable to analysis and to some correction, given adequate control of the interviewing operation.

It is when there is little control over field work that problems in data collection go unnoticed; in such cases steps can seldom be taken to compensate for data of poor quality. In order to cut costs, political campaigns and grass-roots polling operations often enlist the services of volunteer interviewers. For example, as many as a quarter of the interviews conducted for the 1988 Dukakis campaign were conducted by volunteers. This kind of an arrangement is fraught with potential problems: a high turnover in interviewing staff; uneven and often inadequate training of interviewers, which results in lower response rates (less trained interviewers have more difficulty getting an interview started and are less adept at converting refusals); the possibility of bias because of enthusiasm for the candidate; and an inability to pinpoint problems in a timely fashion.

Sampling Error: Essential Information or False Precision?

Media reports of polls usually include a tag line regarding the "margin of error." Initially the practice was a bow to pollsters worried that pertinent aspects of the methodology of polls, including sampling error, were not being covered by news organizations. With time, however, many pollsters have become concerned that the "margin of error" statement is little more than perfunctory and may in fact detract from the intent of acquainting the audience with the probabilistic nature of public opinion polling.

The Concept of Sampling Error

We noted earlier that the variance of a sample depends not only on how many people are in the sample but also how they are selected for inclusion in the sample.

Let us first consider how sample size affects variance. Suppose a question about the approval of the president was asked in an infinite number of polls conducted in the same way at the same time. Suppose further that each sample had 300 cases and that the mean approval rating from each sample that resulted most frequently was 50 percent. The distribution of the separate ratings from the infinite number of samples would appear as in Figure 3-1, around 50 percent and with a gently sloping curve. This is called the "sampling distribution." The gentle slope of the curve reflects the degree to which the results of each separate poll vary from the mean of all the polls. This is expressed as the "standard deviation" of the sampling distribution.

Now suppose the president's approval rating had been tested in an infinite number of polls, each consisting of a sample of one thousand cases. Again, let us assume that the most frequent rating from the samples was 50 percent. In this instance, the sampling distribution of the infinite number of approval ratings, also shown in Figure 3-1, would still be around 50 percent but with a much steeper curve as a greater proportion of the ratings fell closer to 50 percent. That is, there would be less variance in the distribution, hence a smaller standard deviation. In other words, assuming that other sampling and nonsampling factors held constant, the larger the sample size, the closer the approximation of the approval rating that would have resulted if the entire population had

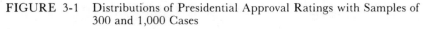

FIGURE 3-1   Distributions of Presidential Approval Ratings with Samples of 300 and 1,000 Cases

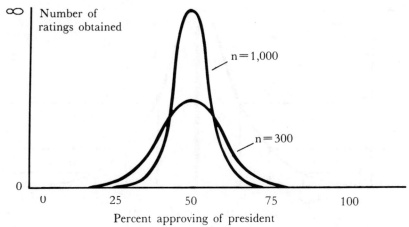

been interviewed, a phenomenon known as the Central Limit Theorem.

Because a single poll does not involve interviews with an infinite number of samples, we do not use the term "standard deviation" to describe a sample's variance. However, we do use the concept of sampling distribution to guide us in calculating the "standard error" of the mean (usually reported as a percentage) of a sample. In the case of our illustration, the mean would be the approval rating. Technically, the standard error of the sample is the standard deviation of the sampling distribution that would theoretically emerge if approval ratings had been obtained from an infinite number of samples of the size specified.

A second factor affects variance. In addition to a sample's size, its variance is also affected if potential respondents become eligible for inclusion in the sample with unequal probabilities of selection. Thus, in the case of commonly adopted sampling procedures for telephone polls, clustering of the sample to increase the cost-effectiveness of reaching residential numbers has the effect of slightly increasing sample variance.

Sampling variance is usually expressed in terms of "sampling error," stated as an interval surrounding a percentage reported in a poll. It is reported at a given "level of confidence" depending on how confident one wants to be that the sample upon which a percentage is based is not one of the fluke samples that is possible among the infinite number of samples that could be drawn.

FIGURE 3-2   Standard Errors at Varying Levels of Confidence

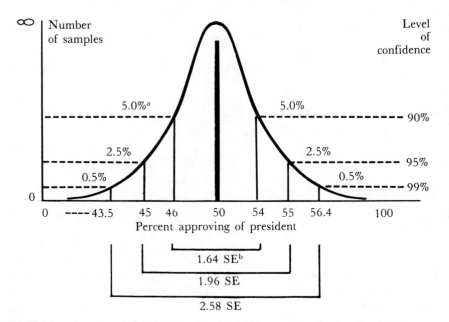

NOTE: Assumes a presidential approval rating of 50 percent and a sample of 400.

[a] Percent of ratings at a given level of confidence. For example, 10 percent of all ratings at the 90 percent level of confidence are outside a range of 1.64 times the standard error from the mean approval rating of 50 percent. That is, 5 percent fall between zero and 46 percent approving and 5 percent between 54 and 100 percent approving.

[b] SE = standard error.

Figure 3-2 shows that the more confident one wants to be in a poll percentage, the larger the margin one needs to allow. Let us again take the example of the president's approval rating and assume a sample of four hundred cases, the standard error for which is approximately 2.5 percentage points.

- An interval or "margin" equal to 1.64 times the standard error on each side of a reported percentage approving the president will ensure protection against chance error for all but ten percent of the infinite number of samples that could be drawn. In this case, an interval of about four percentage points (2.5 x 1.64 = 4.1) is required above and below a reported 50 percent approval rating (46 to

TABLE 3-5 Sampling Error for Percentages of Varying Size for Samples of Varying Size (at the 95 percent level of confidence)

Percentages around	Number of interviews in total sample or subgroup						
	2000	1500	1000	600	400	200	100
5% or 95%	1	1	2	2	3	4	5
10% or 90%	2	2	2	3	4	5	7
20% or 80%	2	3	3	4	5	7	10
35% or 65%	3	3	4	5	6	8	12
50%	3	3	4	5	6	9	12

SOURCE: Warren Mitofsky and Martin Plissner, "A Reporter's Guide to Published Polls," *Public Opinion* (June/July 1980): 19.

54 percent). This is referred to as the "90 percent level of confidence."

• An interval equal to 1.96 times the standard error on each side of a reported percentage will protect against all but five percent of possible fluke samples, referred to as the "95 percent level of confidence." To achieve this level of confidence an interval of about five percentage points (2.5 x 1.96 = 4.9) is required on either side of the reported 50 percent (45 to 55 percent).

• An interval equal to 2.58 times the standard error is needed to achieve the "99 percent level of confidence." Hence, about six-and-a-half percentage points (2.5 x 2.58 = 6.45) is required above and below the reported percent (43.5 to 56.4 percent).

Sampling error is usually reported in the news media at the 95 percent level of confidence.

For ready reference, a sample error chart appears in Table 3-5. It displays the sampling error for samples of different sizes at the 95 percent level of confidence. Note that the sampling error differs depending on the size of the percentage being reported. For example, if a president was lucky enough to have an approval rating of around 80 percent, the sampling error would be three percentage points with a sample of one thousand cases. However, were the approval rating at 50 percent, the sampling error would be slightly larger (four percentage points) assuming the same sample size.

In addition to determining sampling error for an entire sample from

TABLE 3-6   Sampling Error for Differences between Percentages

Size of Sample B	Percentages near 50 (at 95 percent level of confidence)			
	Size of Sample A			
	750	600	400	200
750	6			
600	7	7		
400	7	8	8	
200	10	10	10	12

Size of Sample B	Percentages near 20 or 80 (at 95 percent level of confidence)			
	Size of Sample A			
	750	600	400	200
750	5			
600	5	6		
400	6	6	7	
200	8	8	8	10

SOURCE: The Gallup Organization.

the table, one can also find the sampling error for a portion of the sample, assuming that subsample sizes are known.

Sampling error becomes critical in the analysis of public opinion data in examining the differences between two surveys or between subgroups within a single survey. Consult Table 3-6 on "sampling error for differences" to find the number of percentage points needed before one can conclude (at the 95 percent level of confidence) that the difference between two percentages did not occur by chance. For example, if a candidate goes from 54 percent support to 60 percent in two 400-case polls, one cannot conclude that the difference is statistically significant (eight points being the required allowance for sampling error of the difference between the two percentages). When the Gallup Poll reported on the basis of a 1,000-case sample that there was a ten percentage point difference in approval of Ronald Reagan's job performance between men (59 percent) and women (49 percent), the difference could be regarded as statistically significant (a difference of at least 7 percentage points between two 500-case subsamples being required).

Reporting Sampling Error: Specious Precision?

When sampling error for a poll is reported, the implication is that probability procedures were employed properly at each stage of the sampling process, that every household selected was accounted for, and that the data were processed without error. As we have seen, probability procedures are sometimes not used, especially in selecting respondents at the household level, and response rates can be a problem without enough callbacks. The careful pollster, however, will use some form of probability selection at the household level and will factor response rates into calculations of sampling error.

The larger—and much more important—problem with reports of sampling error is that they imply that sampling is the primary, if not the only, source of possible error in a poll. As we will discuss later in this chapter, there are a host of other reasons why polls can differ, none of which has to do with sampling procedures. The most notable of these are the wording of questions and the order of questions in a poll.

News organizations have adopted the convention of rote reporting of sampling error. With more space available for poll stories, newspapers are more likely to supplement this information with the wording of questions upon which the reported percentages are based. Television seldom presents the wording of questions, although the thrust of a question may be described. The sampling error statement, however, is ever present.

At best, sampling error is important, but partial, information needed in assessing the validity of conclusions drawn from a poll; at worst it conveys a sense of precision to poll percentages that may be specious.

Pollsters differ among themselves on whether sampling error should be reported in releases about polls. The issue emerged in the late 1970s as pollsters were increasing their efforts to get news organizations to report pertinent information about the methodology of polls. Good arguments can be made for each side of the debate:

WARREN MITOFSKY: Sampling error does at least put the findings [of a poll] into some limited context. It's not an absolute answer to the data analysis problem. It is just an indication of one limitation in the data. You cannot withhold knowledge of sampling error by saying there are other errors. It is a disservice not to inform your reader, or your viewer, that there is a known and measurable source of error.[45]

BURNS W. ROPER: The media have overstressed sampling error and understressed the more important and considerably greater sources of error. And in the process of stressing sampling error, they have not warned the reader or viewer of error as they have intended. They have, in effect, said: 'This finding is accurate within three percentage points of what the entire American public thinks on this subject,' when, in fact, a differently worded question might—and often does—produce a result that is 25 or 30 points different from the reported result.[46]

The issue is still alive within the polling community. A "double standard" is the way Irving Crespi characterizes the inclusion of sampling error to the neglect of question wording in reports about polls. He argues: "Until news editors come to appreciate that the meaning of poll results lies as much in the wording of questions asked as in the percentages and their precision, the news media will be unable to do a satisfactory job in reporting opinion polls descriptively, let alone analytically."[47]

Political reporter E. J. Dionne, Jr., thinks the problem is less the failure to present the wording of questions than it is conveying "false precision" about a poll's result. Cliff Zukin of the Field Research Corporation believes that "there ought to be some way for the media to appear responsible other than by citing sampling error when we all know there are a host of other sources of possible error in a poll."[48]

The comments of Dionne and Zukin reflect a consensus that is beginning to form among pollsters: there is danger that specious precision is conveyed by statements of sampling error and that news organizations need to become more attuned to the complexities inherent in public opinion that can seldom be captured in one question.

Tracking Polls

Nothing impels a news organization to examine its ways more quickly than missing a story or getting it wrong. This was certainly the case with the 1980 election. The pollsters of both presidential candidates had better information day by day as to the disposition of the electorate than did the national polls conducted by news organizations. Unlike the major national polls, Richard Wirthlin, polling for Ronald Reagan, and Patrick Caddell, polling for Jimmy Carter, were not surprised by the magnitude of the Reagan victory.

Tracking polls had been in the repertoire of political polling for more than twenty years. Pollsters working for candidates found in tracking polls an immensely valuable tool for picking up the impact of events on public opinion and helping to make tactical adjustments in a campaign, particularly in scheduling the appearances of the candidate.

It was only after the 1980 elections, however, that news organizations began to sponsor tracking polls. The first highly visible demonstration of their utility to a news organization was the scoop earned by the ABC News/*Washington Post* poll in picking up a twelve-point gain by Gary Hart in the three days before the 1984 New Hampshire primary.[49] By 1988 tracking polls were more widely used by news organizations.

The Methodology of Tracking Polls

A "tracking poll" may be defined as a poll conducted as one in a series of polls, usually day by day, whose purpose is to monitor a small number of dimensions of public opinion. Tracking polls are used most often to pick up changes in the relative standing of candidates in an election. In theory they could be applied to any aspect of public opinion in which fluctuations are anticipated.

Methods used in tracking polls vary by pollster and by the situations in which they are used. The more important ways in which they vary are:

- Number of days in the field. Some tracking polls are based on interviews from a single evening. They run a sizeable risk because a single night's interviewing can yield results that are quite skewed, especially if the sample is small. It is for this reason that most tracking polls report the results of several nights' interviewing. Percentages reported from tracking polls will often be two- or three-day averages. When tracking is done day after day, a "rolling average" will usually be reported for the results of interviews conducted over the three most recent evenings. Even when several days' interviews are pooled, the results can be seriously misleading if the interviews from one evening have produced a biased sample.

- Sample size.   One of the major reasons tracking polls are so tricky to conduct and assess is that they usually rest on small samples. Tracking polls conducted by political campaigns can involve as few as 125 completed interviews per night. With centralized interviewing facilities and the financial resources to pay for them, sample sizes can be greatly increased. A large telephone interviewing facility can conduct several hundred interviews simultaneously.[50]
- Callbacks.   Callbacks are usually unworkable when interviewing is confined to a single evening because second attempts to reach a respondent the same evening are seldom productive. Nonetheless they can be built into tracking polls that cover more than one night. For example, the tracking polls conducted by ABC and the *Washington Post* in 1988 distributed interviews over three days as follows: the first night's interviewing would be entirely fresh calls; interviewing the second night would continue with fresh calls but also include callbacks to individuals not reached on the first night; the third night's work would be a mix of fresh calls and callbacks to individuals not reached on the second night.[51]

  When callbacks are built into the design of tracking polls, the cycling of attempts to reach hard-to-find respondents is such that second calls must be made within a day of the initial call and third calls are seldom possible. It is unrealistic to expect response rates in tracking polls to be as high as might be achieved with three or four callbacks. Indeed the amount of elapsed time to achieve such response rates would defeat the purpose of day-to-day tracking of public sentiment.
- Likely voters.   Tracking poll samples can become perilously unreliable as unlikely voters are screened out of samples that are small at the outset. As we have noted, turnout in primaries can be as low as one-third of the voting-age population and caucus turnout even lower. Even under the best of circumstances it is difficult to ascertain which two-thirds of all possible respondents should be eliminated from tabulations of candidate strength.
- Panels.   Reinterviewing individuals, the basic notion of a "panel" study, is a particularly efficient means of assessing changes in opinion. Panels pose two kinds of problems for pollsters: being able to recontact individuals interviewed on an earlier occasion and minimizing the extent to which individuals become self-consciously attentive to their own opinions because they are being reinterviewed. Both of these

problems are mitigated in tracking polls because the reinterview is usually within one or two days and respondents do not expect the second call. The panel approach was used to great advantage in polling done for the 1968 campaign of Richard Nixon by the Opinion Research Corporation. Harry O'Neill, who directed the polls, recalls that "the real benefit of the panel approach is that when you see change, you know it is real change within a good sample. That knowledge far outweighs whatever small panel effect there might be." [52]

Consistency of methodology is vital to the success of any tracking poll. As will be discussed in the next section, question wording and question order can affect the results of a poll. Thus, in successive tracking polls it is essential that questions be asked in the same way and in the same order. Similarly, instructions to interviewers regarding respondent selection at the household and callbacks must be consistent. Otherwise successive rounds of interviewing will yield data that may not be comparable.

Difficulties in Reporting Tracking Polls

With the increased use of tracking polls by news organizations has come the issue of the prudent standard of caution to be used in interpreting such polls. Within a campaign, tracking polls are but one source of information on which to base tactical decisions. Campaign pollsters and strategists are usually aware of the limitations of tracking polls and of the dangers of inferring too much from the results of a single night's interviewing. News organizations tend to report tracking polls on the basis of a rolling average of the last two or three nights of interviews. Even so, news organizations must exercise caution in reporting tracking polls because the reading and viewing audience do not share the political insider's tutored suspicion of even a three-day average. [53]

The value of information from tracking polls is quite different for a political campaign than it is for a news organization. Current intelligence on the thinking of the electorate permits campaigns to fine tune their tactics and occasionally even make changes in basic strategy. The issues to which the candidate speaks can be changed; television advertisements can be initiated, recast, or dropped on the basis of tracking polls; and the candidate's time, the most precious of all resources, can be more effectively scheduled.

Tracking polls are more difficult for news organizations to handle. Although tracking polls satisfy the journalistic appetite for information "as it happens," news reports of tracking polls can be confusing—even misleading. "The tracking survey is something that the public should never see," notes Democratic pollster Peter Hart. "You can't interview 150 people with any sense of real stability. It's too confusing for the public to benefit." [54]

When tracking polls suddenly register a change in voter preference, no matter how small the sample or problematic its reliability, it is easy to attribute more news value to the change than a prudent opinion analyst would indicate is warranted. As Adam Clymer of the *New York Times* puts it: "Tracking polls make more out of a given moment than is warranted. They exaggerate the impression of an event's impact because the politicians will come along and put a spin on the poll as if it was one critical moment. It feeds on itself." [55]

Moreover, many pollsters and journalists fear that release of tracking polls cultivates a general impression that the electorate responds erratically to the twists and turns of a campaign. This is particularly likely to happen if tracking polls are reported too early in a campaign, before the electorate has really begun to focus on the decision that lies ahead.

The public release of tracking polls can also aggravate some of the worst elements in the relationship between news organizations and polling. We noted in the last chapter that "the horse race" is a legitimate part of the news story of an election but it is far from the whole story— especially early on. When tracking polls are overreported, they can drive out other forms of political coverage essential to informing the electorate. "Tracking polls feed in an almost perverse way the focus on the horse race," notes Richard Wirthlin.[56] In so doing, tracking polls as news leave the public with characterizations of its own state of mind that are incomplete and simplistic. Sample sizes are so small that analysis of the views of subgroups is not possible. In addition, the questionnaires used in tracking polls tend to be so short that questions other than those required to conduct trial heats are seldom included.[57]

Preoccupation with the horse race and simplistic depictions of trends can obscure or crowd out reporting of the real dynamics of public opinion. When tracking polls conform to the prevailing consensus among journalists, the result is what Richard Morin of the *Washington Post* calls the "fatal mix where the people reporters trust are saying things the numbers purport to support and, at that point, all the caveats go out the window." [58]

Question Wording and Question Order

One indication of how sensitive an instrument the public opinion poll can be is the impact slight nuances in the wording of questions can have on the results obtained. Research on the wording of questions was part of the early agenda of public opinion research. Then, for some time, interest in aspects of opinion research not related to sampling waned. Since the mid-1970s, however, systematic research has greatly clarified our understanding of how respondents take in the assorted cues embedded in the wording or in the order of the questions they are asked. [59]

Our purpose here is not to summarize an expanding literature on question wording and question order. Rather, it is to highlight some of the considerations poll consumers may find useful as they size up poll reports. Four facets of questionnaire construction merit elaboration here: the presence or absence of balanced alternatives; the inclusion of a middle position between extremes; reference to authoritative names or institutions; and the ordering of questions.

Presence or Absence of Alternatives

The dilemmas of whether and how to spell out various points of view always confront the pollster seeking to gauge the public's thinking on issues. Two common forms of questions do not ask respondents to weigh stated alternatives. In one format a statement is made and the respondent is asked to agree or disagree with it. In the other format the question asks directly about support or approval without the contending view being stated. Both formats have their place in survey research, but with limitations.

"Agree/disagree" questions lend themselves to crisp leads in news reports: a specified percent agree with whatever proposition has been posited. However, this question format has two limitations.

First, a "yea-say" bias can creep in. This occurs because respondents usually try to cooperate with interviewers. Thus, when a proposition is advanced by the interviewer some respondents are reluctant to challenge the premise of a proposition even though they may be slightly uncomfortable with it. Less-educated respondents, those presumably less attuned to both sides of an issue, are more likely to go along with the premise of the statement than are more-educated respondents.[60]

Second, statements posed in agree/disagree questions seldom present respondents with cues concerning the consequences of agreeing with the statement or the legitimate reasons for disagreeing. For example, an agree/disagree question about unemployment got strikingly different results depending on whether or not it provided a plausible alternative:[61]

Form A	Form B
Do you agree or disagree with this statement: Any able-bodied person can find a job and make ends meet.	Some people feel that any able-bodied person can find a job and make ends meet. Others feel there are times when it is hard to get along and some able-bodied people are not able to find work. Whom do you agree with most?

Form A		Form B	
Agree	65%	Can make ends meet	43%
Disagree	25	Sometimes hard to get along	39
No opinion	10	No opinion	18

Although it is not the best way of identifying the proportion of a sample holding a particular point of view, the agree/disagree format can pick up differences in opinion among subgroups and changes in opinion between surveys. It is also a convenient vehicle for building a series of questions on diverse topics for inclusion in various indices and scales. However, in that context, the agree/disagree format is not being used as a comprehensive measure of an issue but as part of a group of questions with a common set of response categories that lend themselves to subsequent analyses.

An illustration from the 1990 elections underscores the limitations of the agree/disagree format. As the 1990 campaign for the Democratic gubernatorial nomination in Massachusetts was heating up, speculation abounded that the popular mayor of Boston, Ray Flynn, would throw his hat in the ring. In this political environment news was made when the *Boston Herald* reported in April the results of a poll of residents of Boston it had just conducted with its polling partner, WCVB-TV: "The poll showed that two-thirds of respondents think Flynn should forget about running for governor and remain as mayor to fight crime in the city."[62]

Wording of the question on which this conclusion was based did not appear in the newspaper, nor was it broadcast. It turned out that the question was of the agree/disagree format, the statement being: "Mayor Flynn should forget about running for Governor and concentrate on fighting crime." Sixty-five percent of respondents agreed. But what was the agree/disagree question really tapping: support for or opposition to the job Flynn was doing as mayor; feelings about crime on Boston's streets; or the relative drawing power of Flynn as against other possible Democratic nominees for governor?

To confuse matters further, the *Herald*'s lead in the story was that the poll had found Flynn with as much support among likely Democratic primary voters in Boston as the front-runner among the declared candidates, Francis Bellotti.

The lesson here is that, without posing alternatives that spell out trade-offs to respondents, the agree/disagree format yielded a percentage that could not be taken as a valid reading of the public's thinking about a possible Flynn candidacy.

A more common approach to wording questions—still without spelling out contending points of view—is to ask simply whether the respondent approves/disapproves, favors/opposes or supports/opposes something. Studies on the effect of varying the wordings of such direct questions are beginning to identify how the presentation of legitimate alternatives makes a difference in the pattern of replies to a question. Four conclusions are emerging from this research.

First, there is little evidence that the mere formality of offering two response categories in a question makes much difference unless a complete exposition of the trade-offs on the issue is also provided. Two examples from the work of Howard Schuman and Stanley Presser, presented in Table 3-7, illustrate this point.

Second, elaborating on both sides of an issue affects the distribution of responses in some cases but not in others. Again, two illustrations from Schuman and Presser make the point. In the abortion example in Table 3-8 the difference between Forms A and B was not statistically significant, but in the gun control question the differences were significant.

Third, whether a counterargument affects the pattern of responses tends to depend upon the intensity with which an individual holds an

TABLE 3-7   Effect of Presenting Balanced Alternatives in Question Wording

Form A	Form B
Do you feel a woman should be allowed to have an abortion in the early months of pregnancy if she wants one?	Do you feel a woman should be allowed to have an abortion in the early months of pregnancy if she wants one, *or* do you feel this should not be allowed?

Yes	68.0%	Should be allowed	65.5%
No	32.0	Should not be allowed	34.5
	100.0		100.0
	n=440		n=429

Form A	Form B
Would you favor a law which would require a person to obtain a police permit before he could buy a gun?	Would you favor *or* oppose a law which would require a person to obtain a police permit before he could buy a gun?

Yes	70.4%	Favor	70.3%
No	29.6	Oppose	29.7
	100.0		100.0
	n=503		n=485

SOURCE: Howard Schuman and Stanley Presser, *Questions and Answers in Attitude Surveys* (New York: Academic Press, 1981): 181-182.

NOTE: The questions appeared in studies conducted by the Survey Research Center at the University of Michigan; the abortion question was included in a February 1975 survey; the gun control question in a February 1978 survey. The differences between Form A and Form B were not statistically significant in either case. In computing percentages, "don't know," no answer, and other responses have been eliminated.

opinion on the issue. That is, when one has firmly held views on an issue such as abortion, hearing the contrary view developed as the interviewer reads the question has little or no impact. Conversely, if the issue is one about which the individual has no intensely held view, the plausibility of countervailing arguments can affect the pattern of responses.[63]

Fourth, the respondent's level of education also affects the degree to which counterarguments affect the pattern of responses, although the intensity with which an individual holds an opinion can offset the effect of education. Referring again to opinions about abortion and gun control, Schuman and Presser found that less-educated respondents were

TABLE 3-8   Effect of Counterarguments in Question Wording

Form A	Form B
Do you feel a woman should be allowed to have an abortion in the early months of pregnancy if she wants one, *or* do you feel this should not be allowed?	Do you feel a woman should be allowed to have an abortion in the early months of pregnancy if she wants one, *or* do you feel a woman should not be allowed to end the life of an unborn child?

Should	65.5%		Should	61.4%
Should not	34.5		Should not	38.6
	100.0			100.0
	n = 429			n = 422

Form A	Form B
Would you favor *or* oppose a law which would require a person to obtain a police permit before he could buy a gun?	Would you favor a law which would require a person to obtain a police permit before he could buy a gun, *or* do you think such a law would interfere too much with the right of citizens to own guns?

Favor	70.3%		Favor	62.0%
Oppose	29.7		Interfere too much	38.0
	100.0			100.0
	n = 485			n = 471

SOURCE: Howard Schuman and Stanley Presser, *Questions and Answers in Attitude Surveys* (New York: Academic Press, 1981): 186-187.

NOTE: In computing percentages, "don't know," no answer, and other responses have been eliminated. Data are from SRC studies in February 1975 and fall 1978.

more likely than better-educated respondents to be influenced by counterarguments on the gun control issue. However, when it came to abortion, the less educated were no more likely than the better educated to be drawn to the counterargument.[64]

Presence or Absence of an Intermediate Position

There are few issues on which public opinion splits into two starkly opposing views. Usually there is a middle ground occupied by a significant proportion of the sample. That the public seldom divides between

TABLE 3-9   Effect of Middle Alternative in Question Wording

Form A	Form B
In your opinion, should the penalties for using marijuana be *more* strict or *less* strict than they are now?	In your opinion, should the penalties for using marijuana be *more* strict, less strict, or *about the same* as they are now?

	A	B	Difference
More strict	49.1%	41.8%	− 7.3 pts.
Less strict	41.8	30.6	−11.2
About same as now	6.1 (vol)	25.8	+19.7
Don't know	2.9	1.8	− 1.1
	99.9	100.0	
	n = 603	n = 562	

Form A	Form B
On most political issues, would you say you are on the *liberal* side or on the *conservative* side?	On most political issues, would you say you are on the *liberal* side, on the *conservative* side, or *middle-of-the-road?*

	A	B	Difference
Liberal	33.1%	16.9%	−16.2 pts.
Conservative	44.4	24.5	−19.9
Middle-of-the-road	16.2 (vol)	53.7	+37.5
Don't know	6.3	4.8	− 1.5
	100.0	99.9	
	n = 507	n = 497	

SOURCE: Howard Schuman and Stanley Presser, *Questions and Answers in Attitude Surveys* (New York: Academic Press, 1981): 165-167.

NOTE: (vol) = volunteered response.

extremes is evidenced by the number of respondents who volunteer an intermediate position on an issue even when one is not provided. The work of Schuman and Presser demonstrates the prudence of providing a middle ground in questions on most substantive issues.[65] The alternative of trying to interpret the significance of volunteered responses is imprecise at best because the analyst never knows how the views of respondents uncomfortable with the extreme positions are recorded. Did they choose the extreme view least alien to their thinking, volunteer a middle alternative, or simply say they did not know?[66] (See Table 3-9.)

Invoking Authority

Authority can be invoked in poll questions in many ways. Reference to revered institutions, widely accepted traditions, and esteemed individuals can affect the pattern of responses.

In 1939 the authority of the U.S. Constitution was invoked in an early experiment in question wording that explored public reaction to the possibility of a third term for Franklin Roosevelt. Respondents were less opposed to "adding a law" to the Constitution than "changing" it.

Form A		Form B	
Would you favor *adding a law* to the Constitution to prevent any president of the United States from serving a third term?		Would you favor *changing* the Constitution to prevent any president of the United States from serving a third term?	
Yes	36%	Yes	26%
No	50	No	65
No opinion	14	No opinion	9

SOURCE: Donald Rugg and Hadley Cantril, "The Wording of Questions," in *Gauging Public Opinion,* ed. Hadley Cantril (Princeton, N.J.: Princeton University Press, 1944), 44.

NOTE: The two forms were asked in a split-ballot in November 1939.

The authority of the American tradition of freedom of expression was shown to affect dramatically an exploration of public attitudes toward communism. People were more likely to say that speeches in its favor should "not be allowed" than that they should be "forbidden."

Form A		Form B	
Do you think the United States should forbid public speeches in favor of communism?		Do you think the United States should allow public speeches in favor of communism?	
Yes (forbid)	39.3%	No (not allow)	56.3%
No (not forbid)	60.1	Yes (allow)	43.8
	99.4		100.1

SOURCE: Howard Schuman and Stanley Presser, *Questions and Answers in Attitude Surveys* (New York: Academic Press, 1981): 281.

NOTE: The questions appeared in split-ballot form in the 1976 Detroit Area Survey.

Use of the names of well-known people can affect response patterns, but not in a predictable direction. The most common effect is to reduce the proportion of respondents without an opinion. It is a well-established pattern for "don't know" and "no opinion" percentages to be higher for less-educated persons. Because prestigious names provide important information, less-educated persons are more likely to venture an opinion when names are included. A collateral effect of prestigious names is that they often increase the political content of a question, a factor that must be taken into account when analyzing the pattern of responses.[67]

Question Order

In addition to the way questions are asked, pollsters have discovered that they must be attentive to the order in which questions are asked. Interviews are more than the sum of several questions. As with regular conversations between two people, carefully planned questionnaires and well-conducted interviews in public opinion polls have an integrity to them. They have a pace and rhythm; they possess a beginning, middle, and end; they evolve as rapport is established between respondent and interviewer.

The context of one question is almost always affected by what has gone before, but that does not mean that answers to the question are always determined by the content of the preceding questions. The extent to which order affects responses is determined by how specifically the answer to one question may bias the answer to another. Thus, for example, when asked about party affiliation, the reply that one is a Republican will almost certainly have an impact on one's expressed preference for a Democratic or Republican candidate. The converse is less often true: an expressed preference for one of the two candidates is less likely to affect one's answer to the party affiliation question.[68]

The most often cited poll results in the media have to do with the standing of candidates and the popularity rating of the president. Experimental work has probed how both types of questions may be subject to question-order effects.

Use of more than one trial-heat measure in a poll can be tricky when cross-pressures may be at work on the voters.[69] There is also some evidence that in single trial-heat questions candidates tend to do better when their names are mentioned first. A vivid example came in one poll by the Roper Organization that asked its trial-heat question in September 1988 using a split-ballot format. Dukakis emerged with a twelve-point lead over Bush when his name was mentioned first and only a three-point lead when his name was placed second. Having interviewers rotate the order of candidate names is one way of mitigating order effects on responses.[70]

When measuring relative support for candidates such question-order problems can be mitigated through the use of the "secret ballot" approach (in personal interviews) and their magnitude can be assessed with split-ballot questionnaires (in which a sample is divided into two comparable subsamples). Question order affects results especially when opinions are weakly held. It is doubtful that the question-order effect in the Roper poll noted above would have been so pronounced closer to election day.

There is some evidence that question order can also affect the measures of presidential popularity. Sigelman conducted a split-ballot experiment in 1979 in which the first half of the sample was presented with the popularity question before questions on any issues (such as items on energy, drugs, pollution, and nuclear power). The second half of the sample was asked the popularity question only after the issue questions.

He found no significant difference in opinion regarding the president's popularity between the two placements of the question. What differed was the proportion of the sample venturing an opinion. Eighty-nine percent of those asked the popularity question after the issue questions offered a rating for the president. By contrast, only 80 percent of those asked the popularity question at the outset offered a rating.[71]

Is the reader to conclude from this discussion that respondents are so susceptible to being influenced by the manner and order in which questions are asked that polls are unable to measure underlying public opinion? On the contrary, it is the attentiveness of respondents to the cues embedded in the way a question is framed that affirms the sensitivity of the poll as a measuring device.

Thus we come full circle to revisit the hypothesis spelled out almost 50 years ago by Hadley Cantril: "Where people lack reliable standards of judgment and consistent frames of reference, they are highly suggestible to the implications of phrases, statements, innuendos or symbols of any kind that may serve as clues to help them make up their minds."[72]

The Crystallization of Opinion

Whether polling on the relative standing of candidates for public office or the disposition of the public on issues, the direction of respondents' opinions cannot be truly understood without some indication of the intensity with which those opinions are held.

The Deciding Voter

In the last chapter we reviewed the evolution of the 1988 campaign in connection with a discussion of variability in poll findings. Underlying that discussion was the fact that the electorate came to know the candidates considerably more slowly than one might expect from a glance at the political calendar, a calendar crowded with primaries, caucuses, conventions, debates, paid advertisements, frequent poll reports, and nonstop candidate appearances. As an indication of how far the electorate had come by election day, when the campaign year was getting underway three-fourths of the public had no strongly held preference among the candidates contending for their party's nomination.

Memorable events of 1988, as in previous election years, often revolved around surprises resulting from unexpectedly solid or unexpectedly soft support for one candidate or another. The shallowness of support for Robert Dole among New Hampshire voters caught the attention of analysts after the primary in that state. The intensity of support for Jesse Jackson that spurred his victory over Michael Dukakis in Michigan's caucuses surprised analysts. Unhappiness with Walter Mondale created a void filled dramatically by Gary Hart in 1984. It was the unanticipated depth of dissatisfaction with incumbent Jimmy Carter that made Sen. Edward Kennedy's victory in the 1980 New York primary so stunning.

In all these cases, the key element was the absence of or inattention to measurements of the *intensity* of public preferences. Such measures can be straightforward. For example, after the standard trial-heat question, three of the major national polls asked the following questions in 1988. CBS News/*New York Times:* "Is your mind made up, or do you think you might change your mind before the election?" Roper: "You may or may not be enthusiastic about [candidate preferred], but assuming those are the candidates, would you say your decision to vote for him is pretty definite, or that you're not at all sure you'll end up voting for him?" Roper: "Will you be voting mostly for [candidate preferred] or mostly against his opponent?" Gallup: "How much of a chance is there that you will vote for [other ticket] instead of [preferred ticket] on Tuesday? "

Some respondents, of course, report that they have not made up their mind. Although recorded by interviewers as "undecided," these individuals can be saying several things. They may truly have no preference; they may have a preference that they do not want to share; or they may not be planning to vote. The proportion of undecided respondents can be reduced in personal-interview surveys by having respondents mark their choice on a ballot that is then put into a box. This "secret ballot" technique can uncover support for candidates that respondents may be reluctant to share with an interviewer.[73] It is a technique that obviously cannot be used in telephone surveys.

Pollsters often ask toward which candidate an undecided individual now leans. Such a question can reduce the undecided proportion by as much as half. Trial heats reported in the news often include these "leaners" as supporters of one candidate or another. However, they do so at the risk of artificially inflating candidates' percentages because, without a good measure of likelihood of voting, many undecided people will be counted as leaning toward a candidate when in fact they will not vote on election day.

Measures of intensity in candidate support go hand-in-glove with measures of the likelihood an individual will vote, particularly in primaries or other low-turnout elections. An understanding of the depth of a candidate's support requires knowledge of the degree of enthusiasm for the candidate among those in the sample who are the probable voters. Although respondents who are deeply committed to a candidate are quite likely to vote, most respondents are not fervent about their candidate, making it essential to differentiate among those more and less likely to cast a ballot.

When final preelection polls are reported in the media, some polling organizations allocate the proportion remaining undecided between the candidates. The theory is that "undecided" will not receive any support on election day and that the percentages for the candidates should add to 100 percent. Even when such allocations rest on rigorous methodology, they vitiate claims by the pollster that the final poll is not a projection but only a measurement "at one point in time."

Of all the ways pollsters can improve the quality of their preelection assessments of voter preferences, few are easier than asking questions to determine how far the electorate has moved toward a coherent and stable sense of the choice available on election day.

Opinions—and Nonopinions—on the Issues

Polling on the issues requires as much attention to the intensity with which opinions are held as does polling on candidate preferences. The division of opinion on an issue may have little significance without an understanding of how important the issue is perceived to be. In the extreme case, feelings on a single issue can run strongly enough to overwhelm opinions on other issues. This was a lesson learned the hard way by Dick Clark, the Iowa senator who lost his bid for reelection in 1978. His pollster, Peter Hart, had picked up the strength of the antiabortion vote against Clark. But the campaign misjudged in thinking that these voters could be appealed to on other issues.

In addition to underestimating the significance of the split of opinion, pollsters must guard against overestimating it as well. This can happen when questions are asked about topics about which few in the population have an opinion or about which few are informed. "Hidden nonattitudes" is the term coined by Philip Converse to describe replies given to poll questions when the respondent has no view on a topic but does not say so.[74]

Those in the political community—journalists, elected officials, campaign consultants, political analysts—sometimes forget that the general public is not as actively engaged as they are in the issues of the day. Ever eager for a reading on the public's sense of an issue, the politically attuned may see more in poll percentages than exists. Many pollsters have had to explain to a client that asking the public narrowly drawn questions about a given issue may not tap opinions in any useful way.

Opinion researchers have three ways of dealing with the problem of nonattitudes. The first is to take enough time in a poll question to explain the background of the issue on which the respondent's opinion is being sought. As an illustration, consider this question asked in a personal-interview poll by the Roper Organization in August 1989:

> On President Bush's recent trip to Poland and Hungary, he promised
> $115 million in aid to Poland and $25 million to Hungary. Some say

TABLE 3-10   Effect of Filtering for No Opinion in Question Wording

Form A	Form B
Here are some questions about other countries. Do you agree or disagree with this statement? Russian leaders are basically trying to get along with America.	Here are some questions about other countries. Not everyone has opinions on these questions. If you do not have an opinion, just say so. The Russian leaders are basically trying to get along with America. Do you have an opinion on that? [IF YES] Do you agree or disagree?

Form A		Form B	
Agree	49.9%	Agree	39.2%
Disagree	34.9	Disagree	23.1
Don't know (volunteered)	15.2	Don't know	37.6
	n = 499		n = 510

SOURCE: Howard Schuman and Stanley Presser, *Questions and Answers in Attitude Surveys* (New York: Academic Press, 1981): 116.

NOTE: These questions appeared in a 1974 survey conducted by the Survey Research Center at the University of Michigan.

we shouldn't give either country anything since they are both communist countries and are members of the Warsaw Pact. Others say we should do a lot more for them in view of the fact that they are turning to the West, to free enterprise and to democracy, and their economic situation is desperate. Do you think President Bush promised them too much or not enough or that what he offered was about right?

A second approach is to ask respondents whether they have thought enough about an issue to have an opinion; only those who respond in the affirmative are asked their opinion on the issue. The proportion thus identified as not having an opinion can be dramatically higher than when no preliminary screening question is asked. In the illustration in Table 3-10, more than a third of respondents replied negatively when asked explicitly whether they had an opinion (Form B). But when confronted with the issue question without an opportunity first to say they had no opinion (Form A), a substantially smaller portion of the sample was recorded as "don't know."

George Bishop, Robert Oldendick, and Alfred Tuchfarber have shown that the less familiar people are with an issue, the more likely they are to say "don't know" when a filter is provided to legitimate the "don't know" response.[75]

TABLE 3-11   Effect of Offering the No Opinion Option in Question Wording

Form A	Form B
We hear a lot of talk these days about liberals and conservatives. I'm going to show you a seven-point scale on which the *political* views that people might hold are arranged from extremely liberal—point 1—to extremely conservative—point 7. Where would you place yourself on this scale?	We hear a lot of talk these days about liberals and conservatives. I'm going to show you a seven-point scale on which the *political* views that people might hold are arranged from extremely liberal—point 1—to extremely conservative—point 7. Where would you place yourself on this scale, or haven't you thought much about it?

	A		B	
Extremely liberal	1.3	⎫	1.6	⎫
Liberal	9.1	⎬ 26.4%	8.6	⎬ 24.4%
Slightly liberal	16.0	⎭	14.2	⎭
Moderate, middle-of-the-road	34.2		31.1	
Slightly conservative	18.6	⎫	15.1	⎫
Conservative	13.9	⎬ 35.0%	9.6	⎬ 26.1%
Extremely conservative	2.5	⎭	1.4	⎭
Don't know (volunteered)	4.4		—	
Haven't thought much about it	—		18.4	
	100.0		100.0	
	n=757		n=768	

SOURCE: Howard Schuman and Stanley Presser, *Questions and Answers in Attitude Surveys* (New York: Academic Press, 1981): 121.

NOTE: These questions appeared in split-ballot format in a 1978 study by the National Opinion Research Center at the University of Chicago.

A third way to handle the nonattitude problem is to indicate in the wording of a question the legitimacy of not having an opinion. Table 3-11 affirms that many respondents welcome the option of saying they have not thought much about the matter under study.

Both Schuman and Presser and Bishop and his colleagues have shown that less-educated respondents are less willing than the better educated to respond "don't know" on issue questions.[76]

Polls on issues can seldom be validated with the same rigor as the results of a preelection poll that can be held up to the election returns. Instead their validation must come from the intrinsic sense they make and degree to which a coherent picture of underlying public opinion comes into focus. Toward this end, multiple measures are essential that help sort out the level of information respondents bring to the matter at hand, how strongly they feel about the issue, and how aware they are of the implications of the opinions they hold.

Focus Groups

Postmortems on the 1988 presidential campaign have identified two focus groups conducted in late May in Paramus, New Jersey, as being decisive events in the evolution of the strategy George Bush used to defeat Michael Dukakis.[77] Focus groups bring together a small number of individuals with known demographic characteristics for an informal and open discussion of issues framed by a pollster and often raised by a moderator. In this case about twenty conservative Democrats were brought together for each of the two groups. They all had voted for Ronald Reagan in 1984 and were leaning to Dukakis in 1988. As the moderator encouraged conversation on a wide range of subjects, two points became clear: neither Bush nor Dukakis was well known and no overarching issue was working to the advantage or disadvantage of either candidate.

To the Bush team watching the groups through one-way glass the strategic implications were clear. There was ample opportunity to define both candidates for the electorate, and the side that seized the initiative would control the agenda of the campaign. The magnitude of the opportunity for the Bush campaign emerged as the focus group moderator acquainted participants with vulnerabilities in the Dukakis record: the furlough of Willie Horton, the veto of a bill mandating the pledge of allegiance in schools, and the pollution of Boston Harbor. Individually, none of these issues dislodged support for Dukakis, but collectively they were devastating. By the end of the sessions, about half of the focus group participants expressed serious doubts about Dukakis.

The Place of Focus Groups in Opinion Research

The prospect of insights like those garnered from the Paramus focus groups leads political analysts to use the technique as a complement to sample surveys of public opinion. By virtue of the free-flowing conversation that is encouraged, focus groups make it possible to explore the terms of reference within which people view an issue, how they react to the views of others, and how people work through an issue that is new to them or with which they may be uncomfortable.

By way of illustration, consider the focus group conducted by Peter Hart for People for the American Way on the problem of AIDS. Participants in the group were selected for their conservative political views. As the group sorted its way through the issues there emerged an underlying sympathy for victims of the disease, even among those who had been explicitly hostile toward the gay community.[78]

Focus groups were heavily used by both the Bush and Dukakis forces toward the end of the 1988 campaign. Relative to opinion polls, focus groups are less expensive, easier to complete logistically, and take less time. Their fluidity permits the researcher to follow the concerns of participants wherever they may lead. They can give participants a chance to view a planned television commercial and react to it. Individuals can be preselected for inclusion in a focus group by rigorous application of demographic criteria or the pattern of responses in an earlier poll.

As alluring as focus groups are, however, they are by definition unrepresentative—even of a small and targeted population. There is no escaping the fact that a dozen or so individuals, no matter how carefully selected, cannot be looked to as a microcosm of a larger population. In addition, bias that may exist in the group at the outset can be greatly magnified by the interpersonal dynamics at work during the focus group. Seldom is there a focus group that does not contain a strong personality and one or more passive individuals.

Even so, focus groups can enrich public opinion research by acquainting pollsters with nuances and dimensions of the public's thinking. This is often a great help as questions are worded for polls and questionnaires are put together. As Humphrey Taylor of Louis Harris and Associates puts it: "You can learn interesting things from focus groups, but they should never be used to reach any definitive conclusions. Their utility is to suggest hypotheses which can then be confirmed or not in a subsequent poll." [79]

The Perils of Focus Groups in Journalism

The use of focus groups by news organizations is a subject on which journalists and opinion researchers are divided. To the extent that news accounts of focus groups are accompanied by the results of a poll, and if no effort is made to quantify the distribution of opinion within the focus group, some pollsters do not object to their being reported.[80]

Other opinion researchers are uneasy about the journalistic use of focus groups on the grounds that caveats about the unrepresentative nature of the group tend to get lost even if the journalist is careful to mention them. Moreover, even though focus groups are better than old-fashioned person-on-the-street interviews, they run the risk of having reporters take journalistic license by imputing to compelling comments heard in a focus group a significance that may be totally unwarranted.[81]

Instant-Reaction Meters

A variant on the focus group, revived in the last ten years, is a technique first used by George Gallup in the 1940s to obtain public reactions to motion pictures. It convenes a small group of individuals at a central location to record their reactions minute by minute on hand-held dials. Gallup used the device, the Hopkins Televote machine, to monitor public reaction to the 1960 Kennedy-Nixon debates.

Instant-reaction meters were a part of the research conducted for the Reagan White House by Richard Wirthlin, who monitored public reaction word by word to the president's speeches, using what he called the "speech pulse" system.

Ratings from such meter systems can provide important political intelligence. They can also be wildly misleading. Like any form of intelligence, the raw information produced by the meter must be carefully assessed by an experienced analyst and conclusions drawn only with extreme caution.

The pitfalls are numerous: first, the numbers involved are small. Thus, even if a homogeneous subgroup within the electorate is sampled, the small number of cases greatly limits one's confidence in the data. Moreover, when the group is subdivided by sex or political point of view, the number of cases dwindles to a fragile few. Yet, the ratings continue to be tallied and arrayed on computer screens with specious exactness.

A second problem with these ratings is that one is never certain what they mean. Simply plotting audience reactions tells little about why the audience reacts as it does. Was it the demeanor of the speaker, the content of what was said, the cutaway shot, or some other facet of the presentation? While favorable/unfavorable reactions can be recorded at a gross level, it is quite another matter to gain insight into the underlying dynamics, especially into variations among subgroups in the sample.

Instant-reaction meters have all of the worst drawbacks of focus groups and none of the advantages. They rely on small samples. They quantify the distribution of reactions, conveying an unfounded impression of precision and reliability. They generate aggregate ratings that oversimplify the complexities of public reaction to events. They also share the principal deficiency of the "instant" poll by elevating the immediate reaction to an undeserved level of importance and implicit validity.

As a source of political intelligence, the instant-reaction meters may contribute important information if complemented by an ongoing polling program and interpreted with great care. However, as a source of news stories, the information from meter systems is too unreliable and partial to be conveyed to the public without an accompanying discussion of the limitations of the information being reported. The responsible reporter faces the task of writing a story in which the caveats make up most of the content and the meter results are relegated to the tag line.

Exit Polls

As useful as preelection polls may be for measuring the evolving disposition of the electorate, they are not nearly as powerful as exit polls in analyzing the message voters have sent by the ballots they cast. By definition, exit polls sample only voters and interview them on election day, thus eliminating two difficulties inherent in preelection polls: the need to identify likely voters and estimate turnout and the challenge of picking up last-minute shifts in opinion. In addition, exit polls can achieve larger samples more cost-effectively than most preelection polls.

Exit polls have become one of the most important sources of insight into what was on voters' minds when they cast their ballots. "They are the most useful analytic tool developed in my working life," is the assessment of the *Washington Post*'s David Broder.[82]

Before exit polling, news analysts would attempt to infer voter intentions from voting patterns in key precincts selected for analysis on the basis of their socioeconomic characteristics. In spite of elaborate selection schemes, these precincts often failed as bellwethers because of the mistaken assumption that individuals with particular social and economic attributes in one precinct would vote the same way as individuals with similar attributes in another precinct. To illustrate, while the concentration of blacks in urban neighborhoods may be high, about two-thirds of blacks do not live in such neighborhoods. Moreover, given heterogeneity within such a subgroup, political preferences for the entire subgroup cannot be inferred from the views of only a third of the subgroup.[83]

A review of the methodology of exit polling helps clarify general principles of sampling, data collection, and data analysis in public opinion research.

With respect to sampling, the key principle is to ensure that every voter has a known chance of being interviewed. As with other sampling, this means knowing the probabilities of selection at each stage of the sampling plan.

Exit poll samples usually start with a list of all precincts in the jurisdiction (usually a state) for which the exit poll is being conducted. A sample of precincts is drawn such that the probability of each precinct's being selected is proportionate to its share of all voters in the most recent comparable election held in the jurisdiction.[84] The number of precincts selected for a state exit poll may range from twenty to sixty.[85]

At each precinct, interviewers are instructed to determine whom to approach by using a "skip interval" so that, for example, every tenth, fifteenth, or twentieth voter leaving the polling place may be selected. The size of the interval is determined by the size of the overall sample desired. News organizations vary in the times interviewers are present at an assigned precinct. Some interview through the entire day, whereas others interview at staggered intervals.

The exit poll questionnaire characteristically contains two to three dozen questions printed on both sides of a "ballot." Questions must be straightforward and present fixed response categories. CBS News has found that the response rate tends to drop the longer the questionnaire. However, it has also found that simply asking how an individual voted yields a less reliable respondent report than asking about the voting decision and posing additional questions.[86]

One advantage of exit polls is that it is possible to monitor patterns of refusal, which range from 25 to 35 percent of all persons asked to participate. The customary practice is for interviewers to record the sex, race, and approximate age on a questionnaire *before* approaching a voter. Should the voter not consent to fill out the questionnaire, the interviewer is instructed to place the incomplete questionnaire in the "ballot box" along with completed questionnaires. It is possible, therefore, to determine the profile of nonrespondents on three important characteristics.[87] Women, blacks, and older persons are more reluctant respondents than others.[88]

The logistical complexity of exit polling is hard to underestimate. The television networks expect to draw on their exit polls as part of their election night broadcasts. In the case of CBS News in the 1988 presidential election, replies to as many as thirty questions from more than 11,000 respondents had to be called into a central location.

Moreover, exit poll data need to be weighted to take into account the probability of each precinct having fallen into the sample and the probability of each voter having been approached within a precinct. The data must then be analyzed quickly. This requires rapid assessment of data quality. Where problems emerge, such as incomplete reports from some precincts, they must be dealt with quickly. Only then can analyses be performed to support points made in election reporting. Preplanning is essential to set up an early warning system to catch and remedy problems in data quality and to anticipate the kinds of analyses that will be needed.

Call-In "Polls": Discredited But Still Alive

After each of the two Bush-Dukakis debates in 1988, viewers in a host of cities across the nation were invited to call one "900" number if they thought Bush had won the debate and another number if they thought Dukakis had won. Their verdict would become part of the overall tally and they would be charged for the call on their phone bill.

The organizer of the call-ins was the American Political Network (APN), the publisher of *Hotline*. APN asked participating television stations to advise their viewers that "the results should not be seen as a scientific survey or as a poll of any kind—but [as] an applause meter only." [89]

The day after the second debate *Hotline* reported among its page one headlines: "Call-in: 65% say Bush won." The caveats APN had urged the TV stations to use in characterizing the results were not mentioned. Meanwhile the same issue of *Hotline* carried the results of two polls conducted immediately after the debate: the *Los Angeles Times* poll found 47 percent thinking that Bush had won; an ABC News poll found 49 percent of the same opinion.

The fact that the *Los Angeles Times* and ABC News polls were so close and at such variance with the APN call-in results indicates how wide of the mark the call-in "applause meters" can be and why they have been so discredited. Eight years earlier ABC News took a barrage of criticism for its use of a call-in after the Cleveland debate between Ronald Reagan and Jimmy Carter. At the time, the National Council on Public Polls, among others, protested. It pointed out that the sample was self-selected; people could call in as many times as they wished; the charge for having one's opinion counted, while modest, was a disincentive for some to participate; a call-in effort could be organized in advance; and technical problems resulted in delays in recording calls from urban areas.

Even after the Cleveland debate provoked widespread complaints, ABC's "Nightline" made repeated use of the "900" call-in. On one broadcast the verdict of 67 percent of 186,000 people calling in was that the United Nations should not be located in the United States. In this instance, Nightline's anchor, Ted Koppel, did close the program by noting that a "scientific" poll asking exactly the same question had found that only 33 percent of the public wanted the United Nations to leave the country.

The troublesome aspect to call-ins is that, caveats aside, they instill in the viewer the notion that a reliable measurement of public opinion is underway. Not only are the sample sizes of scientific polls dwarfed by the thousands of calls, the flow of calls builds a sense of momentum as the tally changes. Even worse, as the tally of calls pro and con is updated during the broadcast, guest experts on the topic at hand are asked to comment on the emerging totals, weighing in with their authority and lending legitimacy to the call-in.

On the evening of the United Nations call-in, for example, Koppel asked the U.S. ambassador to the United Nations how she felt about the purported public opposition to the United Nations on American soil.[90] Another evening, Koppel used the call-in device as the organizing peg for a program on the Soviet downing of a Korean airliner. After several acknowledgments that the call-in was not a scientific poll, Koppel nonetheless turned to his guest, Leslie Gelb, a former Defense Department official, for help in interpreting the data.[91] Not only did discussion of the evolving tally serve as a leitmotif for the entire half-hour broadcast, but inviting comment from an authoritative guest attributed unwarranted legitimacy to the exercise.

AT&T provides the mechanism for the call-ins and markets the service to the broadcast media. Its promotional material notes: "Dial-It's unique polling application is a way your viewers and prospects can tell you what's on their minds *instantly*. . . . For the broadcaster particularly, a Dial-It poll can be an effective way of building audience involvement and getting a feel for his market. Or offering his key advertisers a unique and attention-getting service."[92]

Journalists who should know better, as well as some who do know better, find it all too easy to say, "this is not a scientific survey, but . . . ," and then baldly report the numbers. Just how insidious the process can be was evidenced in *Hotline*'s advisory to its subscribers regarding its intention to use the call-in device after the 1988 debates. After providing phone numbers to record votes for Bush or Dukakis and indicating that each call would cost a dollar, *Hotline* noted: "The results will not be a scientific poll, but could provide a large measure of public reaction." It then noted: "Media outlets who wish to announce the results on Sunday night or Monday are being asked in return to promote the 900 numbers before and after the debate. In exchange they may receive free of charge the national results (updated each ten minutes from 9:40 pm EDT Sunday through 8 pm EDT Monday)."[93]

Concluding Word:
The Complexity of Public Opinion

Few issues wrench individual conscience and national politics like abortion. As our legal and political institutions grope for a principled resolution of the issue, public opinion as measured by opinion polls plays a vital role. But the polls provide no simple cues as to the public's disposition. Public opinion on abortion is an intricate web of definitions, qualifications, conditions, and restrictions applied by both prochoice and prolife advocates.

Consider the diversity of views probed within just a single poll, one conducted by CBS News/*New York Times* April 13-16, 1989.[94] A national sample was asked: "Please tell me whether or not you think it should be possible for a pregnant woman to obtain a legal abortion if. . . ."

	Yes	No	Depends (vol)	Don't know
. . . the woman's own health is seriously endangered by the pregnancy?	87%	7%	4%	2%
. . . there is a strong chance of serious defect in the baby?	69	21	4	6
. . . the family has a very low income and cannot afford any more children?	43	43	4	5
. . . she is not married and does not want to marry the man?	42	50	5	3
. . . the pregnancy interfered with work or education?	26	65	5	4

Simple characterizations of this state of opinion are not easy. When the five questions are analyzed in combination, about a third of the sample held fully consistent views pro or con: 21 percent of the sample approved an abortion under all of the circumstances presented; 10 percent approved an abortion under none of the circumstances. The remaining 69 percent of the sample was ambivalent in varying degrees.[95]

In addition to this kind of division of opinion on an issue, the complexities inherent in public opinion also manifest themselves in apparent inconsistencies in poll findings. A classic illustration is the study of the 1964 election conducted by Lloyd Free and Hadley Cantril, who found that, when approached at the level of ideology, half of the public was "conservative," whereas when it came to support of government programs almost two-thirds of the public qualified as "liberals." [96]

When trying to make sense of a poll's findings it must be remembered that the questions asked and the resulting percentages are attempts by the pollster to measure a complex and dynamic frame of reference unique to each individual. Most people do not think in the issue-specific terms in which questions are asked. Yet the notion persists that public opinion operates on one dimension at a time and that a single question can do justice to the full texture of an individual's opinion.

Respondents generally fulfill their side of the bargain: they do the best they can to answer the questions they are asked. For their part, pollsters have an obligation to make good-faith efforts to phrase ques-

Firsts in the Public Polls

1939   First presidential popularity poll published: by Gallup in July regarding Franklin Roosevelt.

1939   First polling operation within a federal government agency established by Rensis Likert in the U.S. Department of Agriculture.

1940   First media-supported state poll, the Texas Poll, established by Joe Belden.

1940   First archive of public opinion poll data established by Hadley Cantril at the Office of Public Opinion Research at Princeton University.

1940   First routine reporting of public opinion information to a U.S. president: by Hadley Cantril to Franklin Roosevelt.

1947   First association, the American Association for Public Opinion Research (AAPOR), established in the field of opinion research.

1962   First election projections: CBS News, based on Vote Profile Analysis System set up by Louis Harris to tally votes in sample precincts.

1967   First adoption of poll-reporting standards by AAPOR.

1969   First adoption of poll-reporting standards by a newspaper: The *Louisville Courier-Journal.*

1972   First academic program on polling for students of journalism: established by Maxwell McCombs at the University of North Carolina.

1976   First polling collaboration of broadcast and print news organizations: CBS News and the *New York Times* in a poll on New York City's fiscal crisis.

1978   First adoption of poll-reporting standards by a television network: CBS News.

1984   First reported media-sponsored tracking poll: ABC News/*Washington Post* in New Hampshire primary.

tions precisely, not mislead respondents, and guard against overgeneralizing from the results they obtain. Weighing in on this side of the bargain are the news organizations that conduct or report polls. Their challenge is to elucidate, not obscure, the complexity and dynamism of public opinion. It is to these obligations that we now turn.

Notes

1. Readers wishing to know more about the nuts and bolts of polling may consult the following references. For excellent overviews of sampling theory and procedures, see Graham Kalton, *Introduction to Survey Sampling* (Newbury Park, Calif.: Sage, 1983); and Seymour Sudman, *Applied Sampling* (New York: Academic Press, 1976). A comprehensive discussion of question wording and questionnaire development is found in Howard Schuman and Stanley Presser, *Questions and Answers in Attitude Surveys* (New York: Academic Press, 1981). A classic on question wording is Stanley L. Payne, *The Art of Asking Questions* (Princeton, N.J.: Princeton University Press, 1951). The best guide to telephone polling is *Telephone Survey Methodology*, ed. Robert M. Groves, Paul B. Biemer, Lars E. Lyberg, James T. Massey, William L. Nicholls II, and Joseph Waksberg (New York: John Wiley and Sons, 1988). General introductions to survey research are Floyd J. Fowler, Jr., *Survey Research Methods* (Newbury Park, Calif.: Sage, 1984) and Charles H. Backstrom and Gerald Hursch-Cesar, *Survey Research*, 2d ed. (New York: John Wiley and Sons, 1981). Useful guides to the interpretation of polls are Irving Crespi, *Polls, Public Opinion, and Democracy* (Boulder, Colo.: Westview Press, 1989); Norman M. Bradburn and Seymour Sudman, *Polls and Surveys: Understanding What They Tell Us* (San Francisco, Calif.: Jossey-Bass, 1988); and Charles W. Roll, Jr., and Albert H. Cantril, *Polls: Their Use and Misuse in Politics* (New York: Basic Books, 1972; Cabin John, Md.: Seven Locks Press, 1980). Other sources on specialized topics are indicated at appropriate points in these endnotes.
2. A recent and comprehensive exploration of the methodological correlates of accuracy in preelection polls is Crespi's study of 430 polls sponsored or conducted by news organizations from 1980 through the 1984 election. In it Crespi found that 98 percent of those polls were conducted by telephone. See Irving Crespi, *Pre-Election Polling: Sources of Accuracy and Error* (New York: Russell Sage Foundation, 1988), 30.
3. For an excellent overview of telephone sampling, see James M. Lepkowski, "Telephone Sampling Methods in the United States," in *Telephone Survey*

Methodology, ed. Groves et al., 73-98.

4. W. L. Landon and S. K. Banks, "Relative Efficiency and Bias of Plus-One Telephone Sampling," *Journal of Marketing Research* 14 (1977): 294-299.

5. Warren J. Mitofsky, "Sampling of Telephone Households," unpublished CBS memorandum, 1970; and Joseph Waksberg, "Sampling Methods for Random Digit Dialing," *Journal of the American Statistical Association* 73 (March 1976): 40-46. A complementary approach has been developed by Seymour Sudman, "New Uses of Telephone Directories for Survey Sampling," *Journal of Marketing Research* 10 (May 1973): 204-207.

6. Empirical evidence of this is found, among other places, in the work of Hagan and Collier. Almost half (46 percent) of refusals in their experimental study occurred at the respondent-selection stage. See Dan E. Hagan and Charlotte Meier Collier, "Must Respondent Selection Procedures for Telephone Surveys Be Invasive?" *Public Opinion Quarterly* 47 (Winter 1983): 551.

7. See Leslie Kish, "A Procedure for Objective Respondent Selection within the Household," *Journal of the American Statistical Association* 44 (1949): 380-387. M. L. Monsees and J. T. Massey have shown that higher response rates can be achieved when questions regarding the household roster are placed later in the interview. See "Adapting Procedures for Collecting Demographic Data in a Personal Interview to a Telephone Survey," *Proceedings of the Social Statistics Section,* American Statistical Association (1979): 130-135.

8. One of the grids, for example, might stipulate the following:

Number of men in household	Number of adults in household			
	1	2	3	4+
0	Woman	Oldest woman	Youngest woman	Oldest woman
1	Woman	Man	Youngest woman	Man
2		Youngest man	Oldest man	Oldest man
3			Youngest man	Oldest man
4				Oldest man

See Verling C. Troldahl and Roy E. Carter, Jr., "Random Selection of Respondents within Households in Phone Surveys," *Journal of Marketing Research* 1 (May 1964): 71-76. The Troldahl-Carter grid is taken from Hagan and Collier, "Respondent Selection Procedures," 549. (Some bias is introduced for households with five or more adults, but it is negligible.)

9. See Charles T. Salmon and John Spicer Nichols, "The Next-Birthday Method of Respondent Selection," *Public Opinion Quarterly* 47 (1983): 270-276; and D. O'Rourke and J. Blair, "Improving Random Respondent Selection in Telephone Surveys," *Journal of Marketing Research* 20 (1983): 428-432.
10. See Hagan and Collier, "Respondent Selection Procedures," 547-556.
11. See Charlotte G. Steeth, "Trends in Nonresponse Rates, 1952-1979," *Public Opinion Quarterly* 45 (Spring 1981): 40-57.
12. The refusal rates experienced by 55 commercial survey research organizations in September 1988 were:

	Telephone	Personal (in-home)
Refuse before or during interviewer's introduction	27%	33%
Refuse to continue during screening questions	2	*
Refuse to continue after screening questions	3	2
Total percent refusing	32	36

SOURCE: Survey of members of the Council of American Survey Research Organizations, *1988 Refusal Rate Study* (Chicago: Your Opinion Counts, 1989).

* Designates less than one half percent.

Refusal rates were computed as a percent of contacts made with households. It will be noted that the proportion of refusals at the outset is higher for personal interview surveys than for telephone surveys. However, break-offs after the interviewer's introduction are lower for in-person surveys than for telephone.

Corroboration of these data comes from Walker Research, which has conducted annual studies of the public's participation in and perception of surveys. Its 1988 survey, based on 505 telephone interviews conducted in July 1988, found that 34 percent of respondents indicated that they had refused to be interviewed in a survey during the last year. However, Walker also found that of this group, 87 percent indicated that they had participated in a survey at some time in the past. Walker Research, Inc.,

Industry Image Study, 8th ed. (Indianapolis, 1988), 4.

13. See Robert M. Groves and Robert L. Kahn, *Surveys by Telephone: A National Comparison with Personal Interviews* (New York: Academic Press, 1979), 220.

14. Analysis of the completion rates of twenty-eight interviewers in four statewide surveys shows that 33 percent of eligible respondents refused when approached by an interviewer with less than six months of experience in contrast to 23 percent for more experienced interviewers. See Jane Williams Bergsten, "Some Methodological Results from Four Statewide Telephone Surveys Using Random-Digit-Dialing," *Proceedings of the Section on Survey Methods,* American Statistical Association (1979): 242.

15. According to Walker Research, 57 percent of those who had refused to participate in a survey in the last year did so because of the inconvenience or timing of the request for an interview. Walker Research, *Industry Image Study,* 4.

16. The Walker study also found that 42 percent of those interviewed indicated they had received one or more calls in the last year in which a sales pitch was being disguised as an opinion survey. Ibid., 9.

17. Michael J. O'Neil and Robert M. Groves, "Telephone Interview Introductions and Refusal Rates: Experiments in Increasing Respondent Cooperation," *Proceedings of the Section on Survey Research Methods,* American Statistical Association (1979): 252-255.

18. Robert M. Groves and Lars E. Lyberg provide a good summary of this literature in "An Overview of Nonresponse Issues in Telephone Surveys," in *Telephone Survey Methodology,* ed. Groves et al., 203-206. See also A. Regula Herzog, Willard L. Rodgers, and Richard A. Kulka, "Interviewing Older Adults: A Comparison of Telephone and Face-to-Face Modalities," *Public Opinion Quarterly* 47 (1983): 409-412.

19. The response rate in a poll takes into account refusals, terminations after an interview has started, and designated respondents who are not contacted. Of the three, difficulty in completing interviews with hard-to-reach respondents is the largest part of the response rate problem.

20. See Michael W. Traugott, "The Importance of Persistence in Respondent Selection for Preelection Surveys," *Public Opinion Quarterly* 51 (Spring 1987): 48-57.

21. Ibid., 54.

22. The "times-at-home" technique is sometimes used by pollsters to help compensate for the inability to make successive attempts to contact respondents not at home at the time of the first call. Initially suggested by H. O. Hartley and developed by Politz and Simmons, the times-at-home technique asks respondents how many of the three previous days they were at

home at the time of the interviewer's call. Weightings are introduced: the more active a respondent is (the fewer the number of previous days at home) the more he or she is weighted up to compensate for similar people whom interviewers were not able to reach. This technique is seldom used in "instant" polls conducted within several hours of an event. See Alfred Politz and W. R. Simmons, "An Attempt to Get the 'Not at Homes' into the Sample without Callbacks," *Journal of the American Statistical Association* 44 (March 1949): 9-31; Alfred Politz and W. R. Simmons, "Note on 'An Attempt to Get the Not at Homes into the Sample without Callbacks,'" *Journal of the American Statistical Association* 45 (March 1950): 136-137. For a criticism of this technique, see Leslie Kish, *Survey Sampling* (New York: John Wiley and Sons, 1967), 559-560.

23. The most systematic comparison of personal and phone interviewing is by Groves and Kahn, *Surveys by Telephone.* Other useful sources include: Charles C. Cannell et al., "The Effects of Mode of Data Collection on Health Survey Data," *Proceedings of the Social Statistics Section,* American Statistical Association (1981): 1-7; and Herzog et al., "Interviewing Older Adults," 405-418.

24. These data are from the continuous National Health Interview Survey conducted by the U.S. Bureau of the Census. They are reported in Owen T. Thornberry, Jr., and James T. Massey, "Trends in United States Telephone Coverage Across Time and Subgroups," in *Telephone Survey Methodology,* ed. Groves et al., 29. The proportion of nontelephone households was one in five in 1963.

25. Groves and Kahn note that demographic characteristics have elements of choice associated with them. They conclude: "In short, the decision to be without telephone service is a self-selective process and it reflects distinctive characteristics. One cannot assume that the nonsubscribers are like the subscribers. On the other hand, the proportion of nonsubscribers has become small and it continues to shrink." Groves and Kahn, *Surveys by Telephone,* 214-215.

26. These data are also from the National Health Interview Survey. See Thornberry and Massey, "Trends in United States Telephone Coverage," *Telephone Survey Methodology,* ed. Groves et al., 34-35.

27. Ibid., 41.

28. Data from the 1981 National Health Interview Survey show that of those in nonphone households but with access to a phone elsewhere 40.1 percent go to a nonadjacent building, 25.1 percent go to an adjacent building, 13.9 percent use the phone of a neighbor in the same building, 7.7 percent use their landlord's phone, and 13.2 percent have access to a phone elsewhere in their building. See Owen T. Thornberry, Jr., and James T. Massey, "Coverage and Response in Random-Digit-Dialed National Surveys," *Pro-*

ceedings of the Section on Survey Research Methods, American Statistical Association (1983): 655-656.

29. Good descriptions of weighting procedures are found in Steven L. Botman, James T. Massey, and Iris M. Shimizu, "Effect of Weighting Adjustments on Estimates from a Random-Digit-Dialed Telephone Survey," *Proceedings of the Section on Survey Research Methods,* American Statistical Association (1982): 139-144; Howard E. Freeman, K. Jill Kiecolt, William L. Nicholls II, and J. Merrill Shanks, "Telephone Sampling Bias in Surveying Disability," *Public Opinion Quarterly* 46 (1982): 392-407; Kalton, *Introduction to Survey Sampling,* 69-74; and Charles D. Cowan, "Weighting Data from Sample Surveys—Why and How in Brief," *Marketing Research* 2 (March 1990): 76-79.

30. Poststratification rests on the assumption, seldom made explicit, that the people who refused or were not covered by the sample would respond the same way as people who did not refuse or were covered. As Groves and Kahn observe (see note 25), there is an element of choice in whether or not a household has a telephone. Nonetheless, most pollsters are comfortable with the assumption of poststratification because many differences between respondents and nonrespondents are largely explained by the demographic attributes typically built into poststratification weightings.

31. *The FEC Journal of Election Administration* 16 (Summer 1989): 4, 6.

32. Crespi, *Pre-Election Polling,* 178.

33. Ibid., chaps. 4 and 9, passim.

34. Diane Colasanto and Jay A. Mattlin, "Evaluation of Gallup's Methodology for Predicting Likelihood of Voting," *Proceedings of the Social Statistics Section,* American Statistical Association (1986): 136.

35. The nine questions are listed here in order of their efficiency in measuring an individual's likelihood of voting: (1) Do you, yourself, plan to vote in the election this November, or not? How certain are you that you will vote— absolutely certain, fairly certain, or not certain? (2) Are you now registered so that you can vote in the election this November? [If not] Do you plan to register so that you can vote in the November election? (3) Here is a picture of a ladder. Suppose we say the top of the ladder marked 10 represents a person who definitely will vote in the election this November, and the bottom of the ladder marked zero represents a person who definitely will not vote in the election. How far up or down the ladder would you place yourself? (4) How often would you say you vote—always, nearly always, part of the time, or seldom? (5) In the election in [month and year]—when candidate A ran against candidate B—did things come up which kept you from voting, or did you happen to vote? For whom? (6) Where do people who live in this neighborhood go to vote? (7) Have you ever voted in this precinct or district? (8) Generally speaking, how much interest would you

say you have in politics—a great deal, a fair amount, only a little, or no interest at all? (9) How much thought have you given to the coming November elections—quite a lot, or only a little? See Paul K. Perry, "Certain Problems in Election Survey Methodology," *Public Opinion Quarterly* 43 (Fall 1979): 320-321.

36. Another discussion of the Gallup scaling method is found in Andrew Kohut, "A Review of the Gallup Pre-Election Methodology in 1980," *Proceedings of the Section on Survey Research Methods,* American Statistical Association (1981): 41-54.
37. Perry, "Certain Problems," 321. Charles W. Roll, Jr., reports that in his experience, when the sample is limited to registered voters, the difference is seldom more than one percentage point. Interview with the author, Lawrenceville, N.J., July 31, 1989.
38. Warren J. Mitofsky, interview with the author, New York, June 29, 1989.
39. See Kenneth Pins, "Gephardt and Dole Lead Caucus Races in Final Poll," *Des Moines Register and Tribune,* February 7, 1988.
40. Marc Nuttle, manager of the Robertson campaign, described the advantages enjoyed by an underdog candidate whose base is firm: "In the primaries . . . voter apathy produces only about 15 percent total participation. If you know your base and can identify it, you can achieve great election percents with 10 to 15 percent of the voter population. We were on that track." See David R. Runkel, ed., *Campaign For President: The Managers Look at '88* (Dover, Mass.: Auburn House, 1989), 30.
41. Dwight L. Morris, quoted in Barbara Matusow, "Are the Polls Out of Control?" *Washington Journalism Review* 10 (October 1988): 18.
42. In the course of their personal and telephone surveys, Groves and Kahn asked respondents what subjects they were uneasy talking about during the interview. The results:

| | Mode of interview | |
	Telephone	Personal
Income	27.9%	15.3%
Income tax refund	14.1	8.6
Political opinions	12.1	8.5
Racial attitudes	9.2	8.8
Voting behavior	9.1	8.0
Job	3.1	1.9
Health	3.0	1.6

Groves and Kahn, *Surveys by Telephone,* 97-99.

43. Ibid., 221.
44. The strongest race-of-interviewer effects in Virginia were among Democrats, older respondents, and those in the more conservative parts of the state. See Scott Keeter, "Race of Interviewer Effects in the 1989 Gubernatorial and State Legislature Election Polls" (Paper delivered to the 45th Annual Conference of the American Association for Public Opinion Research, Lancaster, Pa., May 17-20, 1990). In addition to possible race-of-interviewer effects in the New York election, Andrew Kohut found higher refusal rates among older persons and less-educated whites, the groups who also were most likely to favor Rudolph Giuliani, David Dinkins's opponent. See Andrew Kohut, "Methodological Problems in Election Polls for the 1989 Mayoral Race" (Paper delivered to the 45th Annual Conference of the American Association for Public Opinion Research, Lancaster, Pa., May 17-20, 1990).
45. Warren Mitofsky in *Polling on the Issues,* ed. Albert H. Cantril (Cabin John, Md.: Seven Locks Press, 1980), 192.
46. Burns W. Roper, "The Impact of Journalism on Polling," in *Polling on the Issues,* ed. Cantril, 16.
47. Crespi, *Public Opinion, Polls, and Democracy,* 113.
48. E. J. Dionne, Jr., interview with the author, Washington, D.C., July 24, 1989. Cliff Zukin, interview with the author, San Francisco, February 9, 1990.
49. James R. Dickenson, "Candidates Put Themselves at the Mercy of an Unpredictable State," *Washington Post,* February 28, 1984, A6.
50. Richard Wirthlin's tracking polls for Ronald Reagan in 1980 rested on nightly samples of five hundred cases nationwide from mid-October until the final week before the election and on one thousand cases in the last three days of the campaign. See Mark R. Levy, "Polling and the Presidential Election," *Annals* 472 (March 1984): 90.
51. Richard Morin, interview with the author, Washington, D.C., July 24, 1989.
52. Harry W. O'Neill, interview with the author, New York, July 31, 1989.
53. This point was made by Charles W. Roll, Jr., interview with the author, Lawrenceville, N.J., July 31, 1989.
54. Peter D. Hart, interview with the author, Washington, D.C., July 25, 1989.
55. Adam Clymer, interview with the author, New York, July 31, 1989.
56. Richard Wirthlin, interview with the author, McLean, Va., July 28, 1989.
57. I. A. Lewis, director of polling for the *Los Angeles Times,* interview with the author, Los Angeles, February 12, 1990.
58. Morin, interview with the author, Washington, D.C., July 24, 1989.
59. In the early 1940s the Office of Public Opinion Research at Princeton

University conducted numerous experiments in question wording and other nonsampling components of opinion research. See Hadley Cantril, ed., *Gauging Public Opinion* (Princeton, N.J.: Princeton University Press, 1944). Two recent books on the subject worth consulting are: Schuman and Presser, *Questions and Answers;* and Seymour Sudman and Norman M. Bradburn, *Asking Questions* (San Francisco: Jossey-Bass, 1982).

60. See George B. Bishop, Robert W. Oldendick, and Alfred J. Tuchfarber, "Effects of Presenting One versus Two Sides of an Issue in Survey Questions," *Public Opinion Quarterly* 46 (Spring 1982): 69-85.

61. A national sample of two thousand personal interviews was divided into two comparable subsamples, each of which was asked one form of the question. The alternate wording of the questions fell at exactly the same point in the questionnaire. See Albert H. Cantril and Susan Davis Cantril, *Unemployment, Government, and the American People* (Washington, D.C.: Public Research, 1978).

62. Wayne Woodlief, "Poll: Flynn, Bellotti in Gov-Run Dead Heat," *Boston Herald,* April 3, 1990.

63. Schuman and Presser, *Questions and Answers,* 246.

64. Ibid., 194.

65. Ibid., 165-167. It might be hypothesized that less-educated respondents would be more drawn to a middle alternative when it is explicitly offered than better-educated persons. However, in a question-wording experiment regarding political philosophy Schuman and Presser demonstrated that less-educated respondents are more inclined to be "middle of the road" than better-educated respondents *regardless* of whether the middle option is presented between "liberal" and "conservative." Ibid., 172.

66. George F. Bishop has shown that "people who select a middle alternative when it is offered would not necessarily answer the question in the same way as other respondents if forced to choose between the polar alternatives. . . ." See Bishop, "Experiments with the Middle Response Alternative in Survey Questions," *Public Opinion Quarterly* 51 (Summer 1987): 227.

67. For an empirical examination of this issue, see Eric R. A. N. Smith and Peverill Squire, "The Effects of Prestige Names in Question Wording," *Public Opinion Quarterly* 54 (Spring 1990): 97-116.

68. Two illustrations from Schuman and Presser elaborate this point. In the 1971 Detroit Area Survey, a seven-item scale on "political efficacy" was presented in different order to two comparable samples. Each item was a statement with which respondents could agree, agree strongly, disagree, or disagree strongly. The content of the statements was specific enough for the order of their asking to make a difference. As can be seen in the examples, respondents were more likely to agree that "sometimes politics and govern-

ment seem so complicated. . ." if they had just been asked about voting as their only way of speaking out than if they had been asked whether they agreed that "people like me don't have any say. . . ."

		Percent agree and strongly agree	
		Form A 1-7	Form B 7-1
1.	Public officials really care about what people like me think.	46.4%	53.4% *
2.	So many other people vote in elections that it doesn't matter much whether I vote or not.	12.7	12.1
3.	People like me don't have any say about what the government does.	31.1	40.1 *
4.	Sometimes politics and government seem so complicated that a person like me can't really understand what's going on.	64.9	73.1 *
5.	Voting is the only way that people like me can have any say about how the government runs things.	61.3	60.2
6.	Given enough time and money, almost all of man's important problems can be solved by science.	29.6	33.7 *
7.	I don't think public officials care much about what people like me think.	48.3	50.6 *

SOURCE: Howard Schuman and Stanley Presser, *Questions and Answers in Attitude Surveys* (New York: Academic Press, 1981): 55.

* Indicates a statistically significant difference between forms.

However, in a survey conducted in 1977, respondents were asked which of five problems presented was most important. The sample was divided into five comparable subsamples, each of which was presented the problems in a different order. The mere formality of changing the order had only a slight effect on the pattern of responses.

		Order of alternatives				
		ABCDE	BCDEA	CDEAB	DEABC	EABCD
A.	Crime and violence	16.8%	14.8%	17.8%	21.6%	25.2%
B.	Rising prices	22.1	28.7	21.2	13.8	15.1

C. Not enough jobs	31.0	29.5	36.4	36.2	31.1
D. Poor quality of government leaders	15.9	7.4	10.2	8.6	12.6
E. Breakdown of morality among people in general	14.2	19.7	14.4	19.8	16.0
	100.0	100.1	100.0	100.0	100.0
	(113)	(122)	(118)	(116)	(119)

SOURCE: Howard Schuman and Stanley Presser, *Questions and Answers in Attitude Surveys* (New York: Academic Press, 1981): 63.

NOTE: These differences were not statistically significant ($X^2=21.07$; df$=16$).

69. Irving Crespi and Dwight Morris, "Question Order Effect and the Measurement of Candidate Preference in the 1982 Connecticut Elections," *Public Opinion Quarterly* (Fall 1984): 578-591.
70. Burns W. Roper, interview with the author, New York, July 20, 1989.
71. Lee Sigelman, "Question-Order Effects on Presidential Popularity," *Public Opinion Quarterly* 45 (Summer 1981): 199-207.
72. Cantril, *Gauging Public Opinion,* 49.
73. The Gallup Poll found in 1964 that Barry Goldwater received two or three percentage points more support in the secret ballot approach than in direct questioning from interviewers about candidate preference. The same obtained in 1972, when George McGovern received more support by secret ballot than in direct questioning. See Paul K. Perry, "Certain Problems in Election Survey Methodology," 316.
74. Philip E. Converse, "The Nature of Belief Systems in Mass Politics," in *Ideology and Discontent,* ed. David E. Apter (Glencoe, Ill.: Free Press, 1964).
75. George F. Bishop, Robert W. Oldendick, and Alfred J. Tuchfarber, "Effects of Filter Questions in Public Opinion Surveys," *Public Opinion Quarterly* 47 (Winter 1983): 532, 540.
76. Schuman and Presser, *Questions and Answers,* 150. In a separate study, Bishop et al. asked respondents whether they approved or disapproved of a fictitious "Public Affairs Act." Wordings of the question that provided variations of a "don't know" filter produced from 4 to 7 percent having an opinion. When no filter was provided 33 percent ventured an opinion. The educational breakdown of responses when the "don't know" filter was omitted showed opinions pro or con being expressed by 26 percent of those with more than a high school education, 36 percent of those having a high school diploma, and 40 percent of those with less than a high school

education. See George F. Bishop, Robert W. Oldendick, Alfred J. Tuchfarber, and Stephen E. Bennett, "Pseudo-Opinion on Public Affairs," *Public Opinion Quarterly* 44 (Summer 1980): 201, 203. Experiments of this genre raise the thorny dilemma of whether respondents should be asked to venture an opinion when the researcher knowingly proffers a false premise in the question.

77. See Jack W. Germond and Jules Witcover, *Whose Broad Stripes and White Stars? The Trivial Pursuit of the Presidency 1988* (New York: Warner Books, 1989), 157-160; and the comments of Lee Atwater in *Campaign for President*, ed. Runkel, 35-36.

78. Peter Hart, interview with the author, Washington, D.C., July 25, 1989.

79. Humphrey Taylor, interview with the author, New York, July 21, 1990.

80. Peter Hart is one who defends reporting of focus groups by news organizations, noting that "in almost every focus group you come away with some new insight." He has been conducting focus groups for the *Wall Street Journal* since 1975. Interview with the author, Washington, D.C., July 25, 1989. Adam Clymer of the *New York Times* concurs: "You can get a sense of what is in peoples' heads far more richly than in a poll, even if with less certainty." Interview with the author, New York, July 31, 1989.

81. Noting that journalistic license is often taken in news stories about focus groups, E. J. Dionne, Jr., observes that "focus groups can be some of the most tendentious research around." Interview with the author, Washington, D.C., July 24, 1989.

82. David S. Broder, *Behind the Front Page: A Candid Look at How the News Is Made* (New York: Simon and Schuster, 1987), 253.

83. Warren Mitofsky makes this point, buttressing it with data from 1972 exit polls that show Sen. George McGovern getting the support of 93 percent of blacks living in "mostly-black city neighborhoods" but support from only 66 percent of blacks living in the suburbs. See Warren J. Mitofsky, "A Short History of Exit Polls," in *Polling and Presidential Election Coverage,* ed. Paul J. Lavrakas and Jack K. Holley (Newbury Park, Calif.: Sage, forthcoming), 85-86.

84. A "two-stage" sample can be drawn by selecting counties in the first stage proportionate to their share of the total number of voters in the last comparable election. Precincts within selected counties are sampled in the second stage, again proportionate to their share of the total electorate within the county in the last comparable election. A two-stage sample is sometimes easier to draw but is less desirable because it has higher variance than a single-stage sample.

85. CBS News, which uses fewer precincts in its sample design than the other networks and the *Los Angeles Times,* has found that it is advantageous to limit the number of interviewers involved in an exit poll. It reports that

improper selection of respondents by interviewers poses more of a problem in increasing sampling error than does limiting dispersion of precincts across a state. See Mark R. Levy, "The Methodology and Performance of Election Day Polls," *Public Opinion Quarterly* 47 (1983): 59.

86. See Mitofsky, "Short History of Exit Polls," 94-95.

87. Refusals can still represent a problem in exit polls because bias may be introduced in measures of attitudes that tend not to be highly correlated with sex, age, or race. Thus *post hoc* weighting by sex, age, and race may not fully compensate for the views of those refusing to participate.

88. Levy, "Methodology and Performance," 61.

89. *Hotline*, September 23, 1988, Item #10.

90. As the tally continued to come in, Koppel asked Ambassador Jeanne Kirkpatrick: "It is still roughly two-to-one favoring those who believe that the United Nations ought to be taken out of the United States. You're our ambassador to the United Nations; how do you feel about that?" See Alvin P. Sanoff, "ABC's Phone-In Polling: Does It Put Credibility on the Line?" *Washington Journalism Review* (March 1984): 49.

91. Koppel: "Les, I've got to ask you, you've seen those results come in, they are more than ten to one in favor of strong action by the administration. Why ... this tremendous feeling of frustration and anger and a call for strong action over an incident like this?" Ibid.

92. From an undated AT&T promotional brochure entitled "Dial-It: The 900 Service." The full description of the service relevant to its use by broadcasters reads:

Americans have strong opinions on many subjects and issues, and they want to be heard. A 900 number will 'listen' to them.

Dial-It's unique polling application is a way your viewers and prospects can tell you what's on their minds *instantly* by merely calling a 900 number that corresponds to the answer of their choice. Each caller can receive vote confirmation *and* an advertising message.

Is it proper for a woman to ask a man for a date? Was that baseball player 'safe' or 'out' in that crucial play? What is your vote for the year's best movie? What's your opinion on our nation's energy policy? Did you love or hate this new pilot program?

For the broadcaster particularly, a Dial-It poll can be an effective way of building audience involvement and getting a feel for his market. Or offering his key advertisers a unique and attention-getting service.

The polling results can be provided minute-by-minute over the subscriber's computer terminal, or delivered within days by mail.

Proof of Dial-It's success as a polling medium was demonstrated on national television most notably during coverage of the Carter-Reagan debate, when some 700,000 viewers—in the space of just two hours—dialed a 900 number to 'vote' for the candidate who gained the most from the debate.

93. *Hotline,* September 22, 1988, Item #9.
94. Complete data for alternative question wordings on abortion from this survey are presented in Appendix A, Table A-5.
95. See E. J. Dionne, Jr., "Poll on Abortion Finds the Nation Is Sharply Divided," *New York Times,* April 26, 1989, A1.
96. Free and Cantril found that 46 percent of those qualifying as "conservatives" in their responses to questions about political ideology also qualified as "liberals" in their responses to questions about specific government programs. See Lloyd A. Free and Hadley Cantril, *The Political Beliefs of Americans* (New Brunswick, N.J.: Rutgers University Press, 1967), chap. 3.

c h a p t e r   f o u r

Polls and the Public Trust:
Standards and Accountability

I will follow that method of treatment which,
according to my ability and judgment, I consider for
the benefit of my patients and abstain from whatever
is deleterious and mischievous.

Hippocratic Oath
Fifth century B.C.

Polling is a transaction of mutual trust. The pollster counts on the respondent to be forthright; the respondent accepts the pollster's seriousness of purpose. So, too, must the pollster and the press trust each other—one to measure with care, the other to report with precision. Understanding the nature of the mutual bonds among the public, the pollster, and the press requires examination of three issues. This chapter considers each in turn.

First, technology has made public opinion polling more accessible. A generation ago conducting opinion research required a network of interviewers, a staff to draw areal samples, and data-processing capability. Today polling can be highly modularized. High-quality samples can be purchased from vendors. Interviewing agencies exist all over the country, some with imposing capacity to field hundreds of phone calls simultaneously. Desk-top personal computers now can handle most data-processing software packages and samples of the size commonly used in polls. As the technological and technical barriers to conducting a poll have been lowered, the criteria of professional competence of those who call themselves pollsters take on even greater importance.

Second, because they have become central to news coverage of politics, polls conducted by and for news organizations ought to be as accountable to accepted norms of good practice as polls conducted outside the Fourth Estate. This is easier said than done, because most reporters and editors eschew criteria of performance defined outside the terms of reference of journalism. However, in conducting and reporting polls, news organizations use the methodology and invoke the authority of an independent field of endeavor having its own criteria of professional competence.

Third, as discussed earlier, the move from an elite-based to a mass-based system of nominating candidates for public office has put pollsters in the front ranks of a new political elite, the campaign consultants. This new elite is less accountable to the public than were its predecessors, the party leaders.

What Should Standards Be About?

From the earliest days of public opinion research, practitioners have wrestled with issues of standards. The desire was to have not only broad guidelines regarding research competence but a means of holding polling practitioners accountable. As the number of polling organizations has proliferated and polling and journalism have become more interdependent, the old formulations have been continually reevaluated.

Standards issues figured prominently in the founding of the American Association for Public Opinion Research (AAPOR) and the National Council on Public Polls (NCPP), the two associations most involved in the professional affairs of opinion research intended for release to the public. The codes of both organizations have undergone periodic revision. As this book is being written, AAPOR is assessing the adequacy of its code.

What should the standards cover? The polling community has long agreed that the term "standards" is appropriately applied to what is disclosed about a poll's methodology. The consensus is that the burden is on the pollster to disclose pertinent methodological information when a poll is released to the public. It is quite another matter, however, to stipulate standards to be applied across the board regarding pollster performance because of the wide range of research needs that polls serve and the circumstances under which they are conducted. We explore this distinction by turning first to standards of disclosure and then to principles of professional conduct and competence.

Disclosure: The Public's Need to Know

As we saw in Chapter 3, a competent news report about the state of public opinion must be more than the recitation of percentages resulting from a poll. We have seen how much the reliability of a poll can be affected by the degree of control exercised over the design and implementation of the sample. We have also noted how the validity of the conclusions drawn from a poll rests on the phrasing and ordering of questions asked, the number of questions used to explore a dimension of opinion, and the subtlety with which the data are described and analyzed.

Because pollsters have a vital stake in the quality of reporting about polls, most spend considerable time talking to reporters and editors about the complexities inherent in public opinion and how far a poll's findings can be generalized. For the public to benefit from these exchanges between pollster and reporter, three conditions must obtain: (a) pollsters must make available pertinent information about the methodology of a poll; (b) reporters must know enough about polling to make sense out of the information given to them; and (c) reporters must include in news stories enough information about a poll's methodology to allow the public to size up the poll for itself. We will look at each of these conditions and the regularity with which each is met.

Pollsters. By and large pollsters make methodological information available to reporters and editors—either at the time a poll is released to the press or later in response to requests for more information. This is a generally accepted part of the professional ethic and is something journalists expect. Benjamin Bradlee of the *Washington Post:* "Just as you attribute to the maximum extent possible in a news story, you should explain the technicalities of your poll. If you are asking people to believe you, you have got to be able to show them why you should be believed." [1]

Both NCPP and AAPOR have formulated a list of the elements of methodology that should be available when a poll is made public. [2] For NCPP, the "principles of disclosure" that form part of its code spell out

The "Principles of Disclosure" of the National Council on Public Polls

- Sponsorship of the survey
- Dates of interviewing
- Method of obtaining the interviews (in-person, telephone or mail)
- Population that was sampled
- Size of the sample
- Size and description of the sub-sample, if the survey report relies on less than the total sample
- Complete wording of questions upon which the release is based
- Percentages upon which conclusions are based

The "Standards for Minimal Disclosure" of the American Association for Public Opinion Research

- Who sponsored the survey, and who conducted it
- The exact wording of questions asked, including the text of any preceding instruction or explanation to the interviewer or respondent that might reasonably be expected to affect the response
- A definition of the population under study, and a description of the sampling frame used to identify this population
- A description of the sample selection procedure, giving a clear indication of the method by which the respondents were selected by the researcher, or whether the respondents were entirely self-selected
- Size of sample and, if applicable, completion rates and information on eligibility criteria and screening procedures
- A discussion of the precision of the findings, including, if appropriate, estimates of sampling error, and a description of any weighting or estimating procedures used
- Which results are based on parts of the sample, rather than the total sample
- Method, location, and dates of data collection

SOURCE: National Council on Public Polls, 1979; American Association for Public Opinion Research, 1986.

NOTE: The full texts of the NCPP and AAPOR codes from which the above points were drawn appear in Appendix B.

eight items to be disclosed. AAPOR's code contains a section on "standards for minimal disclosure" that calls for release of a slightly different mix of eight items. The full NCPP and AAPOR codes appear in Appendix B.

Unlike AAPOR, NCPP does not call for disclosure of sampling error. For the reasons discussed in Chapter 3, many NCPP members are concerned that reference to sampling error conveys a sense of false precision about a poll and neglects other equally significant sources of error or bias.

Reporters. Many pollsters find that reporters today ask more informed questions about poll results and are more attentive to the limits of how far poll results can be generalized than was the case two decades ago.

Several factors have contributed to this favorable trend. In the mid-1970s news organizations realized that without polls of their own or polling savvy among their political reporters they could not assess the quality of polls leaked to them by candidates or special interests. More generally, the social and political turmoil of the late 1960s and early 1970s could not be adequately covered by news organizations without the kinds of information available only from the social survey. Increasingly, the journalist was confronted with quantitative information about political and social trends. In response, schools of journalism expanded their curricula in the applied social sciences.[3]

Even though there is a sense among many pollsters that journalists are more attentive to the nuances of polling than twenty years ago, misgivings persist about the quality of poll reporting.[4] An informal survey of pollsters conducted by Gladys Lang and Kurt Lang in early 1990 found that 86 percent of 119 pollsters contacted were not sanguine that news accounts of polls helped the public distinguish between polls of varying quality.[5]

Readers and viewers. It is difficult to gauge how much information news organizations share with the public about the methodology of the polls they report. Available data on the levels of compliance of news organizations with the NCPP and AAPOR codes are now more than a decade old.

NCPP, in conjunction with the Medill School of Journalism at Northwestern University, examined 270 articles on polls appearing in 60 newspapers in 30 major metropolitan areas from before the New Hampshire primary to the general election in 1976. The degree of

TABLE 4-1   Consistency of Poll Reports with NCPP Principles of Disclosure

Information included	Articles consistent with principles
Population being surveyed	99%
Poll sponsorship	90
Overall sample size	83
Interviewing dates	81
Mode of interview	77
Question wording	31

SOURCE: Albert H. Cantril and Jay T. Harris, "The Reporting of Polls by Sixty Newspapers: Some Preliminary Findings," unpublished report by the National Council on Public Polls and the Medill School of Journalism, November 12, 1976.

compliance with the NCPP principles of disclosure is shown in Table 4-1.

Mark Miller and Robert Hurd took a comparable look at conformity with the AAPOR standards for minimal disclosure. Their review covered 116 stories from 1972 through 1977 in three regionally important newspapers. They were able to compare how the papers treated polls in election and nonelection years (Table 4-2).

From the pollster's standpoint, the most discouraging finding in both these studies is the relatively low proportion of newspaper articles in which readers had an opportunity to assess the wording of questions for themselves.

Regrettably, more recent data are not comprehensive enough to bring these trends up to date. Nor are we able to infer from these data much about the quality of the newspaper articles other than that some items were included. For example, we have no idea how carefully the story leads were written or how considered were the generalizations drawn from the findings. We do know that the television networks seldom provide the wording of questions in poll stories, even though sample size and sampling error generally are reported. As to local television, we have no systematic information regarding how polls are reported. Evans Witt of the Associated Press has found compliance with the NCPP code "far less pervasive" at the state and local level than it is among the national news media. More systematic research in this regard is needed.[6]

Reporter versus pollster.   A tension persists between what pollsters think should be included in public reports about polls and what

TABLE 4-2   Consistency of Poll Reports with AAPOR Standards for Minimal
             Disclosure in Election Years and Nonelection Years

	Articles consistent with standards	
Information included	Election year	Nonelection year
Population	91	66
Sample size	89	81
Sponsor	80	87
Timing	76	48
Question wording	71	34
Method (interview)	62	38
Sampling error	31	2

SOURCE: M. Mark Miller and Robert Hurd, "Conformity to AAPOR Standards in Newspaper Reporting of Public Opinion Polls," *Public Opinion Quarterly* 46 (Summer 1982): 246.

NOTE: The newspapers included were the *Chicago Tribune,* the *Los Angeles Times,* and the *Atlanta Constitution.*

news organizations are willing to report. Thoughtful journalists have expressed doubts about the burdens imposed on reporters by lock-step adherence to the NCPP and AAPOR codes. Philip Meyer has questioned whether all of the items in the NCPP and AAPOR codes need to be reported. He argues that all of this information should be made available by the pollsters, but he would leave to the discretion of the reporter whether items such as question wording and subsample sizes should be included in what is printed or broadcast.[7]

Often frustrated with their colleagues in journalism, the members of the opinion research community continue to advocate inclusion of more, not less, information about polls in news reports. However, they do so with a clear sense of real-world pressures at work. For example, when NCPP revised its code in 1979, it adopted an explicit strategy of limiting the items about methodology that member organizations would be "required" to include in public releases of polls. It did so to elicit a greater degree of compliance and to increase the chances that news organizations would use the information.[8] The code also spelled out how and when additional information would be made available.

AAPOR took a slightly different tack in its code revision in the early 1980s. It was more inclusive in what it said should be disclosed. Whereas the NCPP code specifies that items such as completion rates and sample weightings should be released upon request, the AAPOR code calls for their disclosure at the outset. As a practical matter, many polling organizations do not include these items in their public poll releases. AAPOR members in these organizations, working with the best of professional intentions, and often directing the studies that are released to the public, comply with some of the items on AAPOR's minimal disclosure list while paying little attention to others. It can be argued that this dilutes the authority of the AAPOR code.

The viability and vitality of any professional code rest on an uneasy balance between the real and ideal worlds. A code that stretches beyond professional consensus is as ineffective as one that understates it.

Thus far we have been discussing polls intended for release to the public. But what about private polls leaked to the press? What are the pollster's disclosure obligations under such circumstances? Most private pollsters stipulate in their contracts that they retain the right to release an entire poll if the client leaks partial information that misrepresents the overall picture presented by the poll. Both the NCPP and AAPOR codes consider that a proprietary poll leaked by the pollster has entered the public domain and should be subject to the same disclosure rules as polls intended for public release.

A final issue relating to disclosure standards relates to their effect on competition. It might be argued that by setting standards of disclosure (to say nothing of standards of performance) AAPOR and NCPP make organizations that do not comply with the standards less competitive in the marketplace. To make clear that it intends no restraint of trade, NCPP's code states that "any survey organization, upon providing evidence to the Council of its compliance with this Code, shall be permitted to state that it 'complies with the Principles of Disclosure of the National Council on Public Polls.' "

Disclosure versus Performance: How Good Is Good Enough?

If NCPP and AAPOR are concerned with improving the quality of polls and of poll reporting, the reader may ask, why does neither provide criteria of professional competence to be applied across the board? Are there no straightforward tests to determine whether a poll has been competently conducted?

A simple answer to these questions is difficult because of the diversity of situations in which standards of performance might have to apply. Consider two examples.

- An overnight tracking poll for a campaign based on five-minute telephone interviews of a 200-case sample without callbacks may provide crude, but useful, indications of the impact of an event on the fortunes of the candidate. While the campaign's pollster would be foolish to draw major conclusions from such a tracking poll, the preliminary glimpse into public thinking it provided may alert the campaign to an opportunity or problem that might be corroborated by more polling data.
- Studies of the values of the American people as they bear on electoral choices, such as those conducted by the Gallup Organization for Times Mirror, involve in-person interviews almost ninety minutes in length with a sample of four thousand respondents including an oversample of blacks.

Which study was "better"? The 200-case tracking poll does not begin to approach the 4,000-case personal interview study in terms of data quality or the richness of the analyses it can support. Nonetheless, it should not be faulted as methodologically inadequate *provided* the limitations of a small sample without callbacks and a short interview are clearly spelled out.

In short, the quality of a poll must be assessed in light of the purposes for which it is being conducted. Cut-and-dried criteria for poll evaluation can be misleading. Moreover, requiring standardized procedures for all polls regardless of their purpose would impose a methodological straightjacket that inhibits experimentation with new techniques.

For these reasons, both NCPP and AAPOR have concluded there is no easy answer to the question of "how good is good enough?" While concern about the quality of polling remains central to the purposes of both associations, each group sees imposition of uniform standards of performance across the board as unrealistic and even inappropriate.

NCPP is quite explicit. The preamble to its Principles of Disclosure reads, in part:

> It shall not be the purpose of this Code to pass judgment on the merits of methods employed in specific surveys. Rather, it shall be our sole purpose to ensure that pertinent information is disclosed concerning methods that were used so that consumers of surveys may assess studies for themselves.

AAPOR's code is similar. Its revision in the early 1980s was motivated by concern among many members that the association had to be more aggressive in improving survey quality. After two years of deliberation, AAPOR made its code more specific on many points but did not formulate standards of performance. Although it did elaborate standards of disclosure, in matters of professional practice and professional responsibility it advocated "principles." [9]

It is important to note that, although AAPOR is reluctant to stipulate generic performance standards, it has not refrained from evaluating performance in specific cases. This is because in a specific instance performance can be judged against the objectives for which the poll was conducted and the degree to which the guidelines of professional conduct were followed.

Many of the issues brought before AAPOR's standards committee have had to do with pseudopolls such as the "900" call-ins and with the use of the survey as a ploy by organizations soliciting funds or selling products. In these cases, AAPOR's formal complaint-review process has usually not been used. Instead, AAPOR has responded with a statement of concern or by joining NCPP in issuing a press release.

AAPOR's baptism in the public arena of poll review came in 1955 when Walter Reuther, president of the United Automobile Workers, complained that a questionnaire being used in a survey for General Motors by the Opinion Research Corporation was biased. One result of AAPOR's review of the study was the association's realization that it did not have the machinery to bring a complaint to a definitive resolution.[10] In subsequent years, AAPOR incorporated to protect its leadership against legal actions (1963-1964) and formulated specific procedures to ensure due process in handling complaints (1974-1975).[11]

The standards dilemma for some pollsters has been well put by Warren Mitofsky. After years of advocating standards of performance, he concluded in 1989 that "as much as I believe that in most cases it is possible to write performance standards for specific survey research projects, I no longer believe that it is possible to codify performance criteria that are general enough to meet most needs." At the same time, he bemoaned the fact that "AAPOR today still has no *unambiguous* mechanism in its Code of Professional Ethics and Practices for condemning polls that are outright garbage, let alone so-called legitimate work that cuts corners and lacks scientific rigor." [12]

Others contend that the profession indeed ought to be able to articulate standards of performance that would constitute a minimum threshold of professional competence. They believe that an organization such as AAPOR needs some mechanism for citing as deficient polls that fail to meet rudimentary requirements of proficiency. Beyond the threshold concept, AAPOR would retain a range of discretion for reviewing performance in cases where the minimal standards had been met but other grounds for concern were alleged.

The matter of standards of performance in opinion research is greatly complicated by the proximity of polling to the world of journalism. Even as pollsters work toward consensus on criteria by which to assess one another's work, they have little clout when it comes to the performance of newspapers and broadcasters who conduct or report polls. News organizations are unyielding in their opposition to formally stated criteria of performance or external oversight.

Accordingly, as we turn to the issue of accountability in polling and poll reporting, it is useful to distinguish between issues *within* the polling profession and issues *between* it and journalism.

Pollster Performance and Peer Review

Efforts to institutionalize performance standards and professional accountability within the polling profession are dogged by thorny philosophical, legal, and procedural questions.

The Marketplace and Accountability

In any consideration of professional accountability in the American system the opening presumption is that the market will induce self-regulation of performance. Only in extreme cases is some external intervention needed, such as through the courts. The argument is that professional competence will result from the free entry of practitioners into the market and from the unfettered ability of consumers to choose among those practitioners.[13]

The regulatory literature is extensive on the circumstances under which this ideal marketplace operates for certain professions under certain conditions. As far as opinion polls intended for public release are concerned, some factors point toward the market's ability to sustain quality through competition. Other factors militate against it.

Among factors fostering market competition in a direction that ensures quality in research, four are noteworthy.

Eased entry into the profession.   The modularization of polling has made the tools of opinion research more accessible. Technical and technological hurdles have been lowered and economic costs have been reduced, as the capital investment required to get started in polling is now modest and the wherewithal to sustain a labor-intensive field operation is no longer required. Greater access to the profession enriches and diversifies the talent pool, thus spurring competition.

More competing polling organizations.   A result of eased technological and economic accessibility has been a proliferation of polling firms and polling operations within news organizations. Critics of polls complain of a plethora of polls and poll reports that appear in the news media. But an important dividend has been expanded opportunities for competition among polls and polling organizations on everything from the way questions are phrased to the procedures used to screen respondents for inclusion in a sample.

A more informed consuming public.   As outlined above, the profession continues to make concerted efforts to expand public awareness of the factors contributing to greater reliability and validity in polls. These efforts are important, for they affirm that the public is not being excluded from the process by which polls are evaluated.

Increased opportunities for professional education.   A notable expansion has occurred in the training available to individuals who produce polls and to those who try to make sense of them. Dozens of universities now support survey research centers and laboratories. Courses in quantitative methods cut across disciplines within the social sciences. Programs in journalism education now often provide more than cursory exposure to the theory and techniques of opinion research. In short, anyone interested in learning about polling can find some means of doing so.

As much as these factors may stimulate competition, they are offset by three considerations that limit the effect of market forces when it comes to standards in polling.

A lack of widespread knowledge about polling.   In spite of efforts by associations in the field to expand awareness of the nuances of polling, a stunning degree of ignorance persists not only among the public but among many reporters and editors who turn polls into news and among politicians who commission private political polls. Pseudopolls such as "900" call-ins continue to get much play in the news, especially on local television stations. News reports on the latest in candidate standings based on paltry poll samples abound.

News organizations as poll sponsors. Print and broadcast media tend to judge the value of a poll by its timeliness, the simplicity of the news lead it might suggest, or the newsworthiness of the topic it covers. These may be legitimate journalistic criteria, but they can be at odds with a researcher's concern about the reliability of the data or the validity of the inferences drawn from those data.

The premium on political judgment. Increasingly the performance of pollsters who work for political candidates is assessed as much by the quality of their political judgment as by the quality of their data. While a pollster's counsel is often informed by opinion data, it need not be. To the degree that competition among private pollsters deflects attention from issues of data quality and analysis, the market cannot be relied upon to encourage higher standards in polling.

Weighing these seven factors together we conclude that, left to its own devices, the market alone will not sustain attention in the research community and among consumers of research to issues of reliability, validity, and responsible reporting.

Toward Self-Regulation

What mechanisms might complement the marketplace in moving competition in public polling to an arena having more to do with generally shared norms of proficiency?

The most extreme form of intervention would be licensing, a mode of regulation in which unlicensed individuals are barred from professional practice. Licensing systems, administered by government bodies, are usually reserved for fields where health and public safety are at stake. Most would agree that licensing doctors or airline pilots serves a clear purpose. However, polling poses no threat to life or limb, however uncertain critics may be that polls serve the democratic process. Furthermore, extending the concept of licensing to opinion research would, by implication, threaten the independence of myriad other domains in which government intervention is contrary to our political tradition.[14]

It is also implausible to imagine judicial intervention in the polling business. Even were the polling profession to have a highly codified structure of performance criteria, it is highly unlikely that the courts would rule on the basis of such criteria.[15]

The issue of government intervention was debated in the late 1960s in connection with several initiatives aimed at mandating reporting requirements for pollsters. Legislation was introduced in 1968 by Rep. Lucien Nedzi (D-Mich.) to require pollsters to file information with the Librarian of Congress about the procedures employed in a survey. Failure to comply within three days would expose the pollster to a possible penalty of ninety days in jail. The bill drew little congressional support. It was reintroduced two years later only to suffer the same fate.[16]

Sen. Charles Goodell (R-N.Y.), blaming his 1970 defeat in part on his poor showing in a poll published just before the election, introduced legislation that would provide a civil penalty against any pollster who released a privately commissioned poll without making public information about the procedures used. Like the Nedzi bill, Goodell's "Polls Procedure Disclosure Act" never caught fire.

Occasionally poll-regulation proposals are floated in state legislatures, but they do not attract much interest. As a general principle, many legislatures are reluctant to extend regulatory procedures to new professions out of concern that the practical consequence would be exclusion of qualified practitioners from the marketplace.

External attempts to constrain the activities of pollsters have been most visible regarding exit polls conducted in connection with television network election projections. The objective of such attempts has been to prohibit exit poll interviewing within specified perimeters of voting places to make it difficult for interviewers to monitor the flow of voters leaving polling places, thus compromising the sampling process and the quality of the data upon which the election projections rest.

In one case after another, the courts have stymied these efforts on First Amendment grounds. When the state of Washington was challenged in court regarding its prohibition of exit polling within three hundred feet of polling stations, one justice held that "it is not the business of government to decide what we should and should not know about the political process." [17] Three years later in 1988, the state of Montana was enjoined by a federal district judge from enforcing its ban on interviewing voters within two hundred feet of polling places. In this instance, the judge noted that the Montana law was "seemingly a broadside attack upon significant, traditional and cherished First Amendment freedoms." [18]

More generally, those attempting to regulate polling or constrain polling activities will find little in the First Amendment to differentiate between types of polling activity that should be more or less susceptible to external oversight. As to the fundamental principle, there is little to distinguish between a reporter interviewing a dozen people at a shopping mall and a large polling company conducting a rigorous national sample survey.

Self-regulation of the polling profession remains the only practical approach. However, the degree to which the field is left to monitor its own affairs is contingent upon the credibility of its enterprise in self-regulation. An asset in this regard is that the authority of the field rests on a body of knowledge that has built up cumulatively over the years through professional discourse and publication. Thus, the more solidly judgments by peers about one another's performance are grounded in shared terms of reference and shared knowledge, the less likely they are to be dismissed as arbitrary. Moreover, the greater the specificity of the professional consensus regarding what is "good" and "bad" practice, the greater is the likelihood that the consensus will be observed by practitioners and upheld in those unhappy circumstances when formal peer review procedures must be used.

Four general approaches to self-regulation need elaboration.

Certification. Like licensing, certification is a process that stipulates performance criteria. However, unlike licensing, certification need not be administered by a government agency. A professional association can assume responsibility for certifying practitioners in its field. External authority is invoked only when individuals use a title for which they have not been certified. In such cases they may be sued by the certifying body.

Certification can stimulate competition within a field.[19] First, in contrast to a licensing system, certification does not preclude uncertified practitioners from entering the marketplace but only from using the title protected by the certification system. Second, it is possible for competing certification systems to operate within a field, thereby generating an incentive for certifying associations to monitor performance and to establish the authority of a specific imprimatur. Third, certifying practitioners can have the effect of leveling the competitive playing field by diminishing any advantage larger firms may have over smaller firms in determining competence.

Notwithstanding these spurs to competition, certification could have a stifling effect. If poll consumers come to rely on it too heavily as a yardstick of quality, certification could become a de facto licensing system. While there is some possibility that competing centers of certifying activity within the polling profession would emerge, it is not likely.

There remains the question of how the threshold of knowledge required for certification would be stipulated. This returns us quickly to the issue of how good is good enough and the reluctance of polling associations to codify performance standards. Thus, as inviting as certification is as a vehicle for fortifying the best professional intentions, it remains a weak candidate overall as far as opinion polling is concerned.[20]

Complaint processing. Although the polling community has found across-the-board standards unworkable, it has been mindful of its public obligation to respond when serious allegations are made about a specific poll. The latest code revisions by NCPP and AAPOR were prompted in large part by a perceived need to create a mechanism that could see complaints about a poll through to a definitive conclusion.

To meet this objective it was necessary to build into the NCPP and AAPOR codes explicit due process provisions to ensure that alleged offenders had ample opportunity to respond to allegations.[21] Without such provisions both associations would be vulnerable to legal action and thus powerless.

Cases of alleged unprofessional conduct by polling organizations are seldom unambiguous. Two cases illustrate this point.

In the mid-1970s, a complaint was brought against the Opinion Research Corporation (ORC) by a consumer-advocacy organization, which alleged that the wording of a question about a piece of proposed legislation was biased against the interests of the consumer. With the full cooperation of ORC, AAPOR investigated the matter and concluded that bias probably did exist. AAPOR found some "interpretations which do not appear to be supported by the data made public." However, Ithiel de Sola Pool argued in dissent that it was unreasonable to expect any question to capture all facets of public opinion on anything as complex as proposed legislation and that the matter was one of subjective interpretation rather than ethical misconduct.[22]

A second example came in 1983 when Cambridge Survey Research (CSR) was called to account for using in a political survey a question that alleged marital indiscretions on the part of one of the candidates. CSR noted that the allegations had been in the news several years earlier and that its research objective was to assess aspects of candidate vulnerability. The matter worked its way through the AAPOR review process without unequivocal conclusion. Some involved in the review concluded that some of the respondents in the poll were exposed to information that may well have been false. Others argued that the use of hypothetical situations in a question was an appropriate means of gauging opinion.

Sidney Hollander recounts the final disposition of the matter:

> The full investigation procedure was applied and the case presented in late 1983 to [the AAPOR] Council, some of whose members favored a strong reprimand. Others did not, either because they thought adequate disclosure was all that mattered, because the case had dragged on too long, or because they wondered how AAPOR could defend itself if sued. In the face of a divided Council, it was decided to issue a full statement on the matter, without reprimand, which was eventually published in the *AAPOR Newsletter*.[23]

Post hoc peer review. Without minimizing the steps NCPP and AAPOR have taken gingerly to provide a framework for dealing with the occasional extreme case of alleged misconduct, the real business of a peer review system based on competency is done on a day-to-day basis.

We tend to think of peer review as the critical scrutiny by anonymous "referees" of manuscripts submitted to publishers or proposals submitted to funding agencies. This is the expectation of authors who contribute articles to professional journals or books to reputable publishing houses. However, this kind of rigorous external peer review is seldom found after a poll is released publicly.

For example, polls conducted by the *Boston Globe*/WBZ-TV and the *Boston Herald*/WCVB-TV a few days before the 1990 Massachusetts gubernatorial primary failed to tap the throw-the-rascals-out groundswell that would propel Boston University president John Silber to the Democratic nomination. On the basis of a 400-case sample of likely Democratic primary voters, the *Globe*/WBZ reported Silber with only 31 percent against 54 percent supporting the state's former attorney general, Francis Bellotti. When the ballots were counted, Silber, a newcomer to electoral politics, had won handily with 54 percent of the vote.

As might be expected the polls came in for much criticism. John Silber alleged that the *Globe* "had a poll that was out there slanted in the sample it took, and as a consequence they used the poll to try to hurt my campaign."[24]

The public clearly had a need to know what went wrong with the polls. But instead of casting light on the subject, all that was produced was heat in the round of poll-bashing that ensued. News organizations and the pollsters they employed should obviously have been held accountable for their errors. Instead, in the rush to journalistic judgment, the edge of needed criticism was dulled by loose conjecture as to the sources of polling error.

It is episodes such as this that have spurred some in the polling profession to argue for more formal means of post hoc peer review of polls that enter the public domain. This has not been an easy step for pollsters to take, for they are understandably reluctant to criticize one another's work publicly. Yet without such attribution, criticism lacks credibility and can degenerate into carping that serves little public purpose.

A welcome development is the "poll reviews" section recently initiated in *Public Opinion Quarterly*. Most issues of the journal contain an assessment of an opinion poll reported by the news media. A poll can become the subject of a review because doubt exists about some aspect of its methodology or because the poll itself has received attention in the news. The review process provides ample opportunity for response by the individuals whose work has been assessed. Often a reply to the review is published in a subsequent issue.[25]

Another means of post hoc peer assessment remains grossly under-utilized. This is the opportunity for critical evaluation of polls that news organizations conduct and deposit in archives of opinion and survey research data. Vast amounts of data from the ABC News/*Washington Post*, CBS News/*New York Times*, Field, Gallup, Harris, and NBC News/*Wall Street Journal* polls are available at the Roper Center for Public Opinion Research at the University of Connecticut, the Interuniversity Consortium on Political and Social Research at the University of Michigan, and the Harris archive at the University of North Carolina. Warren Mitofsky, former head of the CBS Election and Survey Unit, is puzzled at the lack of secondary use of these data: "We have taken a good deal of time to archive this material in the hope that scholarly scrutiny would give us some critical feedback; but we get none of it."[26]

Specificity in statements of principles. Despite the consensus that comprehensive generic standards of performance are inappropriate and unworkable for public opinion research, much can be done to raise the sophistication of judgment pollsters bring to their trade. A motivating factor in the revision of the AAPOR code was a perceived need for greater clarity in the relationship between lofty pronouncements of intentions and the reality of professional practice.

Systematic thinking about how general principles of "good practice" can be made more specific is called for as the field of opinion research moves toward more rigorous self-regulation and increased accountability to the public. This would appear a modest burden for a field that plays so prominent a role in our political and social life and for which across-the-board performance standards are inappropriate.

Private Polling and Public Accountability

The renown of many pollsters derives not from their findings but from the importance of the clients for whom they conduct private polls. What stance should the polling profession take toward the accountability of those of its practitioners who work exclusively or primarily for private clients? No one would gainsay the right of pollsters to provide privileged information to their clients; however, it is reasonable to ask to what extent private pollsters can be held accountable to the profession and to the public.

Private pollsters practice in two arenas. On the one hand, they form part of the burgeoning cadre of political consultants. On the other, they ply the techniques of opinion research. To assess how accountable they are, we must look at both aspects of their professional identity.

Pollsters as political consultants. The challenge of public accountability for the field of political consulting was framed by Nelson Polsby in 1983:

> Whatever the professional constraints on the behavior of technicians of political campaigns, ... it cannot be said that they represent anyone. The access they gain to candidates serves no legitimate interest beyond that of their own careers, and presumably the careers of the candidates whom they serve. The peopling of a campaign organization with specialists thus makes no coalitions, cements no alliances, seals no deals in the world of grass roots electoral politics.[27]

The thrust of Polsby's argument is that consultants are accountable only to their candidate clients. However, because word of mouth and referrals are the way most consulting business is developed, consultants have strong incentives to avoid the reputation of being unethical or incompetent.

The American Association of Political Consultants (AAPC), to which many private pollsters belong, is in the midst of its own internal debate about the rules of the road. Since 1983, the organization has been wrestling with a code of ethics. [28] The impetus has come from two sources.

First, as more and more individuals hung out their shingles as "political consultants," concern grew within the association that more concerted efforts were needed to instill peer-driven pressures regarding norms of practice. One of the founders of AAPC, Walter De Vries, notes that as many as four in ten of AAPC's members have been members for less than three years. He also reports a huge turnover in membership in the association, suggesting that few individuals stay with political consulting as a career.[29]

Second, the move toward public financing of elections at the federal and state levels was seen by some AAPC members as a possible point of entry for government regulation of political consulting: public resources should be used for television advertisements and other campaign activities only if such activities were in some way publicly accountable.

AAPC now faces an issue that AAPOR and NCPP have already had to deal with: how to establish a mechanism to consider allegations of bad practice that ensures due process, protects the association and its officers from legal intimidation, and engenders confidence among the public that the field can be self-regulating.

Polling has a major advantage over political consulting when it comes to self-regulation. As pointed out above, polling's credibility in self-regulation is greatly enhanced by its lineage in the social sciences. Even though modern political consulting can call on a proud tradition in public relations extending back to the 1920s, it has not enjoyed the proximity polling has to a body of theory and methodology to which practitioners have been adding for three generations.

One consequence is that the challenge of self-regulation is a good deal more difficult to meet in the world of political consulting than in public opinion polling. Reflecting this difference, the criteria of professional conduct are far more broadly framed in political consulting than in opinion research.

The AAPC "Code of Professional Ethics" now consists of eight standards to which members pledge adherence. Some are quite specific, such as, "I will document accurately and fully any criticism of an opponent or his record." Yet some provisions are so general that it is hard to see how they could serve as the basis for adjudicating a complaint. For example, "I shall not indulge in any activity which would corrupt or degrade the practice of political campaigning." While laudable in intent, the provision may be unenforceable because of the near impossibility of agreeing on what yardstick should be used to assess the corrupting influence of a given activity, for "corruption of practice" is very much in the eye of the beholder. Did the 1988 advertisements on the furloughing of Willie Horton degrade the campaign process? Some would say they did not distort Dukakis's record as governor of Massachusetts and were fair play. Others would point out that the furlough program was initiated by a Republican predecessor of Dukakis and that the advertisements unnecessarily roiled racial animosities.

For all the imperfections of its peer-review machinery, the field of public opinion research is light years ahead of political consulting when it comes to formal standards and mechanisms for ensuring public accountability.

Private pollsters and the polling profession. If there is little near-term prospect that peer review among political consultants will serve to hold private pollsters publicly accountable, we must turn to the second arena in which these pollsters operate, the opinion research community itself.

Nine polling firms worked for candidates vying for their party's presidential nomination in 1988. Of these firms, only three were represented in AAPOR's roster. The others had no officer or principal of the corporation listed as a member of the association. One cannot infer from this fact that the firms not represented in AAPOR are less competent than those that are. But one can conclude that the worlds of private political polling and AAPOR are not in sync.

Both worlds can take steps to redress this condition. The association can make greater efforts to engage private pollsters in its activities through panels at the annual meeting and possibly through creation of an AAPOR section on political polling. For their part, private pollsters can overcome inhibitions to collegiality arising out of the proprietary aspects of their work. They can take a leaf from the book of market researchers, who share information about theory and techniques in the belief that, as the state of the art advances, so does the individual researcher.

The pollster unaffiliated with an association of peers is accountable only to the marketplace. As we have seen, the market's power to ensure professional competence is uncertain. On the one hand, private pollsters often compete with one another more as political consultants than as opinion researchers. The success of some pollsters in generating new business rests primarily on their ability to persuade prospective clients of the savvy and tutored political judgment they can bring to a campaign, regardless of the quality of any opinion data they may collect for the campaign. On the other hand, when the quality of opinion data becomes the basis for competition, the marketplace tends to work: most campaign managers and staffers of the campaign committees of the national parties have seen enough polls to be able to sort the good from the not so good.

Before leaving the issue of the accountability of private pollsters, we must return to a dimension of the pollster-turned-strategist that troubles some in the profession. When a pollster ventures counsel—with or without data upon which to base it—some argue that a luring but pernicious erosion of the pollster's function as researcher has taken place. "You can't wear both hats," contends California pollster Mervin Field. "When you're under pressure to get the guy elected, what gives first are your principles as an objective researcher." [30]

This point of view holds that the mission of the pollster, like that of the military intelligence officer, is to collect and interpret information; it is up to someone else—the equivalent of the military planning staff—to weigh the alternatives. Adherents of this view fear that once the pollster becomes an advocate for a strategic recommendation the premises of that recommendation may no longer be rigorously reassessed and alternative recommendations may not be given equal research attention.

The contrary view is summarized by Humphrey Taylor: "The value of the pollster to the politician is at least as much the value of his or her judgment as the value of the data. Most political questions are not answered directly by a poll. Political questions have a way of becoming complex judgment calls often amid conflicting information." [31]

As a campaign insider, the pollster often becomes close to the candidate. When the candidate wins, the pollster's influence can reach deep into matters having little to do with public opinion research. This raises the issues of the limits of the pollster's competence and, to the extent the pollster trades on the authority of the profession, the role of the larger research community in affirming or disavowing the pollster's performance.

These dimensions of the pollster-client relationship clearly lie outside any process of peer review within the polling community. The fortunes of pollster and client will rise and fall with the quality of the political judgments advanced and with the interplay of competing centers of political power.

As to the larger issues of the role of the pollster in the governance process *after* the election, the question pertains less to the pollster-client relationship than to the appropriate role of public opinion and opinion polling in our democratic system, the subject of our concluding chapter.

Press Performance and Polling Standards

Efforts within the opinion research profession regarding performance have little impact on how adequately polls are reported by many news organizations. Try as they may to tighten standards within the polling profession, pollsters confront a new set of challenges when attempting to get reporters, editors, and news executives to become more attentive to issues of quality in the conduct, analysis, and coverage of polls by the media, especially at the local level.

The First Amendment and Press Accountability

"In every instance where you face the possible irresponsible use of information by news organizations—polls or any other kind of information—you have to come down on the side of a free press as being more fundamental to our democracy even than a responsible press." [32]

This premise of journalism, as stated succinctly by Katherine Fanning, former editor of the *Christian Science Monitor,* is one few would challenge. But its practical implications are often a source of frustration to pollsters, who see the techniques and credibility they have developed over the years appropriated by news organizations which fiercely defend the right to define their own criteria of professionalism.

Thoughtful minds have asked whether a free press can in fact remain free without some form of self-regulation. In 1942, six years before the pollsters erroneously predicted Thomas Dewey's victory over Harry Truman and seven years before the founding of AAPOR, a privately funded "Commission on Freedom of the Press" met under the chairmanship of Robert Maynard Hutchins, chancellor of the University of Chicago.[33] The commission was convened out of concern that press freedoms were in danger unless journalists demonstrated greater attention to the nation's needs and abandoned questionable practices. Its final report, *A Free and Responsible Press*,[34] rejected any form of government oversight but did call for the creation of an organization to monitor press performance. The idea never took hold.

A successor initiative, the National News Council, did get off the ground in 1972. Its creation was the principal recommendation of a Twentieth Century Fund task force that had concluded that a mechanism was needed to hold news organizations accountable. Funded primarily by private foundations, the news council was to investigate complaints of unfairness and inaccuracy in news reporting. It was to have no enforcement power, only the power of suasion resulting from public reports of its findings in particular cases.[35]

A handful of influential journalists lent their prestige and energies to the work of the council. Among them were Richard Salant, former president of CBS News, and Richard Harwood, former managing editor of the *Washington Post*. The consensus among publishers and news executives, however, was that existing institutional arrangements were sufficient for the press to be self-correcting in instances of inaccurate or biased reporting. Arthur Sulzberger spoke the views of many in a 1973 memorandum to the news and editorial staffs of the *New York Times:*

> Press performance is constantly analyzed, criticized and attacked outright and the press reports these attacks on itself. The press virtually alone among American institutions disseminates criticism of itself. Letters in opposition to a newspaper's opinions or contradicting its stories are printed by virtually every newspaper.... Most newspapers take seriously complaints that they are inaccurate or unfair and they publish corrections.... We will continue to be monitored and judged by those whose criticisms are vital to us—our readers in the case of *The Times* and our clients in the case of the News Service. We must earn their trust every day.[36]

The demise of the National News Council has been attributed to the procedures and premise of its operation. The council was criticized for pomposity in its judgments, for focusing its attention on the performance of the best news organizations to the neglect of overseeing the worst, and for ducking some issues.[37] The larger problem, however, was that the premise of the council was so alien to the profession that the council never could establish its legitimacy.

Professional associations within journalism resist any form of standards setting. However, there is reluctant support for "principles" of responsible journalism. The American Society of Newspaper Editors, for example, has a "Statement of Principles," although many members remain uneasy about it. Some members fear the principles might be used to justify libel actions against news organizations;[38] others strongly resist any form of imposed standard.[39]

The Reporting of Polls and Press Criticism

As a practical consequence of this disposition of the Fourth Estate pollsters have few points of leverage regarding standards in the use and reporting of polls by news organizations. However, two approaches deserve some comment. We will examine the efficacy of media criticism in cases of misleading reports of poll findings, reports of pseudopolls, or inappropriate use of polling techniques. We will then consider the efficacy of steps pollsters are taking to acquaint reporters, editors, and news executives with the nuances of poll reliability and validity.

The efficacy of media criticism. One of the by-products of the 1988 presidential campaign was heightened awareness among news organizations that the *process* of politics is increasingly a part of the news that needs to be reported. As polling is now part of the process of politics, it is hoped that this awareness will make news organizations more sensitive to criticism of their polling operations and of their reporting of polls.

Whatever public posture news reporters, editors, and executives may assume when under fire, most journalists are not so impervious to criticism as appearances may suggest. For example, ABC News executives felt the heat when ABC was reproached in 1988 for reporting results of a poll on the eve of the Republican convention when only a third of the sample had been interviewed and for its handling of the fifty-state poll before the second Bush-Dukakis debate (see Chapter 2).

In the first case, ABC's polling partner, the *Washington Post,* disavowed the premature release.[40] The *Washington Journalism Review* recounted the episode in great detail.[41] In the second case, the *Washington Post* again broke with ABC by describing the results as an Electoral College tally rather than a poll of unprecedented scale. Moreover, the

Post's presentation of the data from the fifty-state poll was far more guarded than that of ABC on "World News Tonight." [42] The divergence between ABC and the *Post* was picked up by other news organizations such as the *Boston Globe*.[43] The *Los Angeles Times*'s reporting of the controversy included critical comments about ABC's handling of the survey by a consultant to NBC's polling operation.[44]

Media criticism is not a calling for the impatient. Although its efficacy should not be underestimated, evidence of its impact is usually slow to appear. With that premise in mind, Ben Bagdikian observes that well-taken criticism can work in two directions inside a news organization. On the one hand, despite their protestations to the contrary those at the top are very sensitive to criticism of specific cases of poor judgment or performance. Those at other levels, on the other hand, are not likely to be so defensive. In addition, Bagdikian notes that "in many instances there have been arguments going on within news organizations over what is right and wrong. Your criticism may add weight to those who are on the side of virtue." [45]

Instituting media criticism: some requirements.   When a news organization conducts its own polls, the gatekeeper overseeing the polling operation is ostensibly in a position to offer internal critiques of poll handling by reporters and editors. News organizations without their own polling operations may have a knowledgeable reporter assigned to poll reporting who might take on the assignment. Otherwise the critical judgment must come from other quarters.

It is here that those outside the news business have difficulty marshaling the clout necessary to bring criteria of professional competence to bear within the media. For the opinion research community to have a realistic opportunity to comment on the conduct and reporting of polls by the print and broadcast media, at least four conditions must obtain.

Credibility.   News organizations take criticism seriously when its source is credible on two counts. First, the critic must be an authority on the subject matter. Second, the critic's terms of reference must be broad enough to encompass a realistic appreciation of what the news business is about. (The second requirement probably accounts for the fact that most media critics are journalists or former journalists.)

Quick response.   News organizations operate in real time. They focus on the issues at hand. Yesterday's news is not on today's agenda. Accordingly, the less time spent in focusing critical attention on poll reporting problems the better. Critical assessments of specific cases can take time to come together, particularly if an institutional review mechanism is involved. While the breadth of the consensus implied in such institutional assessments can lend clout, that clout may dissipate if the attention of the news organization has moved on.

High visibility.   News organizations are in the business of highlighting matters they deem worthy of the attention of their publics. Hence, to the extent criticism of poll reporting can command visibility, news organizations are more likely to take it seriously. With characteristic enthusiasm, former White House press secretary Jody Powell describes the problem: "There is a vast difference between being criticized by *CJR* [the *Columbia Journalism Review*] or by your local ombudsman and being pilloried in the lead story of a network news program. The censure of peers is not without some effect, but it can hardly be compared with being held up to disdain and ridicule before a good portion of the entire nation." [46]

Criticism of the small as well as the large.   The National News Council was faulted for spending a disproportionate amount of its resources on complaints about the performance of large news organizations, to the neglect of smaller organizations where problems of fairness and accuracy are at least as frequent and serious. This lesson should not be forgotten in current endeavors to review the handling of polls by news organizations, especially in light of the proliferation of local media-sponsored polls.

Instituting criticism: some alternatives.   Scrutiny of the use and reporting of polls by news organizations has taken many forms over the years. In addition, new approaches have been suggested. Among the major avenues that merit consideration are the following.

Review by the polling associations.   NCPP and AAPOR have some ability to call attention to seriously flawed polls and misleading news stories about polls. However, given their organizational purposes and structure, their clout is modest.

The objectives of NCPP are to work for maximum disclosure of information about public polls and to elevate standards of media reporting about polls. The organization's pursuit of this immensely important function has borne much fruit. Press reporting of polls is much improved from two decades ago. NCPP has spoken out against "900" call-ins and taken issue with misuses of polling techniques. For example, it challenged the decision of the League of Women Voters Education Fund to use poll standings as the criterion by which John Anderson would be included in the 1980 presidential debates.

Nonetheless, NCPP explicitly declines to evaluate the quality of polls. Its code focuses on disclosure, not performance standards. NCPP will insist that pertinent information about a poll's methodology be disclosed, but it is not likely to take on the role of public watchdog passing judgment on the merits of polls.

AAPOR will review poll quality but only in extreme cases and through a deliberative process. Although its broad membership base permits AAPOR to speak with special authority on behalf of the polling community, the association is not structured for the quick response, high-profile role necessary for effective criticism.

Media criticism external to news organizations.   Press criticism has taken hold as a legitimate aspect of the accountability of news organizations, and the portfolio of the critic runs the gamut of issues and activities. Polling issues come to the fore on occasion, such as the *Washington Journalism Review's* account of the tribulations of ABC News in its 1988 polling operation. But these media critics are not able to give polls and poll reporting sustained attention. They also often lack the knowledge and contacts to stay on top of emerging issues.

Media criticism by news organizations.   News organizations, like pollsters, are reluctant to criticize each other. According to Benjamin Bradlee, "it opens the door." Despite this reluctance, Bradlee indicates that the *Washington Post* "would go out of its way to cover a polling issue if it was a legitimate incident in the profession." [47]

Many might get the assignment to cover such an incident, such as the reporter covering the media. A large news organization with an in-house polling operation might give the assignment to its polling editor or reporter. It is even possible that a news organization would assign an investigative reporter to look into its own inadequacies if the issue were serious enough.[48] And there is always the prospect of an internal ombudsman taking up the matter.

Media criticism by news organizations has two merits: it permits expeditious treatment of issues and brings them to the attention of the public. Its principal drawback is that only the exceptional issue is likely to warrant assignment of a reporter and a subsequent story.

When it comes to monitoring treatment of polls by news organizations, the greatest weakness is that television's coverage of media performance is still in its infancy. Television's attention to its own performance and impact is sporadic at best, especially with regard to serious self-criticism of its own polling.[49]

Incentives. Pollster Peter Hart has long advocated a high-profile award to be given for excellence in polling and reporting of polls by news organizations. He observes that virtually all domains of journalism and broadcasting have an award: Pulitzer, Peabody, Emmy, Tony, Grammy.[50] Others are not so sanguine that positive incentives would be effective. Richard Wirthlin, for one, thinks that pollsters need to be more critical of the way journalists treat polls: "We need to publicize cases in which they are fast and loose in their use of data. I don't think there is much you can do by way of incentives; it has to be almost a sanction, a negative inducement to get them to report responsibly." [51]

An "ad hoc committee on poll reporting." Some might argue that current institutional arrangements suffice to monitor the conduct and reporting of polls by the press. At most, they would suggest the existing tools could be sharpened to play a more assertive role.

In 1988, however, current modes of criticism were found wanting. For example, at the time of the event, it was not widely known that ABC's poll release on the eve of the Republican convention was based on an incomplete sample that omitted some parts of the country. Later, after ABC's release of results from its fifty-state poll prior to the second Bush-Dukakis debate, criticism of the poll's methodology was left primarily to a member of the Dukakis campaign staff. Although individual pollsters compared notes on the deficiencies of the fifty-state poll, little public criticism was voiced by pollsters for attribution or from the polling community in general.

Then, after the debate, the American Political Network conducted its "nonscientific" call-in poll and reported the results. *No* public expression of concern was heard from the opinion research community.

Some new mechanism seems needed to fill the void. One possibility would be to create an "ad hoc committee on poll reporting" consisting of a half-dozen individuals drawn from journalism and opinion research.[52] Its membership could rotate periodically, for example, every three years. Members should not be currently affiliated with organizations that sponsor or conduct public polls. On the journalistic side, candidates for inclusion on the committee would be former managing editors of major newspapers, former directors of network or local television news departments who had demonstrated a concern for quality in polling and poll reporting, and seasoned political editors and reporters. On the polling side, leading academic, commercial, and political opinion researchers would be called upon. In contrast to the National News Council, the committee would not seek the sustained participation of major news or polling organizations. Thus the "ad hoc" nature of the committee.

Such an ad hoc committee would possess a number of important attributes. First, the combined polling and journalistic competence of its members would reinforce its credibility by establishing its authority in the realm of research while exhibiting its sensitivity to real-world constraints of news reporting. Second, the committee would be able to act quickly. Third, given the stature of its members, the committee could generate news coverage in major cases of deficient poll reporting and could serve as a resource for media reporters, media critics, and others interested in an independent assessment of the quality of poll reporting.

The hurdles in instituting such a review mechanism would be financial and legal. Independent funding for the committee would be required. However, nothing so elaborate as the National News Council is envisioned.

The vulnerability of the committee or its members to legal action would have to be explored with care. However, the threat of libel suits might not be an insurmountable problem, as news organizations themselves would be the focus of the committee's attention. For a libel action to hold up, the plaintiff would have to prove that the ad hoc committee knowingly made an untrue statement about a newspaper or broadcast station or showed insufficient regard for whether its assertions were true.[53]

Of Evidence and Inference: An Understanding of Polling[54]

A journalist confronted with a hot tip will seek out corroborating evidence to test the limits of the story that may be tomorrow's news. Similarly, with a poll, a journalist confronted with a percentage needs to look further within the poll for information to test the limits of the conclusions that can be drawn from the finding. David Broder has observed that the more a reporter knows, the more a reporter can find out.[55] So, too, in coverage of polls, the more the reporter knows about the nuts and bolts of polling, the greater the quantity and quality of insights that can be extracted from a set of poll numbers.

Pollsters are specific about the sort of information that should be disclosed to the public upon the release of a poll: interview dates, sample size, question wording, and the like. For all their diligence on this score, however, the important point pollsters have yet to make clear to many journalists is *why* the information being disclosed is important. Pollsters may be providing answers to questions about a poll's methodology without spelling out for reporters the questions that are being answered.[56] For example, interviewing dates are important because they answer the following question: "Has anything happened between interviewing for the poll and its release that should be taken into account in interpreting the poll's results?" Sample size and sampling error are key to answering the question: "Does the difference between two polls indicate a real change in public opinion or did it occur by chance?"

But the need for knowledge about polling runs deeper. Technology and the modularization of polling have brought public opinion polling within reach of virtually any news organization, no matter how small or untutored in research methodology. Almost without exception a local newspaper or television station can buy a sample, contract for interviewing, and report results, whether or not the staff is competent to direct and analyze the poll. "Every little newspaper in the world can do a 300-sample poll; that's where the problem is," says Jeffrey Gralnick, an executive producer at ABC News. Summarizing his review of state polls during the 1986 election cycle, the Associated Press' Evans Witt notes that "one of the problems with many state polls is that they are done on the cheap" and that "quick, cheap polls are the equivalent of sloppy reporting and careless writing—just as out of place in a good news operation." [57]

Local television stations have four or five times as much air time to fill as the major networks when it comes to news reporting. Reporting of "exclusive" polls has become one of the ways these news operations compete with each other. In the words of a former news executive of Boston's WCVB-TV: "Nothing in our business can be evaluated unless you include competitive considerations. . . . Had we not done polling . . . our competition would have made [our audience] aware of it through promotion and advertising that would have emphasized the fact that they were doing more." [58]

National pollsters continue to express frustration at the way their releases of polls are edited and rewritten by local news outlets. The Gallup Organization and the *Los Angeles Times* have reported finding news stories of their polls in almost unrecognizable form. Important nuances are slighted or missed, leads are overwritten, and important aspects of the initial release are omitted.

For all of these reasons, it is difficult to underestimate the importance of education in the techniques and theory of opinion research for journalists at all levels. New reporters come along every year; old hands can benefit from briefings on emerging techniques and the latest approaches to opinion measurement.

Many modes of instruction have had great success. These include quantitative methods courses in the curricula of journalism schools; regularly scheduled programs at academic centers (such as the University of Michigan's Institute for Social Research and the Roper Center in conjunction with Williams College); ad hoc seminars by pollsters themselves (such as those given in the mid-1960s by George Gallup and in the mid-1970s by Peter Hart); special sessions such as those conducted by the Bureau of the Census and the American Newspaper Publishers Association on the decennial census; and NCPP seminars at the National Press Club in Washington, D.C.

The Stakes: Public Confidence

Incentives for self-regulation in opinion research come less from the threat of intervention by government or some other authority than from the unique dependence of polling on the public's willingness to participate in surveys.

The occasional call is heard for a campaign of public resistance to pollsters; but these entreaties have had little effect.[59] Nonetheless, refusal to consent to an interview persists as a problem for opinion researchers. In fact, refusal rates have gone up slightly in recent years.[60]

But hostility toward surveys is not what accounts for public refusal to participate in a poll. (Inconvenience is the reason given most frequently by those declining.) What worries pollsters most is the reported increase in the use of surveys as ploys in merchandising products and services.[61] Fortunately, this problem can be solved. The research community, under the leadership of the Council of American Survey Research Organizations (CASRO), is fighting back through chambers of commerce, state attorneys general, and the United States Postal Service.[62]

The overwhelming majority of those who agree to be interviewed look back favorably on the experience. About a third of the American people participate in a survey each year and most (more than three-fourths of those interviewed) report that the experience was pleasant.[63]

The public's perception of the polls was explored by the Roper

Organization in 1985 and the Gallup Organization in 1988. Pertinent data from their studies appear in Appendix A, Table A-6. Two over-arching conclusions emerge from this research:

First, the American people tend to have confidence in public opin-ion polls.

- Approximately three in five Americans think the polls are generally accurate
- Only one in six doubts the honesty of pollsters and only one in seven questions whether people tell the truth when interviewed
- Three in four think that opinion polls work for the best interests of the public

Second, however, the public is not without some ambivalence about polling and the electoral process. The American people came away from the 1988 presidential campaign troubled that the nominating process did not put forward good candidates; the polls were implicated as being part of the problem.

- About four in ten registered voters were uneasy about the influence media consultants and pollsters had on the course of the campaign
- The view of almost half of registered voters interviewed was that the reporting of candidate standing in the polls helps neither press cover-age nor the country

Such public ambivalence about the polls may be understandable but it is worrisome, especially at a time of growing public concern about the quality of our politics. It underscores the need for public accountability of those who presume to take the public pulse. It also forces us to look at the question of what larger public purpose the polls serve. It is this question that we take up next.

Notes

1. Benjamin Bradlee, interview with the author, Washington, D.C., July 26, 1989.
2. A third association, the Council of American Survey Research Organiza-tions (CASRO), also has standards of disclosure for the public release of

surveys. These standards are less pertinent for our purposes because most of CASRO's member firms conduct proprietary commercial research studies that do not enter the public domain.

3. Sixty-four percent of departments of journalism surveyed in 1974 had at least one course in quantitative social science. See Brenda Dervin and Michael Banister, " 'Theory' Has Many Definitions in Journalism Education," *Journalism Educator* 31 (1976): 10-15. Fully 77 percent of master's degree programs in journalism in a 1978 survey required a research methods course. Michael Ryan, "Journalism Education at the Master's Level," *Journalism Monographs* 66 (1980): 1-42. Both studies are cited in David H. Weaver and Maxwell E. McCombs, "Journalism and Social Science: A New Relationship," *Public Opinion Quarterly* 44 (1980): 479, 482.

4. Some serious observers of the political scene remain troubled that as polls become ever more central to political coverage they are assessed ever more casually by the print and broadcast media. For example, Germond and Witcover write of 1988: "This poll mania has been made all the more threatening by an accompanying suspension of standards in judging the quality of polls and what they really measure." Jack W. Germond and Jules Witcover, *Whose Broad Stripes and White Stars: The Trivial Pursuit of the Presidency 1988* (New York: Warner Books, 1989), 56.

5. The question asked: "As far as you can tell, is the way the media report polls helping the public distinguish between polls that follow established procedures for obtaining valid measures of public opinion and polls that fall short of these standards?" Eight percent of pollsters responding replied in the affirmative, 86 percent in the negative, and 6 percent gave a qualified response. Permission to use these unpublished data is greatly appreciated. Source: Gladys Engel Lang and Kurt Lang, "Survey of Pollsters," August 1990. Photocopy.

6. Witt notes: "Many state polls release little methodological information beyond the basics—marginal results, sample size, and interview dates. Exact question wording is often hard to obtain and descriptions of sampling methodology almost nonexistent." Evans Witt, "Poll Wars: State Polls in the 1986 Election," *Public Opinion* 9 (January/February 1987): 43. This is an important area for future research. Studies such as the one done by NCPP and the Medill School of Journalism are not logistically complicated. In the NCPP/Medill study, data were collected by retaining the services of a highly regarded press clipping service. The coding scheme employed could easily have been more elaborate. It is far more complicated to monitor local television, but still feasible.

7. Philip Meyer, "Learning to Live with the Numbers," *Columbia Journalism Review* (January/February 1977): 34-35.

8. Personal recollections of the author, who was president of the National Council on Public Polls at the time of the code revision.

9. For a review of AAPOR's recent deliberations, see Deborah Hensler, "New Times, New Technologies . . . New Standards?" *AAPOR News* 10 (Winter 1983): 3; and Deborah Hensler, "Proposed Ethics Code Revisions Near Vote," *AAPOR News* 13 (Fall 1985): 4-7. A more general review can be found in Sidney Hollander, "Survey Standards," *The History of AAPOR,* ed. Paul B. Sheatsley (unpublished).

10. Report of the AAPOR Standards Committee, April 1955, summarized in Hollander, "Survey Standards," 8.

11. Hollander, "Survey Standards," 8-22.

12. Warren J. Mitofsky, "Methods and Standards: A Challenge for Change" (Presidential address to the American Association for Public Opinion Research, St. Petersburg, Fla., May 20, 1989).

13. For a discussion of this presumption see Alan Stone, *Regulation and Its Alternatives* (Washington, D.C.: CQ Press, 1982), chap. 2, esp. 48-53.

14. Registration is a less stringent form of regulation. Its purpose is to establish a means of tracking down those whose goods or services are fraudulent or potentially injurious to life and limb. Thus it makes sense to require dealers in firearms to register with a civil authority, as it may be necessary at some point to trace a particular weapon to its source. However, registration of pollsters would be inappropriate: one of the last problems pollsters face is a low profile. Moreover, registration has nothing to do with standards of competence.

15. The courts generally avoid being constrained by codes of professional ethics and competence. They frequently overturn findings of professional associations based on their codes. For a discussion of this point, see Ronald Farrar, "News Councils and Libel Actions," *Journalism Quarterly* 63 (Autumn 1986): 509-516.

16. Lucien N. Nedzi, "Public Opinion Polls: Will Legislation Help?" *Public Opinion Quarterly* 35 (1971): 336-341.

17. From the opinion of Judge William A. Norris of the 9th Circuit Court in *Daily Herald Company v. Munro* (1985).

18. From the opinion of Judge Charles Lovell in response to NBC's request that a preliminary injunction be granted to stop interference with its interviewing of voters outside voting places.

19. This discussion draws on the excellent summary of the pros and cons of certification presented in Alan D. Wolfson, Michael J. Trebilock, and Carolyn J. Tuohy, "Regulating the Professions: A Theoretical Framework," in *Occupational Licensure and Regulation,* ed. Simon Rottenberg (Washington, D.C.: American Enterprise Institute for Public Policy Research, 1980), 203-206.

20. In fact, in its code, AAPOR explicitly admonishes that members "shall not cite our membership in the Association as evidence of professional competence, since the Association does not so certify any persons or organizations."

21. In the case of NCPP, the procedures even provide for final disposition of a contentious review through arbitration, a provision with which some members were uncomfortable initially but later concurred in order to preserve the code's ability to follow a difficult issue to conclusion.

22. Hollander, "Survey Standards," 19-20.

23. Ibid., 24.

24. A flavor of the impatience with the polls is seen in the comments of two critics. *Globe* columnist Mike Barnicle wrote that people did "the absolutely proper and predictable thing when asked by pollsters for their thoughts on the election: they lied." (*Boston Globe,* September 22, 1990) Christopher Lydon, co-anchor of the WGBH-TV evening news program, dismissed the possibility of any science in polling. "It's not science," he told viewers. "It's just notes on a page. It takes imagination to make music out of it." ("Ten O'Clock News," September 19, 1990) Silber's remarks were made on "This Week with David Brinkley," ABC News, September 23, 1990.

25. The editor of *Public Opinion Quarterly* is mindful of the importance of due process in these reviews because of the possible impact of the reviews on the individuals or organizations involved. The draft review is shared with the individuals responsible for conducting the poll and often revised in light of their response. Further review within the editorial staff of *POQ* then takes place. For a discussion of the rationale and process of these reviews, see "Note from the Editor: Poll Reviews," *Public Opinion Quarterly* 52 (Fall 1988): 277.

26. Warren Mitofsky, interview with the author, New York, June 29, 1989.

27. Nelson W. Polsby, *Consequences of Party Reform* (New York: Oxford University Press, 1983), 75.

28. In November 1983 Ralph Murphine urged the AAPC board of directors to seize the initiative. Since then he has chaired AAPC's Ethics Study Group. The author gratefully acknowledges the background information he has provided regarding the status of AAPC's consideration of issues of professional ethics and performance standards.

29. Walter De Vries, "American Campaign Consulting: Trends and Concerns," *PS: Political Science and Politics* 22 (March 1989): 21-25.

30. Quoted in Janet Bodner, "How Political Polls Can Mislead You," *Changing Times,* September 1980, 58.

31. Humphrey Taylor, interview with the author, New York, July 21, 1989.

32. Katherine Fanning, telephone interview with the author, April 12, 1990.

33. The commission consisted of Arthur Schlesinger, Sr., Charles Merriam, Beardsly Ruml, and Archibald MacLeish. It was funded by Henry Luce of *Time* magazine and the *Encyclopedia Britannica*. For an account of this period of ferment and the implications for contemporary journalism, see Norman F. Isaacs, *Untended Gates: The Mismanaged Press* (New York: Columbia University Press, 1986).

34. Commission on Freedom of the Press, *A Free and Responsible Press* (Chicago: University of Chicago Press, 1947).

35. For an account of the National News Council, see Patrick Brogan, *Spiked: The Short Life and Death of the National News Council* (New York: Priority Press Publications, Twentieth Century Fund, 1985).

36. Memorandum dated January 15, 1973, quoted in ibid., 120.

37. Ibid., 34, 57-58, 91.

38. Farrar reports that significant voices within ASNE have argued for the withdrawal of the Statement of Principles for this reason. Ronald Farrar, "News Councils and Libel Actions," 516.

39. During her presidency of ASNE, Katherine Fanning wanted to add a principle to the statement. She recalls: "I just didn't realize what a tremendous hornet's nest I had stirred up. There came a vote where the Statement of Principles almost got knocked off altogether." Telephone interview with the author, April 12, 1990.

40. Richard Morin, "Trying to Gauge the Pulse of Public Opinion: Polls Reflect Mood Shifts, Survey Quality," *Washington Post,* August 18, 1988, A25.

41. Barbara Matusow, "Are the Polls Out of Control?" *Washington Journalism Review* (October 1988): 18.

42. Paul Taylor and Richard Morin, "Bush Shows Strength in Electoral College," *Washington Post,* October 13, 1988, A1.

43. Chris Black, "ABC News, Washington Post Joined in Poll but Parted in Conclusions," *Boston Globe,* October 14, 1988.

44. Thomas B. Rosensteil, "Questions About Accuracy Arise As Dukakis Denounces Media Polls," *Los Angeles Times,* October 29, 1988.

45. Ben H. Bagdikian, interview with the author, Berkeley, Calif., February 9, 1990.

46. Jody Powell, *The Other Side of the Story* (New York: William Morrow, 1984), 291-292.

47. Benjamin C. Bradlee, interview with the author, Washington, D.C., July 26, 1989.

48. A model of this kind of investigative reporting is the four-part series by David Shaw, staff reporter for the *Los Angeles Times,* that was highly critical of the way the *Times* had covered the story of molestation of preschool children in the "McMartin case." The series ran in the *Times*

January 19-22, 1990.

49. Evidence on this point was the treatment by ABC's "Nightline" of the controversy surrounding the fifty-state poll broadcast on ABC's "World News Tonight" earlier on the evening of October 12, 1988. Rather than treat the controversy on the merits of the poll by inviting an independent polling expert to comment, "Nightline" treated it as a political matter by inviting criticism of the poll from the beleaguered Dukakis campaign.

50. Peter D. Hart, interview with the author, Washington, D.C., July 25, 1989.

51. Richard Wirthlin, interview with the author, McLean, Va., July 28, 1989.

52. The author is grateful to Ben Bagdikian for his thoughtful critique of this idea.

53. Bagdikian is quite sanguine that such an ad hoc committee would not be held hostage to threatened libel actions: "If the committee did an analysis of a poll, based on what was published, and had made a request for more information (such as the details of sampling) from the polling organization which was denied, the committee would have met the requirement for showing absence of malice. It would have made an honest, good faith effort." Interview with the author, Berkeley, Calif., February 9, 1990.

54. We take the liberty of borrowing Daniel Lerner's title, *Evidence and Inference* (Glencoe, Ill.: Free Press, 1959).

55. David Broder, *Behind the Front Page: A Candid Look at How the News Is Made* (New York: Simon and Schuster, 1987), 321.

56. This point was made by Warren Mitofsky, interview with the author, New York, June 29, 1989.

57. Jeffrey Gralnick, interview with the author, New York, July 20, 1989. Evans Witt, "Poll Wars," 43.

58. Phil Balboni, quoted in Martin Schram, *The Great American Video Game: Presidential Politics in the Television Age* (New York: William Morrow, 1987), 185.

59. Chicago columnist Mike Royko has urged people to lie if approached for an interview in an exit poll. Fred Wickham has founded a nonprofit organization, "Poll Scramblers," whose purpose is to undermine polling by encouraging respondents to lie, mumble, and otherwise garble information. See Bernard Weinraub, "Confusing the Polls and Being Proud of It," *New York Times,* October 31, 1988, B5.

60. A study found that 34 percent of a national cross section interviewed in 1988 indicated they had refused to participate in a survey, a ten percentage point increase from just two years earlier. Walker Research, Inc., *Industry Image Study* 8th ed. (1988): 4. See also Charlotte G. Steeth, "Trends in Nonresponse Rates, 1952-1979," *Public Opinion Quarterly* 45 (1981): 32-49.

61. Of those in the Walker sample who had refused to be interviewed in a survey earlier in 1988, 57 percent cited inconvenience as the reason for not participating, 18 percent feared a sales pitch of some sort, and 16 percent were uninterested in the subject. Walker Research, *Industry Image Study*, 4. Twenty-two percent in the Walker survey reported having been asked to participate in a survey only to find that it was a disguised sales pitch (p. 9). This was a dramatic jump from the 13 to 17 percent ranges that obtained for the previous eight years.

62. For an account of a successful initiative to combat the use of polls to disguise sales pitches, see Diane K. Bowers, "Saga of a Sugger—Part I," *Marketing Research* 2 (March 1990): 68-72.

63. The most recent biennial study of the image of the survey research industry (that is, public opinion and market research) found 36 percent of a national sample reporting they had been interviewed in the last year and 73 percent who had been interviewed at some point in their life. Since 1980 the Walker studies have found that no less than three-fourths of respondents who had participated in a survey earlier in the year recalled the interview favorably and no more than 12 percent recalled the experience as unpleasant. Walker Research, *Industry Image Study*, 3, 5. These findings are corroborated by the Roper Organization in a March 1985 survey in which 51 percent of respondents reported that the experience of being interviewed was "enjoyable and satisfactory." Only 5 percent said it was "annoying and unsatisfactory," and 42 percent felt it fell somewhere in between. *Roper Reports:* 85-4, 53.

chapter five

Polls and Democracy: Serving the Public Purpose

I will give *you* three folders of telegrams; let's not
manipulate public opinion.

*Mikhail Gorbachev's response in the
Congress of People's Deputies when
Andrei Sakharov presented him with a
stack of telegrams urging an end to the
Communist party's monopoly on power
December 12, 1989*

Every field of human endeavor goes through stages in its evolution.
With respect to opinion research, four stages are discernible.

First came the phase of *possibilities,* a period of ingenuous enthusiasm over the potential contributions of the fledgling field of opinion
research. The 1930s and 1940s were years of burgeoning confidence
among commercial and academic opinion researchers that the opinion
poll could uniquely help keep political leadership responsive to the
people.

Then came the phase of *reliability,* a period of consolidation and
preoccupation with technique. Roughly from the late 1940s to the mid-
1970s, the focus was on quantitative methods and issues of measurement.
Reflecting trends in the larger academic social science community, the
field of opinion research concentrated on matters of data reliability and
increasingly complex forms of data analysis. This was a period in which
the bona fides of polling as a science were asserted with growing
confidence.

A third phase, which has characterized much work in contemporary opinion research, might be described as a quest for *validity*. Researchers have been seeking assurance that the conclusions they draw are appropriate given the measures employed. Intense interest in "nonsampling" error has led to systematic research on the effects of the wording and order of questions in a poll. There is also keen interest in the circumstances of the interviewing process as they may affect the data that result. Such circumstances include the sex and race of interviewers, the length of interviews, and the conditions under which interviews are terminated by respondents.

A fourth phase, marked by concern over *legitimacy*, has now emerged as increasing attention is paid to the effect of the polls and to their place in the political process. From this perspective, polling is looked to as an institution in its own right. The question being asked is, "Do public opinion polls serve the public purpose?"

It is to issues of legitimacy that we turn in this chapter.[1] We begin by exploring whether important dimensions of public opinion may be obscured by limitations inherent in the habits of thought of the researcher. That is, can we have confidence in the basic soundness of opinion research as a tool for rendering faithfully such complex and dynamic phenomena as public perceptions of issues, events, individuals, and institutions?

Then we take up the matter of the intrinsic value to the public and the political process of reports about the ebb and flow of these public perceptions. We look at what effects, both direct and indirect, reports of polls may have on public opinion itself. We consider the role polls play in setting the political agenda, their influence on political leadership, and how they bear on the processes by which political interests compete. We conclude with an assessment of how well polling serves the public interest.

Do Polls Reflect Public Opinion?

In the preceding chapters it has been argued that, given control over the quality of data collection and appropriate precision in generalizing from data, the public opinion poll can be an exceedingly sensitive measurement instrument. Nonetheless, even assiduous attention to detail at all stages in the conduct of a poll cannot dispel the charge that the polling technique is inherently flawed and unable to represent public opinion faithfully. The elements of this charge are:

- polling may slight the diversity of the public;
- polling may merely play back opinions on issues not as they exist among the public but in the terms implicit in the pollster's questions; and
- polling may imply erroneously that the public opinion reported is considered opinion.

Dealing with Diversity

Most reports of poll findings take the form of percentages that represent proportions of a sample responding in various ways. News media rely on such percentages as the best way to convey quickly and clearly information that is often quite complex. Private pollsters look to the percentage as a way of getting to "the bottom line" of poll findings for clients.

Although the percentage summarizes important information about the overall sample, it tells little about the diversity in points of view that underlies the reported division of opinion. Imagine, for example, a poll that reported that 50 percent of the American people supported a cut in the capital gains tax. The 50 percent could result from equal levels of support for the tax cut among both Democrats and Republicans or it could result from opposition by the Democrats that was offset by support from the Republicans.

Tabulations of differences among subgroups in the sample (or "demographic breakdowns") appearing in some news accounts of polls are helpful. However, they are too seldom included in poll reports on television and remain underutilized in newspaper and wire service stories. Moreover, the sample sizes on which some media-sponsored polls are based are not large enough to permit statistically reliable comparisons of the views of subgroups in the population. In the case of tracking polls, demographic breakdowns are virtually impossible because of the small sample sizes.

As informative as they may be, demographic breakdowns can also mask diversity by conveying the impression that subgroups in the sample are homogeneous. A particular problem obtains with regard to racial and ethnic minorities, whose representation in national surveys does not permit examination of differences by characteristics other than race or ethnic origin unless the minority has been specifically oversampled. Consequently, attributes of the majority population such as age, education, and income are reported while those of the minority populations are not.[2]

To illustrate what can be gained when heterogeneity within a minority population can be explored, we turn to a survey conducted by the Gallup Organization for Times Mirror in May 1987. The survey included an oversample of blacks and thus permitted analysis of differences among blacks on attributes such as age and education. One question in the survey asked respondents to assess the record of the Reagan administration in a number of areas. Respondents were asked whether the administration had made progress, tried but failed, had not dealt with the problem, or actually had created problems the next president would have to face.

On the matter of race relations the plurality view of both whites and blacks was that Reagan had not dealt with the problem. But whites were more likely than blacks to think progress had been made and blacks more likely than whites to think problems had been created for the next president.

Without taking the analysis to a deeper level, important differences *among* whites and *among* blacks would be missed. Within the white subsample, for example, older respondents were less likely than others to think Reagan had neglected the matter of race relations and more likely than others to feel progress had been made. But within the black subsample, older and middle-aged blacks were more likely than younger blacks to feel Reagan had created problems for his successor. It also turned out that the better one's education, the greater the chance one would feel Reagan had ignored the problem, if you were white, but to feel Reagan had made the situation worse, if you were black. (Data for this analysis appear in Appendix A, Table A-7.)

Aside from differences among demographic groups within a sample, another element of diversity can be lost when public opinion is reported only in terms of summary percentages: the intensity with which opinions are held.

We have already seen how costly it can be to ignore differing degrees of intensity in the measurement of opinion. Many political polls fail to pick up the unexpected strength or weakness of a candidate because intensity of support is not measured. The point is made with equal clarity on issues like abortion or gun control, in which simple measures of the division of opinion tell us little about the potency of the issue. On the other hand, overestimating the intensity with which opinions are held can cause political embarrassment, as President Bush learned in 1990 when pushing for an amendment to the Constitution to outlaw burning the American flag. While support for such a prohibition among the American people was broad, it was not deep. Few felt strongly enough about the matter to provide the political base of support the president needed to prevail.

The consequences of misgauging the amount of energy behind an expressed opinion can be real enough for both politicians and news organizations to provide ample incentives to pollsters to include measures of intensity in their surveys.

Terms of Reference: Pollster versus the Public

The opinion analyst's challenge is to characterize as accurately as possible the full range of the public's perceptions. This necessarily involves judgments about the dimensions of opinion to be explored in a poll and the best ways to explore them. In this respect, there is always a danger that poll findings will be more artifacts of the pollster's terms of reference than valid indications of the public's thinking. Poll questions can be self-fulfilling in the sense that respondents are asked to answer a question whether or not it reflects their own approach to the issue at hand.

The most common vulnerability of polls in this regard is that the public does not follow politics and current affairs as closely as do politicians and journalists. Karlyn Keene of the American Enterprise Institute worries that many polls are driven by a "Washington agenda" that reflects the "sophistication and cynicism of political reporters." [3]

Those immersed in the give-and-take of politics are often animated by issues on which the public has only begun to focus. Journalistic preoccupation with candidate standing months in advance of the presidential primaries is one example of this phenomenon. Another example was the polling conducted on President Reagan's nomination of Robert Bork to the U.S. Supreme Court when Bork was virtually unknown to the American people.

A more subtle bias in the pollster's terms of reference can result from a preoccupation with the issues foremost in the mind of the public at large. One consequence of this concentration can be the inadvertent slighting of the concerns of minorities in the population. Robert Hill illustrates the point:

Polls and surveys have revealed consistently that the goals of equal employment opportunities and voting rights are more important to blacks than are the goals of integrated housing or schools. Yet, because the latter are of utmost importance to whites, the polls have concentrated much more attention on issues of integrated housing and education than on equal jobs or voting rights. [4]

Critics also contend that the opinion research technique itself is artificial in the sense that the polls measure privately expressed views, which may not have been tempered by the respondent's consideration of the consequences of holding the opinion. In making this point, Bill Kovach, curator of the Nieman Foundation at Harvard University, is troubled that what is reported by news organizations as "public opinion" may often lack the critical dimension of a "public context," by which Kovach means the circumstances "within which personal opinion must contest with public responsibility." [5] In his view, public opinion reported in polls may be a commodity quite different from public opinion forged from exchanges of views with others. The latter process yields opinions that are not merely privately held but also publicly tested.

Kovach's concern is legitimate. However, nothing inherent in polling methodology precludes tapping the public context of privately held opinion. Polls are amply able to acquaint respondents with the consequences of holding an opinion. A superb illustration is a survey conducted by Lloyd Free and Charles Roll in 1971 for Nelson Rockefeller, then governor of New York. Rockefeller had proposed a bond to finance improvements in the state's mass transportation system. Early in the questionnaire, Free and Roll posed a general question about the transportation bond. They found 57 percent of New Yorkers approving the idea, 32 percent opposed, and 11 percent with no opinion. Respondents were then taken through a simulated public debate by being asked to assess the relative strength of arguments for and against the bond issue. When the approval/disapproval question was then repeated, support for the bond had dropped by nine percentage points and opposition had risen by eight points. The Free-Roll approach had come close to anticipating the dynamics of public debate because the opinions it tapped had been informed by the most persuasive arguments for the contrary point of view. The bond issue was defeated by the voters not long after.[6]

Although polling can rise to Kovach's challenge, it often does not. Thus his concern remains an important admonition to pollsters. It underscores the importance of posing trade-offs in public opinion poll questions and reminding respondents of the possible costs to them if the views they espouse were to prevail. It also returns us to a major theme: the necessity of asking enough questions to bracket the dimensions of public thinking about an issue, and particularly to determine how much the public may know about it.

Informed Opinion: More or Less?

A founding premise of public opinion research articulated in the 1930s by George Gallup and Archibald Crossley was that the new technique would serve as a counterbalance to entrenched interests. By bringing into public view the thinking of the people on issues large and small, it was argued, those in positions of power would have to listen. The representatives would be put in touch with the people. (See "Some Founding Premises" in Chapter 1.)

The contrary view, presented most influentially by Walter Lippmann, was that there was no way the general public could—or should—be looked to for definitive judgments on issues of the day. He argued that it was unrealistic to expect to find "public opinion" on every issue; people are simply too busy with the demands of their own lives to have sufficient time or capacity to grasp the dimensions or implications of alternative public policies.[7]

Opinion researchers have grappled with this challenge for three generations. They have been reluctant to accept Lippmann's contention that the ideal of the involved citizen, however desirable, was unworkable. Several lines of reasoning have been advanced. One thesis differentiated the public's inability to reckon with specific means of government from its competence in appraising the basic ends of government.[8] A second challenged the adequacy of Lippmann's critique for an era in which television is bringing distant corners of the globe into American homes, enriching the mix of impressions by which an increasingly competent public can make informed judgments.[9] A third response, as expressed in the "two-step flow" conception of political communication, has been that most of the public is comfortable delegating to the better informed the task of staying on top of politics and public issues and will look to them for guidance.[10]

Three decades ago, E. E. Schattschneider chided the opinion research community for worrying about the wrong problem. He complained that pollsters, still attached to the democratic ideal of government "by the people," were spending more time defending the competence of the public than they were using the tools of their trade to identify the dimensions of that competence. Schattschneider called for help from the pollsters in formulating an "operating democratic theory." His charge to opinion researchers is worth noting in some length:

> It is hard to see how anyone can formulate a satisfactory theory of public opinion without meeting this problem [devising an operating democratic theory] head on. What is the function of the public in a modern democracy? What does the public have to know? The failure to understand how the public intervenes in the political process, what the public can be expected to do, what it cannot do, how questions get referred to the public has led to quantities of remarkably pointless speculation. [11]

A useful starting point in updating our conception of "the public" is W. Russell Neuman's characterization of the American population as three publics, each of which possesses a surprising degree of homogeneity in its attitude toward governance and politics. The vast majority of the population—Neuman estimates about 75 percent—"are marginally attentive to politics and mildly cynical about the behavior of politicians, but they accept the duty to vote, and they do so with fair regularity." An "unabashedly apolitical" stratum of about 20 percent shuns the normative virtue of staying politically informed and are consistent nonvoters. The remaining 5 percent constitute the activists who do much of the public's political business.[12]

This conception is important, for it removes us from mechanistic notions about the interaction of an undifferentiated public and its elected representatives. It also reflects an understanding that people in the "marginally attentive" stratum can be mobilized given the right confluence of issues, leadership, and events. Finally, it captures the iterative nature of political discourse as a give-and-take between activists and political leaders that hones the edge of political debate.

However clear we may be regarding our concept of the public, the thorny problem persists for pollsters of when and how to differentiate the more informed from the less informed opinion. Thoughtful critics of the polls are concerned that all poll respondents receive equal weight regardless of how informed they may be about the issue being explored. Would it not be a more faithful rendition of the state of public opinion, they ask, to provide some indication of respondents' familiarity with the issue?

Elmo Roper was alert to this issue when he warned in 1942: "The emphasis in public opinion research has been largely misplaced. I believe its first duty is to explore the areas of public ignorance." [13] From the pollster's standpoint, the matter of gauging the level of public information when polling on issues is far more complex than it may first appear. Does the pollster need to plumb the depths of public understanding on every issue on which polls are conducted? Clearly not. Respondents do not need a grounding in macroeconomics to have valid opinions on whether the cost of living seems to be going up or down. At the same time, however, it is reasonable to expect pollsters to assess public knowledge on issues about which the public has little reason to be deeply informed.

When they attempt to identify the "informed" opinion, pollsters risk imposing their own judgments of what information may be important on an issue. Matters of "fact" used to assess respondents' knowledge about an issue may be criticized by advocates on various sides of the issue as being slanted toward a pro or con position. [14] Stipulating a threshold between "informed" and "uninformed" opinion also imposes a burden of judgment on pollsters with which many are not comfortable.

The most common means of dealing with a lack of information on the part of the general public is to include an explanation of pertinent background in a preamble to poll questions. However, pollsters again open themselves to complaints by issue advocates that the set-up material provided may be loaded in one way or another. [15] Moreover, by providing background information to respondents, some claim pollsters are altering the very property they are trying to measure. Carried to its logical conclusion, this line of argument holds that a question or group of questions in a poll has no prospect of ever assessing the true state of public opinion. [16]

As a practical matter, when polling on issues, pollsters increasingly use the procedure of asking respondents whether they "have read or heard about" the issue or "thought enough about it to have an opinion." The issue question is asked only if the respondent answers a variant of this screening question in the affirmative. As we observed in Chapter 3, the answers of as much as a quarter of the sample can be affected by using this approach in the drafting of poll questions.

We have already touched on another aspect of "informed" opinion: the degree to which the respondent is aware of the possible consequences of taking a stand on an issue. Most important policy questions embody trade-offs. Whether respondents are already aware of such trade-offs or learn about them in the preamble to questions, the respondent's attention to the larger implications of holding an opinion can be an important element in the degree to which that opinion holds up over time.[17]

A final word of caution is in order. While being attentive to the need to differentiate among levels of informed opinion, pollsters and poll consumers must not fail to appreciate the "understanding without recall" quality in the public's way of sizing up issues and public figures. The marginally attentive public may do poorly when quizzed about the particulars of a policy issue. However, it is often shrewd in the opinions it renders.

The competence of what might have been dismissed as uninformed opinion was on display in 1973 as the American people came to terms with the dimensions of the White House cover-up of its complicity in the break-in at the Watergate headquarters of the Democratic National Committee. As the evidence continued to mount that the president might have been involved, the issue was framed in the political community (most notably in Congress) as one of whether Richard Nixon was guilty of impeachable offenses.

For the general public, however, the concept of impeachment was so little understood that early poll questions invoking the term picked up little support for it. According to a Roper poll in November 1973, 48 percent of respondents lacked a basic understanding of what the term "impeachment" involved.

But the finding that nearly one-half of the public might be described as uninformed about the meaning of impeachment in no way diminished the public's ability to render a judgment on the process the word described. Striking substantiation of this point is the response of a national sample to sequential questions posed by the author in a survey in October 1973. The first question asked simply: "Do you think President Nixon should be impeached or not?" Twenty-five percent said "yes," 56 percent said "no," and the remaining 19 percent had no opinion. The next question asked about the concept of impeachment without using the word: "Do you think the entire Congress should begin to look into the innocence or guilt of President Nixon in the Watergate matter or not?" Sixty-three percent favored an initiative by Congress, only 30 percent were opposed, and 7 percent were not sure.

The disparity between a 25-56 split for impeachment on the first question and a 63-30 split for it on the second question is explained by the fact that 49 percent of those who were opposed to having Nixon impeached were in favor of the process that impeachment involves.[18]

Thus, while distinguishing more informed opinion from less informed opinion should be on the agenda of opinion research, pollsters and politicians dismiss "uninformed" opinion only at their peril.

The Challenge

A fundamental contention of this book is that there is nothing intrinsic to the theory or methodology of public opinion research that limits its ability to deal with the challenges we have been discussing.

Diversity can be portrayed in many ways: by using demographic breakdowns to explore differences between subgroups; by gauging the intensity with which opinions are held; and by analyzing the interplay of dimensions at work in public opinion.

The possibility that pollsters' frames of reference impose a self-fulfilling dynamic on the process of measuring public opinion would be more worrisome were it not for the proliferation of polling organizations and the accompanying pluralism in approaches to gauging opinion. The sheer volume of such polls increases the likelihood that disparate approaches to probing public thinking will be employed and that simple divisions of opinion will be complemented by other measures that put the direction of opinion in context.[19]

In addition, academic survey research centers active in opinion research tend to be removed from the rush of the daily news cycle and the terms of reference that rush engenders. As a result, more often than not such centers take a longer view of social and political issues and design questionnaires for more elaborate analyses than those conducted by most news-oriented polling operations.

Survey activities have expanded rapidly over the last two decades within the academic community, just as they have outside it. One tally in mid-1989 counted sixty-six university-based survey research centers in the United States.[20] The work of major centers such as the National Opinion Research Center of the University of Chicago and the Survey Research Center of the University of Michigan is well known. The General Social Survey of NORC and the National Election Studies of SRC are widely disseminated.

Surveys by university-based centers tend to focus on issues of social policy (such as research on health care delivery, employment training, and substance abuse) rather than public opinion and politics. Nonetheless, several centers have organized state polls that are reported by the news media and sometimes cosponsored by the media. A partial list of the states covered includes: Alabama, Connecticut, Florida, Georgia, Indiana, Iowa, Maryland, New Hampshire, New Jersey, New York, North Carolina, Ohio, and Virginia.

Given the pluralism now found in approaches to opinion research in the United States, there is little reason to fear that shared terms of reference within the polling community will systematically distort the portrayal of public opinion.

Much of the burden for realizing the potential of public polling rests with news organizations. As the institutions that finance or conduct most of the polls appearing in the public domain, news organizations determine how elaborate a poll's design should be and how data will be reported. Samples in media-sponsored polls can be large enough to support demographic breakdowns and informative analyses or too small to provide much more than rough estimates of the distribution of opinions. Interviews can be long enough to cover the dimensions of opinion with some care or they may be kept short for purposes of producing a quick story without much depth.

As reading and viewing audiences are exposed to more polls, and as political analysts and commentators draw on polls with growing frequency, it would seem that poll consumers could be treated to more sophisticated forms of poll analysis. While television probably will continue to limit the complexity of the material it presents, news organizations generally should be able to offer more elaborate analyses of poll data.

The value of polls that provide a comprehensive examination of an issue or a cluster of related issues has been clearly demonstrated.[21] Rather than fill a questionnaire with individual questions on a host of unconnected topics, news organizations may see the merit of exploring a single topic in more comprehensive, discriminating, and subtle terms. In addition, scales and indices that draw on several questions to capture dimensions of public opinion can be constructed and conveyed in a straightforward manner to the general audience. Even if news organizations are slow to move toward more comprehensive poll analyses, greater priority could be given to including in reports of poll findings indications of the diversity of the public's view, how familiar the public is with the issue at hand, and how intensely views are held.

The Impact of the Polls on Public Opinion

Pollsters are frequently asked whether the reporting of poll results affects the very thing the polls are trying to measure—public opinion. Do preelection polls impel some people to get on the bandwagon or move others to support the underdog? Do election projections influence whether or how people vote on election day, and how are exit polls likely to be affected by the debate over projections? Do reports of the division of public opinion on issues affect public perception of those issues?

Bandwagon Effects

Over the years, pollsters have tended to dismiss bandwagon effects with confidence. They have pointed out that voters who report making up their minds in the last few days of an election do not decide disproportionately to go with the candidate who is ahead in the polls. They have also noted that final preelection polls would consistently underestimate the strength of the winner if large numbers of voters took their cues from the polls.

As much as the issue has been examined over the years, the difficulty always has been establishing cause and effect in a mix of elements: the results of polls, the events of a campaign, the way candidates come across to the electorate, the reporting of the campaign by the press, and the structure imposed by such factors as the campaign calendar.

One example illustrates the variety of the interactions. It has been suggested that the boost Rep. Richard Gephardt (D-Mo.) got in the polls in New Hampshire prior to that state's 1988 primary resulted from his good showing in Iowa polls conducted before the Iowa caucuses were held.[22] That is, the polls created a self-perpetuating cycle: one set of poll results directly influenced another set of poll results, independently of other events of political significance.

As we saw in Chapter 2, however, the matter is more complex. It is difficult to disentangle the influence of reported Iowa poll standings from other aspects of press coverage of Iowa, including the facts that Gephardt had been campaigning intensively and almost exclusively in Iowa for a year, that he had positioned Iowa as a "must win" state, and that New Hampshire received intense exposure to developments in Iowa as Boston news organizations followed the fortunes of another candidate, the governor of Massachusetts.

We have dealt at length with the ways in which poll results are picked up by the media in political reporting. Reporters invoke poll standings with varying degrees of precision in their assessments of the condition of one candidacy or another. The complex of signals such poll-based reporting sends to the electorate is exactly what research on bandwagon effects has been trying to assess.

In Chapter 2 we reviewed research on the effects of a voter's perception of who is ahead on that voter's candidate preference. We noted that:

- the candidate preferences of probable voters are more highly correlated with their assessment of a candidate's chances of winning than they are with their views of the candidate's ideological orientation, position on issues, or personal qualities;
- voters' assessments of whether a candidate can win tend to be affected by how much they like the candidate;
- at the same time, when the outcome of an election is in doubt and people have little information about the candidates, voter preferences for a candidate can be affected by voter assessments of how well the candidate may do; and
- bandwagon effects evidenced early in the cycle tend to dissipate as the election approaches because there are more important cues for voters to take into account in making up their minds.

Although their impact should not be overestimated, bandwagon effects can no longer be dismissed as unproven. However, we do need more comprehensive research on their effects in electoral settings other than presidential primaries. In addition, research has yet to isolate the degree to which bandwagon effects result directly from the reporting of poll results as against all the other events and images in an election.

Even if it were deemed desirable to ban reporting of all polls for a specified period prior to an election, such a ban would be virtually impossible to enforce. Nothing could prevent polling organizations outside the United States, say in Canada, from conducting surveys of American voter preferences and releasing the results.

Exit Polls

NBC News projected Ronald Reagan the winner of the 1980 election at 5:15 P.M. Pacific standard time, *before* the polls had closed on the West Coast. NBC beat its competition in part because it relied heavily on information from exit polls. It did not take the additional time to wait for vote tallies to come in from sampled precincts in different time zones, the practice used at the time by CBS and ABC. (ABC and CBS have since drawn upon exit poll data in making their estimates of the probable outcomes of elections.)

In the furor that ensued it was alleged that two influential members of Congress went down to defeat because voters, learning of the projected Reagan victory, decided not to go to the polls and thus did not cast ballots in the close House races. Al Ullman (D-Ore.), a twelve-term incumbent, had been chairman of the powerful House Ways and Means Committee. James Corman (D-Calif.), who lost by only 752 votes, had served in Congress for two decades and was chairman of the Democratic Congressional Campaign Committee.

The research done on the impact on the electorate of the 1980 projections was far from definitive. We have no good estimate of the number of potential voters who decided not to vote because of the projections.[23] At the same time, it should be noted that no research has demonstrated that the 1980 projections did *not* have a measurable effect on turnout or the make-up of the electorate that did turn out.[24]

The 1980 experience was revisited on election day 1984 when network projections were aired shortly after 8 P.M., eastern standard time, long before the polls had closed on the West Coast and even in New York State. In anticipation of such projections, research efforts were mobilized in advance to assess the impact of projections on the electorate. William Adams was able to conduct a survey in Oregon on the night of the election. His sample consisted of individuals registered to vote but who precinct records later showed had not voted. He found that 39 percent of his sample had heard about the projections but that fewer than 3 percent reported being influenced by the projections. Adams concluded that no more than one-quarter of 1 percent of the Oregon electorate could have stayed home because of the projections.[25]

After the 1984 election, frustration in the Congress was palpable. Since 1981 it had been searching for a solution that would reassure voters on the West Coast of the value of their votes without depriving the television networks of their right under the First Amendment to broadcast what they know when they know it.[26]

The House Subcommittee on Elections sensed that the Congress might be on a collision course with the television networks. However, impending confrontation ended in accommodation when the Congress agreed to consider closing the polls in presidential elections at a uniform time across the time zones *if* the networks would refrain (voluntarily) from projecting or characterizing the outcome of voting in a state while that state's polls were still open.[27]

The projections controversy will persist as long as polls close at different times across the country. With or without exit polls, votes are counted with increasing speed. As more than three-quarters of the electorate live in the eastern and central time zones, news organizations have enough voting data to project any but the closest presidential races before the polls close in the mountain and Pacific time zones.

If uniform poll closing becomes law, the issue will move from a controversy about projections to a controversy over "characterizations": the reporting of trends or otherwise indicating how an election may turn out. The truce between the Congress and the networks is uneasy on this score.[28]

To the extent exit polls can be uncoupled from the issue of election projections, their value is greatly enhanced. For the reasons examined in Chapter 3, the exit poll provides a unique window on the thinking of the electorate not available with preelection polls, other forms of election day polling (such as phone polls), and postelection studies. The sociodemographic correlates of voter preferences can be reliably measured using exit polls and sufficient sample sizes permit analyses of the electorate's behavior within geographic regions and within subgroups in the population. Voters' views on critical issues can be gauged for their influence on the preference for one candidate or another.[29]

In short, exit polls provide an unparalleled means of assessing what kind of mandate the voters have given a newly elected president, governor, or other official.[30] Moreover, they have been adopted all over the globe and are frequently used as a source of independent information to validate elections, for example, in Eastern Europe.

The Mean and the Mainstream

It is admittedly difficult to assess the impact preelection polls or election projections may have on voters. Even more problematic is the challenge of determining whether reports of the division of public opinion on issues affect what respondents tell interviewers when asked poll questions about those issues.

It has been suggested that opinion polls may serve as a great leveler in the public expression of opinion. The hypothesis is that, in order to avoid social isolation, some people fail to express points of view at odds with what they know to be mainstream thinking, while others who support the prevailing view tend to be more vocal. A "spiral of silence" thus sets in and exaggerates the impression of public consensus. Empirical evidence on this theory is contradictory.[31]

Generalizations about an individual's reluctance to speak his or her mind are tricky because of the many factors that must be taken into account. Social pressures to proffer the consensus view will have varying degrees of success depending on the issue, how much people know about it, how strongly they feel about it, or how stern the social sanctions are for holding a contrary view. People are less likely to be swayed by views of peers when their opinions are rooted in deeply held values and past experience than when they face issues of the day lacking such grounding.

More to the point, however, there are few indications that reports of poll findings directly affect public perception. The Roper Organization, for example, found that respondents were no more inclined to be critics of Jimmy Carter when advised in a poll question that "all of the polls have been showing support for President Carter going down" than when not so advised.[32] To the degree an individual's perception of issues and events is shaped by the broader consensus, polls seem far down the list as influential sources of information about that consensus.

Indirect Effects of the Polls

Polls also may have an indirect effect on public opinion through their impact on candidates for public office, their campaigns, or their contributors.

Candidates and the reporting of polls.   Because they are generally informed by polling data internal to their campaigns, candidates are seldom put off stride by reporters' questions about the latest poll. Depending upon the circumstances, poll results external to a campaign will be touted or discredited.[33] Although campaigns often complain that the polls distract their candidates from other matters, the question of who is ahead in the polls remains a legitimate part of the news. It is only part of the story, however, for there are many other indicators of how a campaign is doing.

Yet there remains the circumstance in which the reporting of a poll by a news organization actually affects the dynamics of a political event. The classic case of intrusive reporting of polls was ABC's evening newscast on the day before the second Bush-Dukakis debate. ABC devoted almost half of its program to reporting the results of its fifty-state poll. Even Dukakis's adversaries conceded that the poll put him on the defensive. Lee Atwater, the aggressive director of the Bush campaign, noted afterward: "I found myself for the first and only time ever feeling sorry for Dukakis. . . . It had to be unnerving." [34]

A parallel example, in a state contest, occurred during the 1990 gubernatorial race in Massachusetts. WBZ-TV and the *Boston Globe* sponsored the first major debate among contenders for the Democratic nomination. Coming just weeks before the state party's convention, the debate had generated great interest. On its evening newscast two hours before the debate's 8:00 P.M. air time, WBZ broadcast the results of a poll it had just completed with the *Boston Globe.* The poll showed that the leading candidate, Francis Bellotti, had dropped 14 percentage points from an earlier sounding. Bellotti was frank to admit the next day that he was off his stride during the debate, saying "I wasn't up for it, physically or otherwise." [35]

There can be little doubt that the poll releases affected the agility of Dukakis and Bellotti in the thrust-and-parry of debate. Few would argue that ABC or WBZ should be constrained from releasing poll findings as they deem appropriate. However, one must ask how the public and the political process benefit when poll releases are timed so that they will almost certainly influence the dynamics of crucial campaign events.

Polls and political money.   Modern campaigns are costly, and poll results play an important role in generating contributions. Although no data have been collected systematically on the role of polls in the decision of supporters to contribute to campaigns, inferences can be drawn from interviews with experts in campaign finance, anecdotal accounts, and other sources of information.

Polls have less impact on contributions to presidential campaigns than on contributions to campaigns for other offices for two reasons. First, federal matching funds go to presidential campaigns that have been able to show a broad base of support, as indicated by the number of individual contributions received. Contributors are generally more motivated by their commitment to a candidate than by that candidate's standing in the polls, which is often at the single-digit level early in the campaign. Second, we saw in Chapter 2 that, as the primary season unfolds, events and the structure of the nominating process interact to create a dynamic that has greater impact on potential contributors than poll standings in upcoming primaries or nationwide.

Where polls play a conspicuous role in fundraising is in races for the U.S. House of Representatives and the Senate. The campaign committees of both political parties, political action committees (PACs), and wealthy individuals turn to polls for guidance, particularly in close races or in the case of a vacancy caused by an incumbent's not running for reelection. As many as 200 of the 435 seats in the House may be the subject of close scrutiny by potential contributors.[36]

Incumbents receive the preponderance of campaign contributions. In the fifteen months leading up to the 1990 House and Senate elections, almost 90 percent of PAC contributions went to incumbents. Only 5 percent of the dollars went to challengers and another 5 percent was spent in races where there was an open seat.[37] Even though favorable poll standings can help show that the challenger has a chance of winning and is worthy of support, challengers face an uphill battle for their share of contributors' dollars.

PACs are eager to commit their resources strategically and produce a good win-loss ratio that they can report to their own contributors after the election. But in spite of the sums they spend, most PACs do not commission extensive polling. Therefore, polls conducted by the campaign committees of the national parties and by larger PACs (such as the Business-Industry Political Action Committee and the PACs of organized labor) become important sources of guidance. PACs with narrow issue agendas may attach less importance to poll standings when deciding how to allocate their funds, but their disbursements represent considerably less than a fifth of the dollars contributed.[38]

As important a role as polls may play, they do not reign supreme. Fears are overblown that potential candidates who do not have "good poll numbers" have no chance of receiving their party's financial support. "Show me a candidate [for the House] who has $100,000 in the bank by January of the election year, and we will back him or her regardless of what the polls show." This observation of Thomas O'Donnell, former political director of the Democratic Congressional Campaign Committee, reflects the importance party operatives attach to other vital signs of a campaign.[39] Most are aware of the limited prognostic value of polls taken early on.

Polling and the Democratic Process

We turn now to the matter of the intrinsic value of polling. What effect does polling have on the way public opinion finds voice and plays a role in our society? How does polling affect the way political interests compete in our system of government?

Among the dilemmas faced by the founders of the American republic, two provide a framework for our assessment of the impact of modern polling on the political process. The first was how to craft a set of institutions that would be sensitive to but not dictated by public opinion. As James Madison put it in *Federalist* No. 50: "It is the reason, alone, of the public, that ought to control and regulate the government. The passions ought to be controlled and regulated by the government." [40] The second dilemma was how to ensure that the views of the majority did not crowd out dissenting and minority points of view.

Schattschneider addresses both dilemmas in his call for a realistic understanding of how the public is sovereign in a modern democratic system:

> The most important thing about any democratic regime is the *way* in which it *uses* and exploits popular sovereignty, what questions it refers to the public for decision or guidance, how it refers them to the public, how the alternatives are defined and how it respects the limitations of the public. A good democratic system protects the public against the demand that it do impossible things. . . .
>
> Above everything, *the people are powerless if the political enterprise is not competitive.* It is the competition of political organizations that provides the people with the opportunity to make a choice. Without this opportunity popular sovereignty amounts to nothing.[41]

Viewed in this context, polling can be seen to affect the way in which issues are brought to the attention of politicians, the way politicians think about the public, and the process by which the competition between politicians is played out.

Polls and the Political Agenda

As a collective expression of individual experiences, hopes, and fears, public opinion holds powerful sway over the political agenda. In this sense, with V. O. Key, we can liken public opinion to a "system of dikes which channel public action or fix a range of discretion within which government may act or within which debate at official levels may proceed." [42]

One agenda-setting consequence of public opinion polling is that it shortens the amount of time required for an issue to come to the attention of the political community. Poll results can tip news organizations to stories by acquainting them with domains of public concern that would otherwise escape their attention. Bill Kovach reflects that while he was Washington editor of the *New York Times* "polling . . . moved us into areas we probably would have avoided without the support of polling data." He cites as examples stories on public attitudes on racial matters, the energy shortage during the 1970s, and changes forced on lifestyles by inflation.[43] In framing questions to ask candidates for public office, reporters often take their cue from public concerns picked up in polls.[44]

Polls also bring issues into political campaigns. Reports from constituency groups, party officials, and others on whom candidates rely for political intelligence can well miss specific issues and themes of concern in the lives of voters. Polls uniquely can assess how salient or pervasive an emerging set of issues is among the public. An excellent illustration from the 1980s was day care: its political importance was missed by many political operatives but registered in poll numbers.[45]

That polls play a role in political agenda setting is not deemed by all to contribute to the vitality of our political process. Benjamin Ginsberg worries that polls provide an early-warning system for politicians regarding public frustrations and grievances. Polling has converted the expression of public opinion from a "behavioral to an attitudinal phenomenon" by shortcircuiting the process by which political leaders come to learn what is on the minds of the people.

Ginsberg is concerned that polls preempt other forms of political expression: "Polls . . . organize and publicize opinion without requiring initiative or action on the part of individuals. With the exception of the small sample asked to submit to an interview, the individuals whose opinions are expressed through polls need take no action whatsoever. Polls underwrite or subsidize the costs of eliciting, organizing, and publicly expressing opinion." [46]

Contrary to Ginsberg's thesis, there is little evidence that the expansion of polling has diminished opportunities for "behavioral" expressions of opinion or weakened nongovernmental leadership.

Opportunities for participation, if anything, have grown. Relative to a generation ago, avenues for individual engagement in public issues have expanded. To traditional opportunities for participation (such as unions, parent-teacher associations, civic clubs, and local political organizations) have been added a host of outlets for expression of concern ranging from neighborhood crime watches to involvement in an assortment of advocacy groups, many of which are membership-based. In fact, advocacy organizations in the United States are distinguished by their number and by the fact that they often compete with one another for the loyalty of those sharing an interest or point of view. For example, competition for the allegiance of educators in the United States has raged between the National Education Association and the American Federation of Teachers.[47]

In the most formal articulation of the role of polls in agenda setting, the opinion poll is likened to a public referendum. The principal proponent of this conception was George Gallup, who believed that polls had unparalleled capacity to highlight the view of the majority to offset the influence of one or another well-connected minority in the political process. He was fascinated with the initiative-referendum process in Switzerland and saw in polling a similar kind of direct involvement of the citizenry in the affairs of government.[48]

The question of whether the initiative-referendum process complements other institutions of a democratic form of government is beyond the scope of this work. However, the fallacy in the concept of polling as a form of direct democracy is that a poll seldom replicates the processes that take place when a ballot question is put before the electorate.[49]

In most jurisdictions the hurdles to placing a proposition on the ballot are sufficiently high that only a handful of issues actually ends up before the voters. Those that are presented to voters tend to be specifically drawn and pertain to matters within the authority of local or state government. Almost always they stimulate weeks of heated debate, as the public is exposed to arguments by proponents and opponents. Finally, only the views of those who are registered and cast a vote on election day are counted. The number who vote on the referendum is often smaller than the number who cast ballots for one or another candidate in the same election.

By contrast, the public opinion poll usually covers a wide range of issues, many of which are national or international in scope. Although topics under investigation in a poll may have been in the news, public discussion about them is rarely focused on provisions as narrowly defined as in a ballot proposition. Without extensive questioning on a topic, it is difficult for a poll to anticipate the arguments that may emerge in public debate or to simulate that debate and its effects on the public's view of the issue. But most important, to ask polls to serve as referenda on issues is to foster the unrealistic expectation that a single poll question can capture all of the nuances of public opinion on a complex matter of public policy and that the results can be seen as determinative.

Soundings of opinion between elections also serve an agenda-setting function by reminding those in public office that it is the public that performs the ultimate oversight function, by bestowing or withholding a mandate in the next election. Popularity and approval rating questions, initiated in the 1930s, have become an institution. Harold Mendelsohn and Irving Crespi have presciently observed that by the late 1960s polling had contributed a fundamentally new dimension to American politics. By keeping the public's assessment of the performance of public officials in the news, the polls have turned "the electoral process [into] an *endless event,* with elections as periodic climaxes." [50]

Polls and Political Leadership

Politics is among other things a kind of semiorganized speculation about the allocation of power down the road. Few tools contribute more to structuring that speculation than the opinion poll. Political opportunities and potential costs of a course of action can be inferred by assessing the importance of an issue to the public, the direction and intensity of opinion on that issue, and the public's response to past initiatives bearing on the issue.

It is argued that polls diminish the quality of political leadership, among both elected officials and individuals appointed to high-level positions in government agencies. There is no doubt that polls can induce caution on the part of politicians who dare not act without considering the public opinion ramifications and dare not venture into new terrain without carefully positioning themselves on the issues according to the latest poll findings.

Former senator John Culver (D-Iowa) spoke eloquently of these dangers: "If one casts each vote on the basis of reelection prospects and thereby steadily erodes his own convictions out of fear of defeat, then he has forfeited his conscience and ignored his own best judgment, which should be the only reason why he or she—rather than someone else—is in office." [51]

These are legitimate concerns. However, a blanket indictment of the polls on this score is as far off the mark as would be an unthinking and indifferent defense of the ennobling function of polls in politics. It is more useful to consider the factors that bear on how politicians use and are influenced by polls.

We must differentiate two ways in which politicians can approach the findings of a public opinion poll. One is the "town crier" model, in which the poll is taken to be the latest public verdict on an issue. The other is the "political intelligence" model, in which the poll is taken into account as but one factor in planning strategy and tactics. The former approach assumes the public has spoken; the latter assumes that the public may be persuadable.

On occasion the town crier model prevails.[52] More generally, however, it is the political intelligence approach to polling that dominates among politicians. This is one reason why private pollsters are often sought by clients as much for their political judgment as for the opinion data they collect.

The manner in which politicians, in the legislative and executive branches in particular, weigh insights from polls varies widely depending on several factors:

- Their confidence in the strength of their political base: in the case of elected officials, assurances of the breadth and depth of their strength with the electorate; and, in the case of government officials, their trust that they will be supported by their superiors
- The political calendar and the proximity of the next election
- The salience of an issue to a wide and diverse constituency
- The extent to which the issue remains salient over time and simply will not go away
- The intensity with which an issue is advocated by a narrow constituency
- The degree to which the general public is familiar with an issue and/or the extent to which public opinion has crystallized on the issue and
- The mix of support or opposition among subgroups within the electorate as coalitions come together and drift apart

As central as poll findings may seem to be in political decision making, in reality they are complemented by a host of political considerations:

- The official's own substantive knowledge of the issue at hand and assessment of the probable consequences of alternative courses of action
- Press treatment of the issue or the official's handling of it
- The range of discretion available to a politician as a result of his or her seniority, committee assignments, portfolio in a government agency, or reputed substantive expertise
- The counsel of staff, long-time political allies, campaign contributors, special interests and lobbyists on the merits of the case at hand
- The strength of partisan leadership that defines and legitimizes a stand on the issue, and in some cases reduces the political risk by taking tough stands that provide cover or show that there is strength in numbers
- The politician's view about the reliability and value of polls themselves

In addition, elected and appointed officials vary greatly in sophistication when it comes to interpreting the results of polls, especially polls on issues. Although generally familiar with polls in a campaign setting, many officials in responsible positions do not have the time, and some may not have the inclination, to reach beyond simplistic characterizations of public opinion on important policy issues such as the federal deficit, AIDS, or abortion.

It is for this reason that competent analyses of public opinion data in magazines, newsletters, and by specialized staffs within legislative bodies and executive agencies are so important. A busy official seeking guidance on "what the American people think" is far better served by a distillation and analysis of disparate poll findings than by the results of a single poll that may be timely but miss important dimensions at work in the public's thinking.

Finally, elected officials retain considerable discretion and room for maneuver, even when under great pressure from constituents and special interests. In their study of the business community's influence over Congress in the matter of foreign trade, Bauer, Pool, and Dexter showed that, because of the number and range of demands made of them, elected officials can be quite selective regarding those interests to which they respond. More often than not, the process by which a member of Congress chooses to attend to one interest and finesse another is a function of the values and predispositions the member brought into office and the points of view with which he or she is prominently identified. When public pressure is brought to bear, the member's position on the issue is less likely to be affected than is the priority the member attaches to the issue.[53]

Polls and the White House

In June 1787, the Constitutional Convention turned its attention to the authority and structure that should be built into the executive branch of government. One of the first issues was whether the executive should consist of more than one individual. Some, eager to avoid the tyranny from which the new republic had fought for independence, thought the executive function should be subordinated to the legislative; one means of accomplishing that objective would be to divide executive power among three individuals drawn from different regions of the country. Others, whose view prevailed, saw this as a formula for ineffective government.

As Alexander Hamilton would later argue in *Federalist* No. 70: "A feeble executive implies a feeble execution of government. A feeble execution is but another phrase for bad execution; and government ill executed, whatever it may be in theory, must be, in practice, a bad government." Hamilton also observed that *"energy in the executive* is a leading character in the definition of good government." [54]

The checks and balances built into the American form of government have evolved over the years as the competitive branches of government probe weaknesses in each other's perimeter. But the "energy" of the presidency has been preserved and the president remains uniquely autonomous in framing the issues facing the nation.[55]

It is little wonder that the White House is an avid consumer of public opinion poll data. Through such data the president can identify areas in which lack of information or public resistance must be overcome if policy initiatives are to succeed. The sustained monitoring of disparate dimensions of public opinion has become integral to the modern presidency. Such monitoring involves more than following the trends of opinion at critical junctures on issues in which the president has invested energy and prestige.

Of the trends followed, none is looked at more closely than the president's popularity. Staffers see it go up with favorable developments on the international front and with decisive presidential actions, even where the public may be somewhat ambivalent.[56] They also see popularity erode if doubt sets in regarding the president's judgment or integrity.[57]

The use made of information from public opinion polls by presidents and their staffs varies widely. It is one of many reflections of the style and substance of presidential leadership. We can illustrate by recalling episodes from several presidencies.

FDR and lend-lease. Aware that the United States would sooner or later have to enter the war against the Axis powers, President Roosevelt was concerned that the American public was not prepared for the burdens it would soon be asked to shoulder. As his reports to the nation prepared the public incrementally for involvement, Roosevelt wanted to make sure he was not getting too far ahead of the public. He wanted to balance public opinion around the course he believed the nation needed to take. Thus he followed trends in the polls closely.

Over the second half of 1941, a question was included in monthly polls being done for Roosevelt by Hadley Cantril. It asked: "So far as you personally are concerned, do you think President Roosevelt has gone too far in his policies of helping Britain, or not far enough?" The proportion volunteering that the president's actions were "about right" held firm in the 50 to 55 percent range month after month. The proportions saying that Roosevelt was going "too far" or "not far enough" each stayed in the range of 20 percent. Cantril recalled: "This was precisely the situation [Roosevelt] wanted to maintain during these critical months." Meanwhile U.S. aid to Britain through the Lend-Lease program increased steadily.[58]

Richard Steele described Roosevelt's disposition toward public opinion: "He saw public attitudes not as a mandate for initiatives generated outside the White House, but as potential obstacles to courses he had already decided upon." Cantril concurred: "Roosevelt regarded the reports sent him the way a general would regard information turned in by his intelligence services as he planned the strategy of a campaign. . . . He utilized such information to try to bring the public around more quickly or more effectively to the course of action he felt was best for the country." [59]

Eisenhower and international opinion. Dwight Eisenhower is not usually associated with an interest in public opinion polls. However, he was an attentive consumer of reports about the state of public opinion in other countries. Drawing on polls conducted by the United States Information Agency as well as other sources, Lloyd A. Free wrote a biweekly memorandum to the White House on foreign public opinion. These reports focused on reactions around the globe to U.S. foreign policy. Since then, with varying degrees of regularity, presidents have kept abreast of developments in international public opinion, particularly before meetings with other heads of state.

LBJ and civil rights.   As the nation worked its way along the tortuous path to expanded civil rights in the early and mid-1960s, President Lyndon Johnson paid close attention to the results of a question asked frequently by the Gallup Poll regarding the public's sense that he was pushing civil rights too fast, not fast enough, or about right. As in the case of FDR and Lend-Lease, the preponderance of public opinion remained balanced around the "about right" alternative as the months progressed.

Meanwhile history was being written, with the violent interruption by police of the march from Selma to Montgomery, Alabama, in 1963; the Freedom Democratic Party's claim to seats at the 1964 Democratic Convention; the signing of the Civil Rights Act of 1964 and the Voting Rights Act of 1965; and rioting in Watts, Chicago, and Detroit. A steady and reliable measure of the public's reaction was essential intelligence as the president led the nation through what was nothing less than a social revolution.

LBJ and Vietnam.   No case proves as dramatically as Vietnam that presidents cannot prevail without public support. As a trusted aide who was at the president's side through the early phases of U.S. involvement and who later broke with Johnson, Bill Moyers's reflections have particular poignancy:

> It should be obvious that a President faces no quest more difficult than the search for an accurate reading of how far and how fast he can lead the people. As difficult as the task is, he must try. He must try because there are questions on which governments dare not act without evidence of genuine support. When policies and laws outdistance public opinion, or take public opinion for granted, or fail to command respect in the conscience of the people, they lose their "natural" legitimacy. . . . Vietnam has proven that good intentions on the part of a nation's leaders will not substitute for the conscious involvement of the people in the decision to go to war. [60]

Carter and "malaise." Regular reports on public opinion also alert presidents to currents in public sentiment they may find worrisome. In late 1978, President Carter was alarmed when his pollster, Patrick Caddell, picked up what was judged to be a serious downturn in public confidence in the health of the nation. Using a polling technique called the "self-anchoring striving scale" on a regular basis, Caddell found a majority of the public fearing that the nation was worse off than it had been five years ago.[61]

Within a matter of months, the president would deliver what became known as the "malaise speech" in which he spoke of a "crisis of confidence" in the nation that "strikes at the very heart and soul and spirit of our national will." While others had corroborated Caddell's findings, few in the opinion research community went as far as Caddell in diagnosing a national malaise gnawing at the American soul.[62] Just one year later, Ronald Reagan challenged Carter with ironic familiarity as he asked audiences across the country whether they were better off than they had been four years ago.

Reagan and education. In April 1983 a national commission appointed by Ronald Reagan's secretary of education released *A Nation at Risk,* a report that rang the alarm about the deteriorating quality of public education in the United States. The report received wide attention and was jarring when juxtaposed against the cuts that had been made by the Reagan administration in federal funding for education.

Polling by Richard Wirthlin confirmed that the president was potentially vulnerable regarding the cuts in education, especially with the 1984 election just around the corner. At the same time, Wirthlin's polls mapped the arguments most and least compelling with the public regarding steps that could be taken to improve the quality of education. As Wirthlin put it, "We tested and found where the hot buttons were. . . . We couldn't beat them [the critics] on the issue of money. We had to change the terms of the debate."[63]

Soon thereafter, the president took his case to the public in a high-profile swing across the country, driving home the elements of his view that Wirthlin's polling had shown were most acceptable to the public: tougher standards for students, more discipline, and holding teachers more accountable for the performance of their students. At no time did the president budge from his own position that the federal government's involvement in public education should be scaled back. In his account of this episode, Hedrick Smith notes that Michael Deaver, the orchestrator of the president's foray, "scored a stunning success, changing the public's perception and attitudes toward Reagan's policy position, *without Reagan's changing his policy.*" [64]

Reagan and the "gender gap."   Regular reports on public opinion also help a president better understand problems with particular constituencies. Illustrative are the difficulties Ronald Reagan had during his first term with the "gender gap," the relative lack of confidence in his presidency among women. Contrary to the counsel of the president's staffers, who were mostly men, polls showed that the problem could not be addressed simply by focusing on what were assumed to be "women's issues" such as family policy and day care. The polls demonstrated that the problem women had with the president originated in their misgivings over his budget priorities and the bellicose tone of his foreign policy. With no change in policies, significant improvement in his standing with women was never to take place.[65]

Popularity as an "asset."   During the second Reagan term, the president's popularity was referred to as "the bottom line" in the "account of the president's political capital." [66] The balance-sheet metaphor usefully conveys the importance in the modern presidency of strategic thinking about the president's standing with the public. As Samuel Kernell has observed, strategic calculations are made about conserving and spending the power that inheres in the personal popularity of the president. Popularity may be traded for policy goals deemed important but likely to be unpopular. Other actors in the president's party and in the congressional opposition may make strategic judgments against the same standard, reinforcing the importance of presidential popularity as a form of legal tender with which the nation does its political business.[67]

The modern president's clout in Washington is now more contingent than ever on his influence outside of Washington. Congress is far more compliant toward the president's agenda when the president's ratings hold up than when they begin to decline.

But the political opposition need not be cowed by a president with imposing approval numbers. As Ronald Reagan's tenure in the White House was to demonstrate so vividly, a president's popularity should not always be construed as public concurrence with the direction of a president's policies and the public's unwillingness to listen to contrary voices.

During his first year in office, Reagan appeared ten feet tall to congressional Democrats. They were intimidated by his high popularity and the magnitude of his victory over Jimmy Carter, even though they harbored profound doubts about the wisdom of his budget priorities and economic policies.[68]

The historic irony is that, while it saw Reagan as a stronger leader than his predecessor, the public had the same doubts about his policy agenda as the Democrats. Adding to the irony is the fact that public reservations about the substance of the president's initiatives were picked up in the same polls that registered his popularity in the first place. The White House made much of the "mandate" bestowed by the voters in the 1980 election, but the pollsters told us that the situation was more complex. Even though the public was drawn to Reagan's "get-the-government-off-your-back" rhetoric, it did not want cuts in many of the programs he had targeted for reduction or elimination. What Reagan had done was highlight Free and Cantril's 1964 finding that the American people tend to be conservative at the level of political ideology while continuing to support an activist government when it comes to specific programs.[69]

As telling an indicator as presidential popularity is, these approval ratings are not complemented by indicators of equal sensitivity regarding public perception of the institutions and interests juxtaposed against the president. Ratings of the other major political actors are not comparable. Questions about confidence in Congress characteristically pick up public cynicism about politicians generally. Leaders of the political opposition (such as the Speaker of the House or the Senate Majority Leader) are relatively unknown to the public. In short, there is no personal or symbolic embodiment of the opposition equal to the public persona of the president.

It is in part to compensate for this inability to monitor public perception of the opposition that pollsters start asking trial-heat questions at what seems an early date. Although such pairings often have little prognostic value, they may be the pollsters' best attempt to deal with the fact that, in accordance with the wishes of the founders of the republic, the "energy" resides in the executive.

A postscript. Pollsters have long had much to say to presidents about when and how the president brings his message to the American people. However, a new dimension to the role was added during the Reagan years: the use of instant-reaction meters to assess the public's reaction to the president's speeches (see Chapter 3).

During the 1984 campaign, Richard Wirthlin convened small groups to watch Ronald Reagan campaigning. Using the hand-held meters, participants would record their positive and negative reactions moment by moment. Public response could then be analyzed on a word-by-word basis. With what he called the "speech pulse," Wirthlin was able to identify "power phrases" and "resonators" to describe especially persuasive words, phrases, and images that could be repeated to the president's advantage.[70] Individuals from the worlds of advertising and marketing have been well represented on presidential staffs for years. But if the choice of presidential words and phrases is now to be determined by ratings of public reaction to "resonators" and "power phrases," have not the politics of substance been replaced by the politics of rhetorical manipulation?

The arbiter of this issue ultimately is the American public. In our system we have no alternative but to wait for effective political opposition and for the public to bring its uncanny judgment to bear.

Polls and Political Competition

Eager to avoid the pitfalls that brought down earlier experiments in self-government, the founders of the American republic worried that an overbearing majority in public opinion might smother competition in the political process. It was James Madison's insight that the new nation possessed a quality unknown in ancient Greece and Italy: social and economic diversity that comes with scale. Madison wrote in *Federalist* No. 51: "Whilst all authority in [the United States] will be derived from and dependent on the society, the society itself will be broken into so many parts, interests and classes of citizens, that the rights of individuals, or of the minority, will be in little danger from interested combinations of the majority." [71]

One wonders what Madison might have made of the modern public opinion poll. Would he have been quite so sanguine that the overbearing majority he feared could be held at bay in light of polling's ability to determine the majority view on virtually any issue facing the nation?

Or would he have seen in the results of polls reassuring evidence that "interested combinations of the majority" are in constant flux, as issues cut across segments of the population in varying ways and as groups making up a majority on one issue will diverge on another?

Madison would have been reassured by research that reveals the heterogeneity of public opinion. His worry about the dominance of a combination of interests or citizens would have been allayed if he had known how difficult it can be to predict an individual's political values from his or her social or demographic characteristics. No doubt he would have been interested to learn that "yuppies" (broadly, the group of college-educated individuals now entering middle age) are not homogeneous in their political dispositions. They do not agree among themselves when it comes to a basic philosophy of political life: some hold to the agenda of the peace and civil rights movements of the 1960s, others are preoccupied with their own well-being, while still others are worried about the health of an unfettered private sector.[72]

With the advent of polling, much of the competition that is the business of politics takes place in terms of a search for public legitimacy. Myriad interests attempt to identify themselves with some facet of the "public interest" as they fight for scarce public resources, special consideration from a public agency, or a special provision in pending legislation.

The decline in party discipline within Congress also reflects and reinforces the role of public opinion polling in national policy making. Kernell has observed that, because members of the House and Senate are less bound by the constraints of partisan agendas, they have become more attentive to public pressure in setting their own agendas. One result is a new-found latitude in the issues they take up. Thus, it is now consistent with an individual member's strategic political interests to entertain the cause of an organization outside the partisan mainstream, behavior that rarely would have been sanctioned in the past. It also means that members can participate in a smorgasbord of coalitions that defy easy categorization in conventional political terms.[73]

In Kernell's view, political competition in Washington has been transformed. Where it once was a process of advocates jockeying for attention by highlighting the potential effect of a law or agency decision on their particular constituencies, it is now a process of pressure groups establishing the legitimacy of their cause by demonstrating support *among the public at large.* The fulcrum of political leverage in Washington is often found outside Washington in the grass-roots mobilization of the public. This heightens the importance of the polls.

Similarly, struggles at the highest levels of the executive branch can be played out in public opinion terms. In 1981, for example, Secretary of State Alexander Haig spoke provocatively about the need for an embargo of Cuba as part of an effort to place Central America higher on the agenda of the Reagan administration. James Baker, then White House chief of staff, shared the alarm of other senior officials that Haig's rhetoric would deflect attention from other issues of higher priority, such as beefing up U.S. defenses and the budget. Baker turned to the president's pollster, Richard Wirthlin, for a quick poll on the public's response to Haig's initiative. The anticipated negative public reaction was picked up and shared with President Reagan to underscore the political costs of the direction in which Haig was headed.[74]

The use of polls by advocates to acquaint decision makers with the public opinion dimension of issues before them has led to what has become known as "advocacy polling." Its purpose is to provide proprietary public opinion data that a client can use in making the best case for its point of view.

A proponent of advocacy polling, Harry O'Neill, insists that such research be methodologically sound and meet generally accepted standards of public disclosure.[75] However, although many advocacy polls meet these standards, advocacy polling as a whole remains susceptible to the problems we have discussed, such as biased question wording, skewed sampling (to overrepresent a particular subgroup), and partial release of findings.

This is further reason why consumers of polls in the political community must have some familiarity with the factors contributing to poll reliability and validity. It also affirms the need for systems of public accountability, as discussed in Chapter 4. Finally, it reminds us of the importance of polling organizations that are not entirely dependent on special interests for their financial support.

Polling and the Public Interest

We have touched on many aspects of the question with which we began this book: how do public opinion polls contribute to the well-being of the body politic and to the democratic process?

To restate the argument advanced in these pages: the public opinion poll—expertly conducted and well reported—can be a uniquely sensitive tool for gauging the usually complex, sometimes ineffable, and always dynamic qualities of public opinion. But, the promise of the public polls is realized only to the extent both partners—pollsters and news organizations—uphold their side of the bargain.

For their part, pollsters must make progress in instituting more effective forms of peer review. When a poll fails to pick up an important undercurrent in public thinking or misreads the preelection disposition of the electorate, there is usually a good explanation. The problem is that, although public disclosure of information about a poll's methodology is now an accepted part of the professional ethic, many pollsters remain uncomfortable using that information to review the work of a colleague for public attribution.

News organizations have reciprocal obligations. At a minimum, those in the Fourth Estate who deal with polls have a responsibility to learn enough about polling to understand why all polls are not equal. It is also incumbent on news executives and editors to think strategically about the way polls are handled in their organizations. Such a strategic approach to polling involves four elements: explicit consideration in planning a poll of how the reading and viewing public might best be informed by it; commitment of sufficient resources to the poll so readers or viewers may have a basis for confidence in its reliability; subordinating editorial to research criteria when determining how far the results can be generalized; and ensuring that the pollster reviews the content of a news story before it is published or broadcast. The burden for such strategic thinking is greater as the vise of financial constraints tightens on all facets of news operations.

Pollsters and news organizations have a common interest in uncovering the source of polling errors when they occur. Where a poll falls short of the mark and its methodology is subjected to review, its shortcomings are less likely to raise doubts about the intrinsic soundness of polling than they are to reflect a shortage of time, resources, or expertise committed to the poll.

But polls sponsored by news organizations often get caught up in the swirl of events and too seldom are subjected to the scrutiny they may deserve. When a poll is in error and no effort is made to uncover the sources of error, both opinion research and journalism suffer. For, if poll consumers are left with the impression that the pollsters and sponsoring news organizations do not know why the poll was wrong, there is less reason for the public to believe them when they say they are right.

Pollsters and news organizations have much at stake. So do the American people. When polls are competently conducted and responsibly reported, they perform an immensely important function by bringing the public's agenda into the political process in a form that is relatively unmediated by advocates for one point of view or another.

Polls serve an important public purpose to the extent they operate as a reality check on representations about the public's disposition by reminding us of the dimensions and underlying dynamic of public opinion. In this capacity polls can anchor the conjecture of the pundits. Polls can rein in the "spin doctors" who try to characterize the public's verdict on an issue in which their clients have an interest. Polls can help delineate the liberties elected leadership may take when proclaiming a mandate from the public. And polls can constrain disingenuous assertions by special interests about where the public stands.

In sum, polls contribute to the give-and-take of politics by acquainting one constituency with the points of view of others, by reminding all constituencies of the prevailing view among the public at large, and by making the public integral to the competition among political interests.

Notes

1. Our concept of legitimacy derives in large part from Max Weber's writings on the sources of the legitimacy of a political order. See Talcott Parsons, ed., *Max Weber: The Theory of Economic Organization* (New York: Free Press, 1947), 130-132.

2. Robert B. Hill, "The Polls and Ethnic Minorities," *Annals* 472 (March 1984): 159.

3. Karlyn Keene, interview with the author, Washington, D.C., July 25, 1989.

4. Hill, "Polls and Ethnic Minorities," 159-160.

5. Bill Kovach, address to plenary session of the annual conference of the American Association for Public Opinion Research, Lancaster, Pa., May 18, 1990.

6. Charles W. Roll, Jr., telephone interview with the author, April 19, 1990.

7. Walter Lippmann, *Public Opinion* [1922] (New York: Free Press, 1965) and *The Phantom Public* (New York: Macmillan, 1925).

8. Harwood L. Childs, then editor of the *Public Opinion Quarterly*, reflected this thinking in his text, *Public Opinion: Nature, Formation and Role* (Princeton, N.J.: Van Nostrand, 1965), 350.

9. Charles W. Roll, Jr., and Albert H. Cantril, *Polls: Their Use and Misuse in Politics* [1972] (Cabin John, Md.: Seven Locks Press, 1980), 145-146; see also George H. Gallup, "Preserving Majority Rule," in *Polling on the*

Issues, ed. Albert H. Cantril (Cabin John, Md.: Seven Locks Press, 1980), 170.

10. The two-step flow of political communication was among the major findings of Bernard Berelson, Paul Lazarsfeld, and William McPhee, *Voting* (Chicago: University of Chicago Press, 1954).

11. E. E. Schattschneider, *The Semisovereign People: A Realist's View of Democracy in America* [1960] (Hinsdale, Ill.: Dryden Press, 1975), 129.

12. W. Russell Neuman, *The Paradox of Mass Politics: Knowledge and Opinion in the American Electorate* (Cambridge, Mass.: Harvard University Press, 1986), 170-171.

13. Elmo Roper, "So the Blind Shall Not Lead," *Fortune,* February 1942, 102.

14. The Gallup Poll was criticized for using three "factual" questions to identify informed opinion about treaties signed by President Carter to return the Panama Canal to the Republic of Panama. The facts were alleged to be "pro-treaty," resulting in what the critics contend was an overstatement of the public's willingness to support the treaties. See Ted J. Smith III and J. Michael Hogan, "Public Opinion and the Panama Canal Treaties of 1977," *Public Opinion Quarterly* 51 (Spring 1987): 22. For other discussions see Bernard Roshco, "Polling on Panama—Si; Don't Know; Hell, No!" *Public Opinion Quarterly* 42 (Winter 1978): 551-562; and George D. Moffett III, *The Limits of Victory: The Ratification of the Panama Canal Treaties* (Ithaca, N.Y.: Cornell University Press, 1985).

15. An illustration is the difficulty pollsters had regarding questions on arms negotiations with the Soviet Union. See William J. Lanouette, "Polls and Pols—With a Grain of SALT," in *Polling on the Issues,* ed. Cantril, 99-114.

16. Howard Schuman and Jacqueline Scott have so concluded in "Problems in the Use of Survey Questions to Measure Public Opinion," *Science* 236 (May 22, 1987), 957-959. For a response see Eleanor Singer, "To the Editor," *Public Opinion Quarterly* 52 (Winter 1988): 576-581.

17. A superb illustration of this point came in a 1971 Gallup Poll that found 66 percent of the public answering the following question in the affirmative: "A proposal has been made in Congress to require the U.S. Government to bring home all U.S. troops [from Vietnam] before the end of this year. Would you like to have your Congressman vote for or against this proposal?" Support for withdrawal dwindled to 41 percent, however, when a follow-up question to those favoring the proposal asked: "Some people say that the U.S. should withdraw all its troops from Vietnam by the end of this year, regardless of what happens there after U.S. troops leave. Do you agree or disagree?"

18. The Roper question asked: "There has recently been talk of impeachment

of the president, and people seem to have different understandings of what impeachment means. Some say that if a president is impeached it means he is thrown out of office. Others say if a president is impeached it only means that he is put on trial by Congress for the charges brought against him to determine whether or not he is guilty. What do you think impeachment means—that a president is thrown out of office, or that he is put on trial by Congress?" The responses: 37 percent, thrown out of office; 52 percent, put on trial; and 11 percent without an opinion. Source: *Roper Reports,* 73-10.

The author's survey involved 1,500 personal interviews with a national sample conducted by the Gallup Organization in early October 1973. Timing of the study turned out to be felicitous for interviewing; it followed many revelations about the cover-up but preceded the "Saturday night massacre" in which Attorney General Elliot Richardson resigned rather than comply with the White House order that he fire Special Prosecutor Archibald Cox. The data are from a specially commissioned, unpublished study by the author and Susan Davis Cantril.

Pollsters themselves contributed to confusion about the public's thinking regarding whether and how Nixon should be brought to justice. The Gallup Poll was first out with the results of a question on impeachment in June 1973 reporting only 19 percent in favor of it. The question asked: "Do you think President Nixon should be impeached and compelled to leave office or not?" Critics quickly pointed out that this formulation mistakenly defined impeachment as a president's being forced from office rather than the House of Representatives setting in motion the process of determining whether or not there is sufficient evidence for a president to be tried by the Senate.

19. A study along these lines was conducted by the Gallup Organization for Times Mirror in September 1987. By asking dozens of questions about the basic values of respondents, the authors were able to divide the electorate into eleven groups, each of which had a distinctive orientation toward politics. This research was publicized by Times Mirror during the 1988 presidential campaign, serving to heighten awareness of the diversity of vantage points from which people were approaching the election. See Norman J. Ornstein, Andrew Kohut, and Larry McCarthy, *The People, Press, and Politics: The Times Mirror Study of the American Electorate* (Reading, Mass.: Addison-Wesley, 1988).

20. Compilation by Mary A. Spaeth, *Survey Research* 20 (Summer-Fall 1989): 17-21.

21. Examples of this kind of polling are: the "State of the Nation" series supported by the Institute for International Social Research and Potomac Associates; the "American People and Foreign Policy" series supported by the Chicago Council on Foreign Relations; and the "Americans Talk

Security" series supported by Massachusetts businessman Alan Kay. Underscoring our point, however, none of these studies was financed by a news organization.

22. Jack Corrigan of the Dukakis campaign made this argument. See David R. Runkel, ed., *Campaign for President: The Managers Look at '88* (Dover, Mass.: Auburn House, 1989), 146.

23. Four studies suggested that the projections could have had an impact on the electorate. Each has been criticized on methodological grounds.

Drawing on the postelection supplements to the Current Population Survey conducted by the U.S. Census Bureau in 1972 and 1974, Wolfinger and Linquiti found a decline in voter participation after 6 P.M. local time in the 1972 Nixon landslide. Their ability to generalize to 1980, however, was inhibited by a lack of time-of-vote data for 1980, the amount of time that had elapsed between the election and interviewing for the postelection CPS supplement, and the unreliability of respondent reports of their own voting. Raymond Wolfinger and Peter Linquiti, "Tuning In and Turning Out," *Public Opinion* 4 (February/March 1981): 56-60.

Leonard Panish, then registrar-recorder of Los Angeles County, routinely recorded the number of votes cast by hour in all national elections. Comparing 1980 to 1978, he found a decline in the proportion of the vote cast after 7 P.M. local time. However, the absence of comparable data for 1976 precluded comparison of the 1980 pattern with another presidential election cycle. LACRRO, "Report to the Los Angeles County Election Commission: Early Network Projections" (Los Angeles: Los Angeles County Registrar-Recorder's Office, 1980).

Jackson and McGee conducted follow-up interviews to the 1980 National Election Study. Using statistical modeling they concluded that turnout dropped by 20 to 25 percent among those likely to vote who had not voted at the time of the projections. Their research came under close scrutiny and has been faulted for resting on a small sample and relying on the veracity of respondents' reports two months after the election. John Jackson and William H. McGee III, "Election Reporting and Voter Turnout," Report of the Center for Political Studies, University of Michigan, Ann Arbor, 1981.

California poll interviewed a cross section of voters and nonvoters in January 1981. The initial sample size was substantial. But by the time respondents had been identified who were registered, reported not voting in November, and cited the projection as the reason for not voting, the analysis rested on only 71 cases. Additionally, the problem of self-reporting of past voting behavior was encountered. While much was made of the finding by California politicians, the poll's director, Mervin Field, cautioned against drawing any conclusions from the data regarding the impact of projections.

242   *The Opinion Connection*

For criticism and discussion of these studies see Seymour Sudman, "Do Exit Polls Influence Voting Behavior?" *Public Opinion Quarterly* 50 (Fall 1986): 331-339; and Warren J. Mitofsky, "A Short History of Exit Polls," in *Polling and Presidential Election Coverage,* ed. Paul J. Lavrakas and Jack K. Holley (Newbury Park, Calif.: Sage, forthcoming), 82-98.

24. While the research community was at work assessing the impact of the projections, the Congress was moving toward its own solution. A variety of legislative solutions was introduced in short order. Hearings were held in the House and Senate during 1981 and 1982, resulting in calls by both chambers for the television networks to delay any projections of the election's outcome until polls had closed on the West Coast (Hawaii and Alaska excepted).

The controversy was rekindled at 8:12 P.M., February 20, 1984, when CBS News projected the outcome of the Democratic caucuses in Iowa. Six minutes later, NBC made its projection. The first of several stages of caucus balloting was not scheduled to take place until 8:30 P.M. The next day a new round of congressional hearings was called to elicit from the networks a commitment to refrain voluntarily from similar projections in the New Hampshire primary, just a week away. By late June the House of Representatives had passed a resolution urging the networks to exercise restraint.

A good summary of the projections controversy is a report of the House Subcommittee on Elections, *Single Poll Closing Time for Presidential General Elections in the Continental United States,* Report 101-15, Part 1, 101st Cong., 1st sess., 1989. See also Committee on House Administration and Subcommittee on Telecommunications, Consumer Protection and Finance of the Committee on Energy and Commerce, *Early Election Returns and Projections Affecting the Electoral Process,* 97th Cong., 1st sess., 1981; and Task Force on Elections, *Election Day Practices and Election Projections,* 97th Cong., 2d sess., 1982. Subsequent hearings on "uniform poll closing" were held by the House Subcommittee on Elections during the summer of 1985.

25. William C. Adams, "Early TV Calls in 1984: How Western Voters Deplored But Ignored Them" (Paper delivered to the annual conference of the American Association for Public Opinion Research, May 1985).

26. It should be noted, their protestations notwithstanding, that the television networks do not always broadcast what they know when they know it. For example, they have the capacity to issue reports on how the vote is going by noon on election day because of the speed with which exit poll data can be collected and raw vote tallies can be aggregated. Yet, the networks have delayed release of this information to the public.

27. The legislatures in nearly a dozen states passed laws designed to inhibit the ability of the networks to conduct exit polls. The principal provision in most

laws restricted exit poll interviewing within a certain distance of polling places, making it more difficult to interview voters according to an assigned "skip interval" and thus causing serious sampling problems. The legislation was challenged in the courts as an abridgment of the First Amendment rights of news organizations. The first court challenge was to the law passed by Washington State. The networks, joined by the *New York Times* and the *Daily Herald* of Everett, Washington, prevailed and were upheld on appeal in 1985 by the Ninth Circuit Court of Appeals. Armed with this victory, the networks went on to defeat exit poll restrictions in other states.

28. It must be assumed that the networks and the Congress reached their understanding in good faith. But as Warren Mitofsky, then of CBS News, was frank to admit with regard to characterizations: "There will be transgressions." Interview with the author, New York, June 29, 1989. The experience of 1988 was a case in point. Five minutes into ABC's "World News Tonight" on March 8 ("Super Tuesday"), coverage of the day's sixteen primaries included the comment that it might be a bad night for Rep. Richard Gephardt "if trends continue." Polls had yet to close in several primary states, including Texas. Six weeks later, WNBC-TV in New York City broadcast word that Governor Dukakis appeared to be winning the New York primary. The announcement came just after 5:00 P.M.; the polls did not close for another four hours. The *New York Times,* parting on the issue with its colleagues in the news business, editorialized on April 25, 1988: "The networks say that the only real answer is a uniform poll closing time for national elections. Yet even if the country took that expensive step, the networks could *still* project the winner before everyone had voted. The public would still need the networks to give their word—and, even more, need confidence that the networks would keep it."

29. Due to cutbacks in their news budgets, the television networks decided in 1989 to pool their exit polling activities. A new company, Voter Research and Surveys (VRS), was formed to provide ABC, CBS, CNN, and NBC with exit poll data and election projections. A benefit of the VRS consortium, some anticipated, was that competition among the networks would not be in terms of early projections but in using the exit poll data most imaginatively in reporting the election outcome. Doubts have been expressed by others, however, about the wisdom of centralizing the exit polling function. Absence of internetwork competition deprives the public of a diversity of approaches that might be taken, especially regarding design of the questionnaire. In addition, reliance on a single capability puts all four news sources in jeopardy in the event of an erroneous projection, a slip-up in some aspect of data collection or analysis, or a system breakdown. For an account of problems of the consortium in the 1990 election see Richard L. Berke, "TV Networks Join on Voter Surveys," *New York Times,* Novem-

ber 7, 1990, A1.

30. Exit poll data are now routinely placed in polling archives by the research units of the television networks. It is curious, and unfortunate, that exit polls are so underutilized by the academic research community. An occasional article will refer to exit poll data, but few present secondary analyses of these data.

31. The theory has been developed by Elisabeth Noelle-Neumann in *The Spiral of Silence* (Chicago: University of Chicago Press, 1984). Several recent studies have not borne out the hypothesis. See Cheryl Katz and Mark Baldasarre, "Using the 'L-Word' in Public: A Test of the Spiral of Silence in Conservative Orange County, California"; and William J. Gonzenbach, "The Abortion Issue: Framing, Media Use and Speaking Out" (Papers delivered at the annual conference of the American Association for Public Opinion Research, Lancaster, Pa., May 17-20, 1990).

32. A split sample was asked the standard Roper question about being a supporter or critic of the president. There was a mere one percentage point difference (not statistically significant) between the rating of the half of the sample given the preamble about the president's sagging poll standings and the rating of the other half. Reported by Burns W. Roper in *Polling on the Issues,* ed. Cantril, 53. An informative treatment of these issues is found in Kurt Lang and Gladys Engel Lang, "The Impact of Polls on Public Opinion," *Annals* 472 (March 1984): 129-142.

33. Harrison Hickman has developed a typology of how campaigns deal with varying public poll results. See Harrison Hickman, "Public Polls and Election Participants," in *Polling and Presidential Election Coverage,* ed. Lavrakas and Holley, 99-132.

34. Quoted in Jack W. Germond and Jules Witcover, *Whose Broad Stripes and Bright Stars? The Trivial Pursuit of the Presidency 1988* (New York: Warner Books, 1989), 412.

35. Quoted in Renee Loth, "The Landscape Shifts for Democratic Gubernatorial Hopefuls," *Boston Globe,* May 16, 1990, A1.

36. The author is indebted to Herbert Alexander for guidance about ways in which polls may bear on the nuances of campaign finance. Telephone interview, June 21, 1990.

37. Distribution of PAC contributions from January 1, 1989 through March 31, 1990 were:

	To Democratic candidates	To Republican candidates	Total contributions
Senate Incumbents	$10,383,052 91.6%	$ 9,594,347 73.3%	$19,977,399 82.8%

Challengers	7.8	16.7	12.1
Open seats	0.6	10.0	5.1
House	$30,188,718	$13,396,243	$43,584,961
Incumbents	92.8%	91.8%	92.5%
Challengers	1.9	1.8	1.9
Open seats	5.3	6.4	5.7
Total	$40,571,770	$22,990,590	$63,562,360
Incumbents	92.5%	84.1%	89.4%
Challengers	3.4	8.0	5.1
Open seats	4.1	7.9	5.5

SOURCE: Federal Election Commission, "PACs Contribute over $63 million to 1989-1990 Congressional Campaigns," News Release, May 27, 1990.

38. "Nonconnected" PACs are those not having a sponsoring organization such as a corporation, labor union, or trade association. They tend to be the ideologically oriented PACs. In the fifteen-month period from January 1, 1989, through March 31, 1990, these nonconnected PACs disbursed $34,653,105 to candidates for the House and Senate, just 20 percent of total PAC disbursements of $172,981,961. (Of total PAC disbursements, $63,562,360 went to candidates for the House or Senate; the balance of disbursements went to party committees involved in federal elections or to candidates in nonfederal elections.) Source: Federal Election Commission, "PACs Contribute Over $63 Million to 1989-1990 Congressional Campaigns," News Release, May 27, 1990.
39. Thomas J. O'Donnell, telephone interview with the author, July 17, 1990.
40. Alexander Hamilton, James Madison, and John Jay, *The Federalist Papers,* ed. Clinton Rossiter (New York: New American Library, 1961), 317.
41. E. E. Schattschneider, *Semisovereign People,* 137. Emphasis in original.
42. V. O. Key, *Public Opinion and Democracy* (New York: Knopf, 1964), 552.
43. Bill Kovach, "A User's View of the Polls," *Public Opinion Quarterly* 44 (Winter 1980): 569.
44. NBC's John Chancellor has made the same point: "We read the polling data and that motivates us to go look for stories." In *Campaigning on Cue,* ed. John D. Callaway (Chicago: The William Benton Fellowships Program in Broadcast Journalism, 1988), 13.
45. Celinda Lake, "Political Consultants: Opening Up a New System of Political Power," *PS: Political Science and Politics* 22 (March 1989): 28.
46. Benjamin Ginsberg, *The Captive Public: How Mass Opinion Promotes State Power* (New York: Basic Books, 1986), 64.
47. Kay Lehman Schlozman and John T. Tierney, *Organized Interests and American Democracy* (New York: Harper and Row, 1986), 393.
48. George Gallup, "Preserving Majority Rule," in *Polling on the Issues,* ed.

Cantril. Applying communication technology to the referendum process has led to experiments with electronic feedback mechanisms, though not without difficulty and vigorous critique. See Ted Becker, "Teledemocracy: Bringing Power Back to the People," *Futurist,* December 1981. For a discussion of the limitations of such feedback systems see Michael Malbin, "Teledemocracy and Its Discontents," *Public Opinion* 5 (June/July 1982), 58-59; and Jeffrey B. Abramson, F. Christopher Arterton, and Gary R. Orren, *The Electronic Commonwealth: The Impact of New Media Technologies on Democratic Politics* (New York: Basic Books, 1988), especially chap. 5.

49. For a discussion of the pros and cons of the initiative-referendum process, see Thomas E. Cronin, *Direct Democracy: The Politics of Initiative, Referendum, and Recall* (Cambridge, Mass.: Harvard University Press, 1989), especially chap. 8; and David Butler and Austin Ranney, *Referendums: A Comparative Study of Theory and Practice* (Washington, D.C.: American Enterprise Institute, 1978), especially chap. 2.

50. Harold Mendelsohn and Irving Crespi, *Polls, Television and the New Politics* (Scranton, Pa.: Chandler Publishing, 1970), 16-17. Crespi has elaborated on the idea of politics as "continuing elections" in his book, *Public Opinion, Polls, and Democracy* (Boulder: Westview Press, 1989), 18-20.

51. John C. Culver, "Challenges of an Elective Career: Values, Compromise, and Conscience" (Address to the Lord Harlech Memorial Conference on Ideals and Values in Politics and Public Service, Institute of Politics, Harvard University, May 9, 1987), 5.

52. In the 1978 Senate race, Virginia Republican candidate John Warner, pressed for an opinion on whether statehood should be granted to the District of Columbia, turned to his pollster, Arthur Finkelstein, and asked, "Art, where do we stand?" See Alan Baron, "The Slippery Art of Polls," *Politics Today* 6 (January/February 1980), 21, cited in Larry J. Sabato, *The Rise of Political Consultants: New Ways of Winning Elections* (New York: Basic Books, 1981), 82.

53. Raymond A. Bauer, Ithiel de Sola Pool, and Lewis Anthony Dexter, *American Business and Public Policy: The Politics of Foreign Trade* (New York: Atherton Press, 1963), 414-424.

54. Hamilton, Madison, and Jay, *Federalist,* 423. Emphasis added.

55. Neustadt, in his 1980 reappraisal of presidential power, notes that persuasion remains the principal weapon in the president's arsenal. He also observes that, while the presidency has not escaped unscathed from the excesses of Watergate and Vietnam, the president retains relative freedom "to deal with [Congress] on his terms, not theirs." See Richard E. Neustadt, *Presidential Power: The Politics of Leadership from FDR to Carter* (New

York: John Wiley and Sons, 1980), 176.

56. Cases in point from trends in approval ratings kept by the Gallup Poll:

- Kennedy: five-point jump (to 83 percent) after the ill-fated Bay of Pigs invasion; twelve-point jump (to 73 percent) after the Cuban Missile Crisis.
- Johnson: six-point jump (to 70 percent) after the dispatch of troops to the Dominican Republic; eight-point jump (to 56 percent) after the first U.S. bombing of North Vietnam.
- Nixon: sixteen-point jump (to 67 percent) upon signing the peace agreement with Vietnam.
- Ford: eleven-point jump (to 51 percent) after the Marine rescue of the crew of the *Mayaguez* freighter seized by Cambodia.
- Carter: eight-point jump (to 47 percent) with the signing of the Camp David Accords.

An invaluable summary of presidential popularity ratings dating back to Roosevelt is found in the *Gallup Opinion Index* 182 (October-November 1980).

57. Cases in point, again from the records of the Gallup Poll:

- Johnson: When it became clear that bombing of North Vietnam would not end the war and pessimism set in, Johnson's popularity dropped steadily from the high 50s in early 1966 to a point in August 1967 when more people disapproved of his presidency than approved.
- Nixon: Whereas 65 percent approved in February 1973, only 30 percent approved eight months later, as the Watergate investigations came to a head.
- Carter: As the nation rallied upon learning that hostages had been taken in Iran, Carter's popularity jumped from 32 percent to 61 percent in the span of a month. However, his ratings soon headed downward as public anxiety about the cost of living set in and as the unresolved hostage crisis in Iran frayed the nation's nerves.
- Reagan: After details of the Iran-Contra scandal began to seep out, Reagan's popularity dropped from 63 percent in October 1986 to 47 percent only six weeks later.
- George Bush enjoyed extraordinarily high approval ratings from the American people for the first two years of his presidency. His standing with the public was buoyed by the historic changes in Eastern Europe and deferral of steps to address the federal deficit. With the dispatch of U.S. troops to the Persian Gulf in August 1990, Bush's approval rating rose fourteen points. But within two months he had suffered a twenty-one point drop in public approval. Many forces were at work: Bush was

viewed as offering little consistent leadership in negotiating a deficit reduction package with Congress; the economy was on the verge of a recession; and public uneasiness was growing about the rationale for the commitment of U.S. armed forces in the Persian Gulf.

A discussion of the correlates of popularity is found in Samuel Kernell, "Explaining Presidential Popularity," *American Political Science Review* 72 (June 1978): 506-522.

58. Hadley Cantril, *The Human Dimension: Experience in Policy Research* (New Brunswick, N.J.: Rutgers University Press, 1967), 44. For a chronicle of Cantril's polling for Roosevelt, see chaps. 6-8 and 11-13.

59. Richard W. Steele, "The Pulse of the People: Franklin D. Roosevelt and the Gauging of American Public Opinion," *Journal of Contemporary History* 9 (October 1975): 210-212; cited in Samuel Kernell, *Going Public: New Strategies of Presidential Leadership* (Washington, D.C.: CQ Press, 1986), 20. Cantril, *The Human Dimension*, 41-42.

60. Bill D. Moyers, "One Thing We Learned," *Foreign Affairs* (July 1968): 661-662.

61. The "self-anchoring striving scale" was developed in the late 1950s by Hadley Cantril for purposes of measuring the hopes and fears of publics in diverse cultures. Respondents are first asked to describe what life would be like in an ideal state of affairs, then, what it would be like in the worst possible state of affairs. They are then shown a picture of a ladder, the top and bottom rungs of which represent the ideal and worst state of affairs, respectively, and asked on which step they stand at the present time, where they stood five years ago, and where they will stand five years in the future. The series is then repeated with respect to the state of the nation. See Hadley Cantril, *The Pattern of Human Concerns* (New Brunswick, N.J.: Rutgers University Press, 1967). For Caddell's account, see Patrick H. Caddell, "Trapped in a Downward Spiral," *Public Opinion* 2 (October/November 1979): 2-7, 52-55, 58-60.

62. An independent national survey using the striving scale found in mid-1978 that the general public's perception was of a decline from past to present in the nation's well-being, with *no* expectation of a recovery in the next five years. See Albert H. Cantril and Susan Davis Cantril, *Unemployment, Government, and the American People* (Washington, D.C.: Public Research, 1978). Warren E. Miller contests Caddell's "malaise" finding in "Misreading the Public Pulse," *Public Opinion* 2 (October/November 1979): 9-14, 60.

63. Richard Wirthlin, quoted in Hedrick Smith, *The Power Game: How Washington Works* (New York: Ballantine Books, 1988), 413.

64. Ibid., 411. Emphasis in original.

65. An account of this contribution of polling to the Reagan White House is found in Richard S. Beal and Ronald H. Hinckley, "Presidential Decision Making and Opinion Polls," *Annals* 472 (March 1984): 79-81.

66. Reagan's chief of staff, Donald Regan, adopted the parlance of his native Wall Street to underscore the importance of the popularity ratings. See Jane Mayer and Doyle McManus, *Landslide: The Unmaking of the President, 1984-1988* (Boston: Houghton Mifflin, 1988), 44-45.

67. Kernell, *Going Public*, 184-200, passim.

68. Within a week of President Reagan's appeal for bipartisan support for his budget before a televised joint session of Congress, the Speaker of the House, Thomas P. O'Neill, Jr. (D-Mass.), abandoned all hope of making the case that Reagan's budget proposals were unsound and the House endorsed a budget along the lines the President had called for. For accounts of this sequence of events see Dale Tate, "Congress Shapes Strategy for Reagan Economic Plan," *CQ Weekly Report,* February 28, 1981, 376-378; Dale Tate and Gail Gregg, "Congress Set for Showdown on First Budget Resolution," *CQ Weekly Report,* May 2, 1981, 743-746; and Dale Tate, "House Provides President a Victory on the 1982 Budget," *CQ Weekly Report,* May 9, 1981, 783-786.

69. A good recapitulation of this public ambivalence in 1981 is found in Andrew Kohut, "Public Attitudes on Domestic Issues, 1981," *Public Opinion* 4 (December/January 1982): 41-43. At the time, Crespi faulted the pollsters for not doing a better job of explaining the contradictions in the public's perception of Ronald Reagan. See Irving Crespi, "Does the Public Approve of Ronald Reagan?" *Public Opinion* 4 (October/November 1981): 20, 41. Discussion of the "ideological/operational" ambivalence of the American electorate in the 1964 election can be found in Lloyd A. Free and Hadley Cantril, *Political Beliefs of Americans* (New Brunswick, N.J.: Rutgers University Press, 1967).

70. See Mayer and McManus, *Landslide,* 43-45.

71. Hamilton, Madison, and Jay, *Federalist,* 324. For a discussion of this point see Marvin Meyers, ed., *The Mind of the Founder: Sources of the Political Thought of James Madison* (Hanover, N.H.: University Press of New England, 1981), xxvii-xxix.

72. These three orientations have been labeled "60s Democrats," "Seculars," and "Enterprisers" and constitute three of eleven types of voters identified in the 1987 Times Mirror study conducted by the Gallup Organization. See Ornstein, Kohut, and McCarthy, *The People, Press, and Politics,* chap. 11.

73. Kernell, *Going Public,* 219-222.

74. This episode is recounted in Smith, *The Power Game,* 347-348.

75. "It is our responsibility [as pollsters] to establish the guidelines for both the research and the release of findings; and if they are not acceptable to our

client, we should refuse the assignment; or, if the results are used in an unethical or inaccurate manner, we have an obligation to take whatever steps are necessary to correct the situation." See Harry W. O'Neill, "The Pollster and the Advocate," in *Polling on the Issues,* ed. Cantril, 182.

a p p e n d i x   a

Tabular Data

TABLE A-1   Percentage of 1988 Primary Voters Deciding in Last Three Days

State	Date	Among Democratic primary voters	Sample size	Among Republican primary voters	Sample size
N.H.	2/16	39%	1,510	34%	1,567
S.D.	2/23	36	837	25	918
Ala.	3/8	28	1,344	18	790
Ark.	3/8	37	910	18	440
Fla.	3/8	33	1,460	20	1,347
Ga.	3/8	31	1,294	24	954
La.	3/8	32	1,391	17	800
Mass.	3/8	21	457	21	672
Md.	3/8	29	649	—	—
Miss.	3/8	25	1,255	20	728
Mo.	3/8	26	706	23	883
N.J.	3/8	8	1,114	—	—
N.C.	3/8	33	1,419	18	989
Okla.	3/8	38	762	28	663
Tenn.	3/8	12	383	21	387
Texas	3/8	31	1,641	19	1,185
Va.	3/8	27	1,290	19	957
Ill.	3/15	22	1,593	20	854
Wisc.	4/5	26	2,056	—	—
N.Y.	4/19	16	2,101	—	—
Pa.	4/26	13	2,116	—	—
Ind.	5/3	12	1,363	—	—
Ohio	5/3	11	1,532	—	—
Calif.	6/7	9	3,101	—	—
N.J.	6/7	8	1,114	—	—

SOURCE: CBS News exit polls.

TABLE A-2 Primary Responsibility in Phases of Polling Among Newspapers Conducting Own Polls

	1978	1986	Change
Determining questions			
News staff alone	67%	49%	−18pts[a]
News staff with consultant	24	40	+16[a]
Paper's market research dept.	9	8	− 1
Commercial polling firm	2	5	+ 3
Academic polling organization	2	4	+ 2
Conducting interviews			
News staff alone	59	28	−31[a]
News staff with consultant	10	7	− 3
Paper's market research dept.	14	10	− 4
Commercial polling firm	17	30	+13[a]
Academic polling organization	4	21	+17[a]
Analyzing results			
News staff alone	67	42	−25[a]
News staff with consultant	17	31	+14[a]
Paper's market research dept.	9	9	—
Commercial polling firm	7	15	+ 8[b]
Academic polling organization	3	12	+ 9[a]
Number of newspapers	162	144	

SOURCE: David Pearce Demers, "Use of Polls in Reporting Changes Slightly Since 1978," *Journalism Quarterly* 64 (Winter 1987): 841.

[a] $p < .01$ (significant at the 99% level of confidence).

[b] $p < .05$ (significant at the 95% level of confidence).

TABLE A-3 Composition of Sample in Successive Callbacks

	\multicolumn{5}{c}{Cumulative completed calls by attempt}
	One	Two	Three	Four	Full sample
Age					
18-30	23%	26%	26%	28%	30%
31-54	44	42	42	42	43
55 and over	33	32	32	30	27
Race					
White	89	88	87	87	86
Nonwhite	11	12	13	13	14
Sex					
Male	34	39	41	43	44
Female	66	61	59	57	56
Education					
High school or less	52	53	54	55	54
Some college or more	48	48	46	45	46
Party identification					
Republican	36	35	37	36	38
Independent	14	15	15	15	15
Democrat	51	50	46	47	46
Other, apolitical	0	*	1	2	2
Interest in presidential campaigns					
Good deal	38	37	37	36	34
Somewhat	40	43	45	46	47
Not much	22	20	18	18	18
Presidential approval					
Positive	47	49	51	52	58
Neutral	16	14	14	14	15
Negative	31	33	28	27	28
Don't know	6	6	6	7	9
Presidential trial heat					
Reagan	48	51	51	52	52
Mondale	45	45	42	40	39
Other	2	3	5	4	2
Don't know/no answer	4	4	6	5	7

SOURCE: Michael W. Traugott, "The Importance of Persistence in Respondent Selection for Preelection Surveys," *Public Opinion Quarterly* 51 (Spring 1987): 54-55.

NOTE: Data are from the state of Michigan, 1984. An asterisk designates less than 0.5 percent.

TABLE A-4   Persons in Nontelephone Households by Selected Characteristics and Region: 1985-1986

	All regions	North-east	Mid-west	South	West
All Persons	7.2%	4.1%	4.8%	11.0%	6.9%
By sex					
Male	7.6	4.3	4.9	11.8	7.4
Female	6.7	3.9	4.7	10.2	6.4
By age					
Under 6 years	12.3	6.8	9.2	18.5	10.6
6-16 years	8.5	5.0	5.1	13.6	7.2
17-24 years	11.2	6.2	7.9	16.7	11.4
25-34 years	8.0	4.4	5.2	12.1	7.9
35-44 years	5.0	3.0	2.9	7.5	5.1
45-54 years	4.2	2.6	3.0	6.2	4.3
55-64 years	3.7	2.5	2.5	5.5	3.6
65-74 years	3.2	2.0	2.5	4.7	3.1
75 years and over	3.3	2.4	2.1	5.3	2.5
By race					
White	5.8	3.4	4.2	8.8	6.0
Black	15.6	10.5	10.1	19.9	10.1
Other	10.9	3.2	5.5	10.8	14.3
By poverty index					
Above poverty	3.7	2.3	2.3	5.5	4.0
Below poverty	27.4	17.8	20.3	35.1	27.8
By employment status[a]					
Currently employed	5.2	2.0	3.0	8.0	5.5
Unemployed	16.0	9.4	11.8	22.9	15.8
Not in labor force	7.2	4.2	5.7	10.4	6.7
By household income					
Less than $5,000	29.2	16.8	22.7	36.9	31.9
$5,000-$6,999	20.0	16.5	16.4	25.1	18.5
$7,000-$9,999	18.8	12.7	12.3	23.6	18.7
$10,000-$14,999	12.9	7.2	8.4	19.0	13.2
$15,000-$19,999	7.7	3.7	4.8	11.4	8.5
$20,000-$24,999	3.6	2.6	1.8	5.9	3.2
$25,000-$34,999	1.8	1.5	0.8	2.5	2.4
$35,000-$49,999	0.9	0.5	0.5	1.0	1.4
$50,000 or more	0.4	0.4	0.1	0.4	1.0
By education of adult responsible for household					
8 years or fewer	18.1	12.0	11.2	23.3	19.6
9-11 years	19.2	12.7	15.4	24.4	17.5
12 years	8.0	4.1	5.4	12.3	9.0

TABLE A-4 (continued)

	All regions	North-east	Mid-west	South	West
13-15 years	4.1	2.2	2.5	5.9	4.6
16 years	1.8	0.8	1.0	2.7	2.3
17 years or more	0.8	0.6	0.4	1.1	1.0
By marital status					
Married, spouse in household	4.8	2.4	2.8	7.8	4.7
Married, spouse not in household	16.2	10.9	8.7	20.5	21.4
Widowed	4.5	2.9	3.2	6.5	4.5
Divorced	9.8	4.8	7.9	13.5	10.0
Separated	18.8	13.5	16.6	24.8	15.3
Never married	8.1	5.1	5.9	11.8	8.2
By Hispanic origin					
Puerto Rican	22.1	22.8	33.4	11.8	18.4
Cuban	4.5	2.0	3.3	5.1	4.7
Mexican	18.1	16.7	15.0	24.6	13.7
Other Latin American origin	12.6	14.9	3.9	7.2	17.9

SOURCE: Owen T. Thornberry, Jr., and James T. Massey, "Trends in United States Telephone Coverage Across Time and Subgroups," in Robert M. Groves et al., eds., *Telephone Survey Methodology* (New York: John Wiley & Sons, 1988), 34-35.

NOTE: These data are from the continuous National Health Interview Survey conducted by the Bureau of the Census. The data presented are from the 1986 survey, which involved 153,048 personal in-home interviews. In the course of the interview, the interviewer ascertained the telephone status of the household, either by direct questioning or by observation.

[a] Eighteen years of age and over.

TABLE A-5　Varying Distribution of "Opinions" on Abortion

Question	Total	Clearly Pro-choice	Qualified	Clearly Pro-life
Should a legal abortion be possible if . . . the woman's own health is seriously endangered by the pregnancy? [a]				
Yes	87%	87%		
No	7			7%
Depends[b]	4		4%	
Don't know	2			
Should a legal abortion be possible if . . . there is a strong chance of serious defect in the baby? [a]				
Yes	69	69		
No	21			21
Depends[b]	4		4	
Don't know	6			
If a woman wants to have an abortion, and her doctor agrees to it, should she be allowed to have an abortion or not?				
Yes	63	63		
No	24			24
Depends[b]	10		10	
Don't know	3			
Should abortion be legal as it is now, or legal only in such cases as rape, incest, or to save the life of the mother, or should it not be permitted at all?				
Legal as now	49	49		
Legal to save mother, rape or incest	39		39	
Not permitted	9			9
Don't know	3			
If the Supreme Court changes its view of the law so each state could make its own decision on abortion, would you want your state to permit abortions under all circumstances, or to only allow abortion in cases of rape, incest, or to save the life of the mother, or to outlaw all abortions?				
All circumstances	43	43		
Only in cases of rape, incest or to save mother	43		43	
Outlaw all abortions	10			10
Don't know	4			

TABLE A-5   (continued)

Question	Total	Clearly Pro-choice	Qualified	Clearly Pro-life
Should a legal abortion be possible if . . . the family has a very low income and cannot afford more children? [a]				
Yes	43	43		
No	49			49
Depends[b]	4		4	
Don't know	4			
Should a legal abortion be possible if . . . she is not married and does not want to marry the man? [a]				
Yes	42	42		
No	50			50
Depends[b]	5		5	
Don't know	3			
Would you approve or disapprove of someone you know having an abortion?				
Approve	39	39		
Disapprove	32			32
Depends[b]	25		25	
Don't know	4			
Should a legal abortion be possible if . . . the pregnancy interfered with work or education? [a]				
Yes	26	26		
No	65			65
Depends[b]	5		5	
Don't know	4			

SOURCE: CBS News/*New York Times* poll, April 13-16, 1989; 1,412 telephone interviews.

[a] These questions followed the general preamble: "Please tell me whether or not *you* think it should be possible for a pregnant woman to obtain a *legal* abortion if. . . ."

[b] Volunteered response.

TABLE A-6   Public Perception of the Polls

The Roper Organization

Now I'd like to ask you some questions about polls in general, based on what you know or have read or heard about them, and not just your experience in this interview. First, do you think most public opinion polls work for or against the best interest of the general public?

For	75%
Against	8
Don't know/no answer	18

How much do you think poll results affect or change things—would you say polls usually have almost no influence, or some influence, or quite a lot of influence, or have too much influence?

Almost no influence	9%
Some influence	58
Quite a lot of influence	21
Too much influence	5
Don't know/no answer	7

Do you think polls are almost always accurate, usually accurate, accurate only sometimes, or accurate very seldom?

Almost always accurate	10%
Usually accurate	46
Only sometimes accurate	32
Very seldom accurate	6
Don't know/no answer	6

Do you think pollsters are almost always honest about their polls, are usually honest, honest only sometimes, or honest very seldom?

Almost always honest	25%
Usually honest	51
Only sometimes honest	14
Very seldom honest	3
Don't know/no answer	7

Do you think nearly all people who are interviewed in polls tell the truth, or most people do, or only some do, or that very few in a poll tell the truth?

Nearly all	28%
Most	53
Only some	13
Very few	3
Don't know/no answer	3

The Gallup Organization for Newsweek

In your opinion, did this year's presidential primaries produce the best candidates or do you think there were better qualified candidates who should have been selected?

Produced good candidates	26%
Better qualified candidates should have been selected	66
Don't know	8

In your opinion, are the polls conducted by news organizations to measure support for the presidential candidates mostly accurate or mostly inaccurate?

Mostly accurate	60%
Mostly inaccurate	26
Don't know	14

Do you think that the results of presidential preference polls should or should not be reported during the final weeks of a presidential campaign?

Should be reported	43%
Should not be reported	52
Don't know	5

The Gallup Organization for Times Mirror

How much influence do you feel advertising consultants and pollsters have on which candidate becomes president. Would you say they have:

Too much influence	43%
Too little influence	8
About the right amount of influence	44
Don't know	5

In your opinion, does the reporting of who is ahead in the polls improve the press coverage of the election or not?

Improves press coverage	38%
Does not improve press coverage	47
Has no effect (volunteered)	7
Don't know	8

In your opinion, is the reporting of who is ahead in the polls a good thing or a bad thing for the country?

Good thing for the country	38%
Bad thing for the country	45
Neither good nor bad (volunteered)	12
Don't know	5

SOURCE: The Roper Organization, *Roper Reports* 85-4, 2,000 personal interviews, March 23-30, 1985; the Gallup Organization, telephone interviews with 1,013 registered voters, October 20-21, 1988 (the *Newsweek Poll,* copyright 1988 by Newsweek Magazine Inc.); the Gallup Organization, telephone interviews with 2,006 registered voters, October 23-26, 1988 (used with permission of Times Mirror Center for the People and the Press).

TABLE A-7   Assessments of Reagan Administration Progress on Race Relations by Race, Education, and Age

Question:[RESPONDENT HANDED CARD] For each of these areas of national interest, tell me if you think the Reagan administration has *made progress* in solving problems, *tried but failed* to solve problems, *did not deal with* problems, or *created* problems for the next president.

	Made progress	Tried but failed	Did not deal with problem	Created problems	Don't know
Full sample	25%	13%	40%	11%	11%
Whites	28	12	39	9	12
Blacks	14	14	43	23	7
Among whites					
Some college	24	12	49	10	6
HS graduate	29	12	36	8	14
Less than HS	29	14	28	9	20
Under 30 years	25	10	43	9	14
30-39 years	23	12	47	9	9
40 years and over	31	14	34	9	13
Among blacks					
Some college	11	10	45	33	2
HS graduate	13	14	47	18	7
Less than HS	16	16	37	20	11
Under 30 years	17	16	48	15	5
30-39 years	9	10	45	28	7
40 years and over	14	14	38	26	9

SOURCE: 4,244 personal interviews, including 755 with blacks, conducted by the Gallup Organization in May 1987 (used with permission of Times Mirror Center for the People and the Press).

NOTE: Percentages may not add to 100 due to rounding.

a p p e n d i x   b

Professional Codes

National Council on Public Polls
Principles of Disclosure

We, the member organizations of the National Council on Public Polls, hereby affirm our commitment to standards of disclosure designed to ensure that consumers of survey results that enter the public domain have an adequate basis for judging the reliability and validity of the results reported.

It shall not be the purpose of this Code to pass judgment on the merits of methods employed in specific surveys. Rather, it shall be our sole purpose to ensure that pertinent information is disclosed concerning methods that were used so that consumers of surveys may assess studies for themselves.

Any survey organization, upon providing evidence to the Council of its compliance with this Code, shall be permitted to state that it "complies with the Principles of Disclosure of the National Council on Public Polls."

To the above ends, we agree with the following Principles of Disclosure and procedures to be followed in the event question is raised about compliance with them.

All reports of survey findings of member organizations, prepared specifically for public release, will include reference to the following:

- Sponsorship of the survey;
- Dates of interviewing;
- Method of obtaining the interviews (in-person, telephone, or mail);
- Population that was sampled;
- Size of the sample;
- Size and description of the sub-sample, if the survey report relies primarily on

less than the total sample;
- Complete wording of questions upon which the release is based; and,
- The percentages upon which conclusions are based.

When survey results are released to any medium by a survey organization, the above items will be included in the release and a copy of the release will be filed with the Council within two weeks.

Survey organizations reporting results will endeavor to have print or broadcast media include the above items in their news stories and make a report containing these items available to the public upon request.

Organizations conducting privately commissioned surveys should make clear to their clients that the client has the right to maintain the confidentiality of survey findings. However, in the event the results of a privately commissioned poll are made public by the survey organization, it shall be assumed that they have entered the public domain and the above eight items should be disclosed. In the event the results of a privately commissioned poll are made public by the client and the client acknowledges the release, the survey organization (a) shall make the information outlined above available to the public upon request and (b) shall have the responsibility to release the information above and other pertinent information necessary to put the client's release into the proper context if such a release has misrepresented the survey's findings.

Revised September 1979

American Association for Public Opinion Research Code of Professional Ethics and Practices

We, the members of the American Association for Public Opinion Research, subscribe to the principles expressed in the following Code. Our goals are to support sound and ethical practice in the conduct of public opinion research and in the use of such research for policy and decision-making in the public and private sectors, as well as to improve public understanding of opinion research methods and the proper use of opinion research results.

We pledge ourselves to maintain high standards of scientific competence and integrity in conducting, analyzing, and reporting our work and in our relations with survey respondents, with our clients, with those who eventually use the research for decision-making purposes, and with the general public. We further pledge ourselves to reject all tasks or assignments that would require activities inconsistent with the principles of this Code.

I. Principles of Professional Practice in the Conduct of Our Work
  A. We shall exercise due care in developing research designs and survey instruments, and in collecting, processing, and analyzing data, taking all reasonable steps to assure the reliability and validity of results.
    1. We shall recommend and employ only those tools and methods of analysis which, in our professional judgment, are well suited to the research problem at hand.
    2. We shall not select research tools and methods of analysis because of their capacity to yield misleading conclusions.
    3. We shall not knowingly make interpretations of research results, nor shall we tacitly permit interpretations that are inconsistent with the data available.
    4. We shall not knowingly imply that interpretations should be accorded greater confidence than the data actually warrant.
  B. We shall describe our methods and findings accurately and in appropriate detail in all research reports, adhering to the standards for minimal disclosure specified in Section III, below.
  C. If any of our work becomes the subject of a formal investigation of an alleged violation of this Code, undertaken with the approval of the AAPOR Executive Council, we shall provide additional information on the survey in such detail that a fellow survey practitioner would be able to conduct a professional evaluation of the survey.

II. Principles of Professional Responsibility in Our Dealings with People
  A. The Public:
    1. If we become aware of the appearance in public of serious distortions of our research, we shall publicly disclose what is required to correct these distortions, including, as appropriate, a statement to the public media, legislative body, regulatory agency, or other appropriate group, in or before which the distorted findings were presented.
  B. Clients or Sponsors:
    1. When undertaking work for a private client, we shall hold confidential all proprietary information obtained about the client and about the conduct and findings of the research undertaken for the client, except when the dissemination of the information is expressly authorized by the client, or when disclosure becomes necessary under terms of Section I-C or II-A of this Code.
    2. We shall be mindful of the limitations of our techniques and capabilities and shall accept only those research assignments which we can reasonably expect to accomplish within these limitations.
  C. The Profession:
    1. We recognize our responsibility to contribute to the science of public

opinion research and to disseminate as freely as possible the ideas and findings which emerge from our research.

  2. We shall not cite our membership in the Association as evidence of professional competence, since the Association does not so certify any persons or organizations.

D. The Respondent:

  1. We shall strive to avoid the use of practices or methods that may harm, humiliate, or seriously mislead survey respondents.

  2. Unless the respondent waives confidentiality for specified uses, we shall hold as privileged and confidential all information that might identify a respondent with his or her responses. We shall also not disclose or use the names of respondents for nonresearch purposes unless the respondents grant us permission to do so.

III. Standards for Minimal Disclosure

Good professional practice imposes the obligation upon all public opinion researchers to include, in any report of research results, or to make available when that report is released, certain essential information about how the research was conducted. At a minimum, the following items should be disclosed:

  1. Who sponsored the survey, and who conducted it.

  2. The exact wording of questions asked, including the text of any preceding instruction or explanation to the interviewer or respondent that might reasonably be expected to affect the response.

  3. A definition of the population under study, and a description of the sampling frame used to identify this population.

  4. A description of the sample selection procedure, giving a clear indication of the method by which the respondents were selected by the researcher, or whether the respondents were entirely self-selected.

  5. Size of sample and, if applicable, completion rates and information on eligibility criteria and screening procedures.

  6. A discussion of the precision of the findings, including, if appropriate, estimates of sampling error, and a description of any weighting or estimating procedures used.

  7. Which results are based on parts of the sample, rather than the total sample.

  8. Method, location, and dates of data collection.

Revised March 1986

American Association of Political Consultants
A Code of Professional Ethics

As a member of the American Association of Political Consultants, I believe that there are certain standards of practice which I must maintain as a representative of my profession. I, therefore, pledge to adhere to the following Code of Ethics:

- I shall not indulge in any activity which would corrupt or degrade the practice of political campaigning
- I shall treat my colleagues and clients with respect and never intentionally injure their professional or personal reputations
- I shall respect the confidence of my client and not reveal confidential or private information obtained during our professional relationship
- I will use no appeal to voters which is based on racism or discrimination and will condemn those who use such practices. In turn, I will work for equal voting rights and privileges for all citizens
- I shall refrain from false and misleading attacks on an opponent or member of his family and shall do everything in my power to prevent others from using such tactics
- I will document accurately and fully any criticism of an opponent or his record
- I shall be honest in my relationship with the press and answer questions candidly when I have the authority to do so
- I shall not support any individual or organization which resorts to practices forbidden in this Code

Adopted 1969

Index

ABC News, 31, 47, 64, 65, 74, 78, 88, 190, 193, 217, 243
  call-in polls, 144-145
  handling of fifty-state poll (1988), 88, 187, 220
  poll releases before 1988 Republican convention, 1-2, 72-74, 187, 191
ABC/*Washington Post* poll, 1, 36, 39, 72, 81, 84, 121, 122, 148, 180
Abortion, 3, 128, 129, 136, 146, 206, 227, 256-257
Abramson, Jeffrey B., 246
Academic resistance to polling, 12, 13, 27, 28
Accountability
  of political consultants, 6, 15, 265
  of pollsters, 2, 6, 261-264
  See also First Amendment and press accountability
"Ad hoc committee on poll reporting," 191-192
Adams, William C., 217, 242
Adatto, Kiku, 31
Advocacy polling, 236, 249, 250
Age

and measurement of public opinion, 100-105, 108, 110, 143-144, 156, 253, 254-255
  and nonphone households, 104-106
  and turnout, 108, 110-112, 122
  as variable in poll analysis, 98, 161, 205-206
Ailes, Roger, 21-22, 23
Alderman, Jeff, 61, 74
Alexander, Herbert, 244
American Association for Public Opinion Research (AAPOR), 183
  Code of Professional Ethics and Practices, 148, 165-173, 178, 198, 262-264
  founding of, 13, 148, 164, 185
  reviews of released polls, 172, 178-182, 189-190
American Association of Political Consultants (AAPC), 16
  Code of Professional Ethics, 181-183, 265
  Ethics Study Group, 198
  founding and growth of, 16
American Federation of Teachers, 224

Hogan, J. Michael, 239
Hollander, Sidney, 179, 197-198
Horton, Willie, 26, 32, 139, 183
Hotline, 34-36, 71, 88, 144
Hume, Brit, 64-65
Humphrey, Hubert H., 14, 22, 64, 85
Hurd, Robert, 168-169
Hursch-Cesar, Gerald, 149
Hutchins, Robert Maynard, 185
Hyman, Herbert, 7

Indianapolis Star, 32
Initiative-referendum process. *See* Polls, as issue referenda
Instant polls, 2, 47-48, 52-53, 102, 142, 152
Instant-reaction meters, 141-142, 233-234
Institute for International Social Research, 240
Intensity of opinion. *See* Opinion, intensity of
Interest groups
  number and make-up of, 17, 29, 223-224
  polls in competition among, 2, 6, 9, 13, 17, 222-224, 226-227
  use of polls by, 17, 29
International public opinion, 229-230
Interuniversity Consortium on Political and Social Research, 180
Interviewing
  just before an election, 41-42, 49-50, 58, 79
  race of interviewer effects, 112-113, 156
  refusal conversion, 99-100, 113
  relative merits of telephone and personal, 93, 100, 102-103, 112, 135, 151, 152, 153, 155

supervision of, 97-100, 106, 112-113, 152, 161
use of volunteers, 99, 113
Interviewing dates, disclosure of, 74-75, 166, 192, 261, 264
Iowa caucuses, 38, 55-58, 111, 215
Iowa poll. *See Des Moines Register and Tribune*
Iran-Contra scandal, 68, 247
Iran hostage crisis, 49, 247
Isaacs, Maxine, 65
Isaacs, Norman F., 199
Isaacs, Stephen, 78
Iyengar, Shanto, 30

Jackson, Henry M., 85
Jackson, Jesse, 40, 71, 113, 134
Jackson, John, 413
Jennings, Peter, 1, 47, 72-74
John, Kenneth E., 84
Johnson, Lyndon B., 14
  monitoring of public opinion by, 230
  popularity of, 427
  and war in Vietnam, 230-231
Johnston, Richard, 59, 61, 63, 84-85
Jordan, Hamilton, 59
Journalism and campaigns, competition between, 24-26, 31-32, 70
Joyce, Ed, 86-87

Kahn, Robert L., 151, 153, 155
Kalton, Graham, 149, 154
Katz, Cheryl, 417
Kauff, Denis, 69
Kay, Alan, 411
Keenan, Kevin, 78
Keene, Karlyn H., 207
Keeter, Scott, 156
Kemp, Jack, 22, 63
Kennedy, Edward M., 62
Kennedy, John F., 75, 247